A History of AUSTRALIAN SCHOOLING

CRAIG CAMPBELL AND HELEN PROCTOR

ALLEN&UNWIN
SYDNEY • MELBOURNE • AUCKLAND • LONDON

Published by Allen & Unwin in 2014

Allen & Unwin
83 Alexander Street
Crows Nest NSW 2065
Australia
Phone: (61 2) 8425 0100
Fax: (61 2) 9906 2218
Email: info@allenandunwin.com
Web: www.allenandunwin.com

Cataloguing-in-Publication details are available
from the National Library of Australia
www.trove.nla.gov.au

ISBN 978 1 74237 182 5

Set in 11.75/15 pt Minion Pro by Bookhouse, Sydney

10 9 8 7 6 5 4 3 2 1

Contents

List of tables		v
Acknowledgements		vi
The authors		viii
Introduction		ix
1	Precarious endeavours: to 1820	1
2	School entrepreneurs: 1821–1860	31
3	Inventing public school systems: 1861–1900	64
4	Towards universal provision: 1901–1925	106
5	The socially useful school: 1926–1950	142
6	Equality of opportunity: 1951–1975	178
7	Towards a market of schools: 1976–2000	211
8	The present and future school	248
Select bibliography including references		271
Index		281

List of tables

2.1 Trained teachers in the publicly funded schools of New South Wales 45

2.2 Schools and enrolments in three colonies, 1861 62

3.1 Education laws systematising colonial and state systems of public education 74

3.2 Foundations of corporate schools, mainly church owned, that continued to exist in 1985 90

4.1 Growth of different kinds of public schools and public school enrolments in New South Wales, 1901 and 1925 111

6.1 Enrolment growth in each education sector in comparison with population and labour force, Australia, 1955, 1965, 1975 (indexed as percentage increase) 185

7.1 Number of schools in Australia by sector, 1976–2001 213

7.2 Changes in the numbers of full-time Australian secondary students enrolled in government and non-government schools, 1976 and 2000 213

7.3 Female teachers as a proportion of all teachers in Australia, 1976 and 1999 by school sector (%) 240

7.4 Comparative retention rates of Indigenous and non-Indigenous students in Australian schools to Year 12, 1994 and 2000 (%) 243

8.1 Students in Australian schools by school sector, 2012 260

8.2 Change in shares of school sector enrolment (full-time students), 2001–2012 (%) 261

Acknowledgements

A book such as this depends on the research of many scholars over many decades. Though it is impossible to name everyone here, we acknowledge their work and thank them for it.

A number of colleagues and friends have assisted us by reading our drafts and offering commentary. Special thanks must go to John Cleverley, Tom O'Donohue and Kay Whitehead, who spent many hours on our behalf. Phillip Cashen, Lyndsay Connors, Julia Horne, Stuart Macintyre, Paul Kilvert and Geoffrey Sherington have also been generous with their time and suggestions. Regardless of all this assistance, the authors are fully responsible for the final text.

Others assisted us in other ways, sometimes with little notice. Tanya Fitzgerald, Tom O'Donoghue and Richard Selleck were encouraging readers of our original book proposal. We thank Simone Alcorso, Tim Allender, Dianne Bloomfield, Reg Butler, Mary Carroll, Phil Cormack, Alison Elliott, Hannah Forsyth, Deb Hayes, John Hughes, Kate Keeley, Rebecca Kummerfeld, Tony Loughland, Alison Mackinnon, Jo May, Julie McLeod, Jim McMorrow, Gabrielle Meagher, Lesley Preston, Rosalie Trioli and Katie Wright. Rennel Lope and Clare McCarty generously helped us with two of our brief school studies.

The Faculty of Education and Social Work at the University of Sydney provided us with generous allocations of time and resources. Helen Proctor was a recipient of the University's Brown Fellowship, which assisted with her research and writing.

This book originated in correspondence with our publisher, Elizabeth Weiss of Allen & Unwin. In his ABC Boyer Lectures of 2008, Rupert Murdoch had suggested that Australian schooling remained mired in the nineteenth century. Elizabeth asked us what we thought of that. When we offered to write a book saying why Murdoch had it wrong for the most part, Elizabeth said 'Yes!'. We thank her for the opportunity.

Our families have provided welcome distractions throughout the research and writing. Helen thanks Peter, Anna and Louisa Studman. Craig thanks Keith Foulcher, Gabrielle Green, and Tim and April Foulcher.

The authors

Craig Campbell is an honorary associate professor in the history of education at the University of Sydney. Following a school teaching career in South Australia, he wrote a doctorate on the history of adolescence and the rise of the Australian high school. He has taught and researched the history and sociology of education at the University of Sydney from 1994. In recent times, he has written a school history and co-authored books on education in the South Pacific, the history of childhood, the sociology of education, and the rise and decline of the comprehensive government high school.

Helen Proctor is a historian of education in the Faculty of Education and Social Work at the University of Sydney and a former high school teacher. Her published research includes work on gender relations in public and non-government schools. With Alison Mackinnon, she has contributed a chapter on education in twentieth-century Australia to *The Cambridge History of Australia*. She is currently researching the history of parents' engagement with their children's schooling.

The authors, with Geoffrey Sherington, co-wrote *School Choice: How Parents Negotiate the New School Market in Australia* (Allen & Unwin, 2009). They are also co-editors, with Kay Whitehead, of the research journal *History of Education Review*.

Introduction

The last substantial efforts to write comprehensive histories of Australian schooling occurred in the 1970s—a period of radical educational reform. There was good reason to review the history of Australian education at that time, as great questions associated with access to educational opportunity and the renewal of funding to non-government schools after a century of non-funding came to dominate policy debates. The ways in which teaching occurred, the architecture of schools, school and teacher management, assessment practices, relationships between school credentials and the labour market, the ways in which students, parents, teachers, educational institutions, school systems and policy-makers related one to another—all of these issues and more were subjects of reform.

Since the 1970s, the pace of change has never slowed. With the rise of neoliberal-influenced education policies, continual transformation has become a permanent feature of Australian education. There are new school markets. Families are encouraged to think of themselves as informed consumers in competition for educational services, both non-government and government. This post-1970s reform effort has been going long enough now for it to have its own history. Knowledge of this history, along with earlier phases of Australia's educational history, is essential for those who seek to understand present arrangements—and to plan for the future.

Since the 1970s, there have been important developments in how the history of education has been written. One was to take seriously the differences between histories of *education* and histories of *schooling*, which are not the same thing. There are many agencies and processes that educate populations besides schools—in fact, what schools do often looks narrow by comparison. The distinction between education and schooling is especially important in making sense of the history of Indigenous education, for example. For some Indigenous children living in remote areas, education and schooling were often separate until late in the twentieth century. Nevertheless, schools have provided highly significant interventions in the lives of young people. During the period covered by this book, the routines, procedures and knowledge associated with schooling eventually came to define childhood in very substantial ways, touching even those who had only brief contact with actual schools.

Another important movement in the historiography was the development of a critical stance towards schools and classrooms. Before the 1970s, most histories of schooling tended to equate the building and modernisation of schooling systems with enlightenment and progress. Since the 1980s, though, it has been difficult for historians to ignore the role of schools in the production or reinforcement of social hierarchies and inequalities. Their role in 'social uplift' remains an important theme, but it is not the whole story.

As this history shows, schools were quite marginal in the lives of most young people for much of the eighteenth century, and even well into the nineteenth century. Schools grew in their significance for all groups in the population in the late nineteenth and twentieth centuries, though at very different rates for communities differentiated by social class, gender, religion, place of residence, and ethnic and racial designation. Explaining how this occurred is an aim of this book. If we have an overriding concern in interpreting the history of Australian schooling, it is to show how schools eventually became universal, powerful and highly intrusive institutions in the organisation and ordering of the lives of children, youth and families. A popular way to think about schools and society is to see schools as merely 'reflecting' society. We prefer the perspective that schools are an integral part of society; rather than reflecting it, they are often powerful agents in its 'making'.

This argument leads us to write a little differently from many of our predecessor historians in the education field. Our research backgrounds are rather more in social history than in institutional and administrative history. The latter areas are hardly neglected in this book, but we take a strong interest in the experience of different social groups in schools. We pay more attention to what goes on within the four walls: to teachers, curriculum and occasionally the mundane daily rituals of the school day. We differ from our predecessors in terms of our attention to the local, and the relationships between the local and national, peripheries and centres.

Besides attending to the clear need to develop a narrative and analysis of the last half-century, we look at topics that have tended to be neglected in previous general histories of schooling and education. We insist that the school experiences of Aboriginal and Torres Strait Islander peoples need to become a significant part of the national story. We pay more attention to the private providers of schools, especially before the large church collegiate schools, and government and Catholic school systems, dominated provision. We incorporate Catholic schooling into the national story. Inattention to its development produces a very weak understanding of why Australian schooling has such peculiar characteristics, including the strength of the non-government sector in comparison with similar nations.

Issues surrounding compulsory schooling have been a preoccupation of Australian policy-makers since the *Education Acts* of the late nineteenth century. They are an important issue in this book. The lower and upper ages of compulsion varied from colony to colony in the nineteenth century, and from state to state in the twentieth. Significant social consequences—especially for families and household economies—have resulted from compulsory schooling.

The idea of a path through schooling beginning with 'primary', followed by 'secondary' and perhaps aiming for 'tertiary' education—a well-ordered three-stage process—is, at the earliest, a rather late nineteenth-century idea in Australia. The experience of a routine three-step educational path was not common until well after World War II. In the nineteenth century, the 'elementary' schools were mostly stand-alone institutions, with no expectation that pupils would progress beyond them. In this book, we pay most attention to the history of the primary and secondary school, but we also track the development of early childhood education in its various institutional forms.

Fulfilling our intentions with a limited number of words means that the text occasionally suggests a range of schooling relationships rather than providing explication in detail. Where readers require more, at the end of each chapter they will find recommended further reading. However, as we explain below, there are areas within the history of Australian schooling that remain under-researched.

We had other aims in writing this book. We wanted to shift the locus of our history away from an over-concentration on Victoria and New South Wales. The colonies and states of Australia have common and uncommon histories. We wanted to show that small localities often have unique schooling histories. We also wanted to attend to the experiences of children and youth within schools. This last intention has been difficult to fulfil. We have subsequently made young people the main subject of the illustrations used in the book. They look out at us as readers and authors, often suggesting that there are great gaps between the published narratives of schooling and the lived experiences of its participants.

In all this, we have been very dependent on scholarship in the history of education field over the past 40 years or so. During this period, attention shifted from institutional and system histories, and biographical studies of significant founders and leaders, towards studies of localities, schooling cultures, school populations and biographical studies of ordinary teachers and sometimes young people. In this project, we point to the evolving nature of teaching and teachers. We point to the changing gender relations and expectations both within and of schools. Teachers, teaching, curriculum, childhood, youth and families—each of these has radically changed its character and social significance over time, and it is one of the challenges of this book to show how this has occurred in relation to the school.

In Australia, a number of historians—especially a group of social and feminist historians—have mined hitherto neglected archives to write rich accounts of particular incidents or experiences of ordinary individuals or groups, thereby illuminating the ways in which nineteenth- and early twentieth-century teachers, students and families operated within schools and school systems. However, the published research on which we have depended in writing this history remains patchy. Two areas that have received some attention, yet require much more, are histories of the curriculum and histories of the daily lives of children, youth, teachers and parents as they experienced schooling. Perhaps the most alarming absence in the field is the lack of consolidated and reliable histories of Aboriginal and Torres Strait Islander schooling.

In the writing of this book, we have not undertaken any new search of the archives. We have seen our main job as the reinterpretation of the existing published record, and bringing new perspectives to old controversies. We have been particularly dependent on those historians of an earlier generation who published great collections of documents relating to educational history. We have listed these separately as the first part of this book's bibliography. The re-reading of these document collections is highly fruitful, even though the questions we asked of the material were not necessarily those that their compilers originally had in mind. We have organised our story on a chronological basis, giving more words to the period after 1901 than before. This has allowed us to create more unified portraits of particular periods than otherwise would have been possible.

In this book, we argue that schools as institutions, and what happened inside them, have been highly significant in the lives of Australians. The school signifies purposeful, organised and concentrated effort in the shaping of young people. School founders and operators had and have multiple and ambitious purposes, despite the various reforms that appear to narrow their impact, such as the 'back to the basics' movement in curriculum. We also note that, despite the various attempts in the 1960s and 1970s to imagine societies that might be de-schooled, schools remain a significant feature of Australian social life. Some essentially nineteenth-century institutions, such as the lunatic asylum and orphanage, mainly failed to survive the twentieth century, but schools—like hospitals and prisons—apparently remain institutions without which life in Australia can barely be imagined.

The ambitions of those who built schools, or created systems of schools, have always been great. For most, it was not simply about inculcating literacy and sometimes numeracy, or 'transmitting' high culture or religious truths; it was also about reforming and civilising unruly populations, about inculcating new behaviours, and new ways of thinking and interacting with others. Sometimes it was about forming character, creating citizens, producing leaders or forming loyal subjects, good mothers or productive, compliant or creative workers.

The inventors and managers of schools were rarely content with sharp boundaries that might mark out what schools did from what families and the rest of society were supposed to do. Although this book is about schooling, it asserts the impossibility of clear boundaries between what schools have done and do, and what occurs elsewhere.

Schooling often produces unintended consequences—or intended outcomes that are not always explicit in official documents. An example is the role of schools over the last two centuries as an instrument of colonisation and assimilation, a means of breaking down surviving Indigenous cultures and the remaking of Indigenous society. Another is the aim of some schools to consolidate and foster social elites. Some social groups have not always experienced schools as positive. Schools can confine, can undermine family and local cultures, can oppress populations in many different ways—but the same groups who experience schools in this way may also see them as a way out of their difficulties. The discourse of opportunity, self-improvement and reform also wields power. Opposing discourses can operate as a paradox, working simultaneously on and in the same individuals or social groups.

Individuals, families and other groups often have private requirements of what schools should do for them. Private purposes can rub up against public statements about what schools are supposed to be doing. This is another theme that is pursued in this book.

Australian schooling has never been isolated from global developments, especially those that occurred in Britain, Europe and North America. In some periods, the influences from abroad have been very great indeed. The transnational movements in persons and educational ideas, of curriculum and inspirations for institutional reform, condition our argument—although one country, Australia, and the unique characteristics of its emerging school arrangements are our clear focus.

As authors of this book, we believe that it is time for another good look at the national story. Each generation needs to look afresh at the institutions that organise their lives. Schools as they exist in Australia today are not comprehensible without a strong understanding of their history.

A note on terminology

We have made some careful decisions in this book about the use of terms to describe different kinds of schools. For example, we do not use the commonly recognised term 'private school' to refer to those non-government schools that are owned and run by churches and other incorporated organisations. There are several reasons for this. First, in a work of history it would cause confusion with nineteenth- and early twentieth-century usage. In the nineteenth century, 'private' schools, owned and run by a sole proprietor or a single family, were important providers of schooling. These were usually small schools, and they died out in the competition with larger church and state schools. The use of the word 'private' to denote all non-government schools confuses both narrative and analysis.

All terms have their drawbacks. The term 'independent school', for example, is quite misleading—especially for the international reader. Australian 'independent' schools are currently subsidised by governments, and are part of a regulated education system. Their real independence is limited. When writing about the high-fee 'independent' schools, we have tended to default to the term 'corporate', as used by Sherington and co-authors (1987), which recognises that these schools are usually governed by corporate bodies—that is, they are not part of the bureaucratic systems directly run by government or by the Catholic Education Offices.

Most of our treatment of Catholic schools in this book refers to the parochial schools, which in the wake of the 1973 Karmel Report became 'Catholic systemic' schools. There are corporate or 'independent' Catholic schools as well.

We are aware that different parts of Australia follow different conventions in the naming of government schools. We have used the terms 'public' or 'government' school in this book, while bearing in mind that in the early colonial period the 'public' schools were not necessarily run directly by governments. A further complication is that in some contexts 'public' refers to an altogether different kind of school—that is, a specific small group of high-fee corporate or wealthy 'independent' schools that use the term in the same way that non-government British schools like Eton and Harrow do.

The historical terminology of schooling can be confusing, especially when the same words carry different meanings in different historical periods. A 'grammar' school in the nineteenth century was a school that quite literally taught Latin and often ancient Greek grammar, dominating the curriculum. More recently, it has been used in the names of newer non-government schools as a declaration of academic seriousness.

Finally, the naming of the different kinds of institutions that comprise the early childhood sector remains, in twenty-first century Australia, a historical work in progress. The sector is still very much under construction, with shifting boundaries between 'care' and 'education'. Current nomenclature includes (in chronological order of coinage) infant school, kindergarten, pre-school, child-care centre and early learning centre. In this book, the terms we use for pre-school institutions depend on their immediate historical context.

Further reading

Discussions of the historiography of Australian education occur in W.F. Connell (1987), Miller and Davey (1990), Bessant (1991), Blackmore (1992), Hunter (1994), Theobald (1998), Campbell (1999) and Campbell and Sherington (2002). The previous generation of general histories of Australian education and schools include Austin (1972), Cleverley and Lawry (1972), Hyams and Bessant (1972) and Barcan (1980). The main publication that essayed new interpretations of the historical record arising from the revisionist movement in social history and beyond was edited by Theobald and Selleck (1990). The main record of more recent historical research into Australian schooling occurs in the *History of Education Review*, the journal of the Australian and New Zealand History of Education Society (see <www.anzhes.com>).

CHAPTER

1

Precarious endeavours to 1820

For several decades from 1788, the year of the first British settlement in Australia, schools were of remarkably little consequence for the education of most young people. This was true for both the Aboriginal and British populations. By starting the story in 1788 with the first rude British schools, an injustice is done to the educational work that had proceeded among the peoples of Australia for thousands of years previously.

Even for the children of British settlers, at the end of the eighteenth and into the early nineteenth century, 'schools' with four walls and persons whose profession was that of 'teacher' were usually marginal to their lives. For those who were to be schooled, there was no agreed age for starting and finishing. The education of most young people in the 'real business of living' usually took place elsewhere. Nevertheless, attempts were made to establish schools—usually with government assistance—in the first colony, New South Wales, and then the later settlements in Van Diemen's Land (Tasmania) and on Norfolk Island.

By attending first to the common ways of educating young people, we can then show how organised schooling became more important over time. The significance of schools increased during the nineteenth and twentieth centuries, but the rates at which schooling became important for different populations varied. Social class, ethnic, religious and 'racial' identities, as well as gender helped govern the take-up of schooling. Consequently, the institution of the school remained alien to many for a long time. The growing coincidence of 'education' and the 'work of the school' is mainly a story of the mid-nineteenth century onwards.

To understand developments in schooling, it is also necessary to note new ideas about human development that increasingly saw childhood as a distinctive life-stage requiring special attention. During the first half of the nineteenth century, most children did not experience the kind of prolonged and protected childhood that was common a century later. Making the modern child was an historical project. New laws were part of the process. Early in the period, the registration of births was haphazard. Childhood finished at the age of 7 years for some—that was the age at which children could be sent to prison. There were no child labour laws. A girl could marry with her parents' consent at 14, a boy at 16; child prostitution was common, according to the documents of the Molesworth Committee on convict transportation (1837). No law required children to attend school.

In this chapter we look at four main topics. The first concerns the education of young Indigenous children before settler contact. Second, we provide a brief survey of the ideas and practices of schooling that the British settlers brought with them. Third, we present a survey of the early schools of Australia. Finally, we look at curricula and teaching methods before 1820.

Educating the young before European contact

Our understanding of education for Aboriginal children and youth before British settlement is usually dependent upon the efforts of Aboriginal people to communicate with missionaries and other Europeans who took an interest. Their understanding of what they heard and saw was limited. For example, the term 'traditional education' is often used, but it suggests a lack of dynamism in Indigenous educational practice. Trade, travel and cultural exchange occurred between different groups from the beginnings of Indigenous occupation, some 50 000 to 60 000 years earlier. Indigenous communities in northern Australia and the Torres Strait interacted with traders from Sulawesi from the eighteenth century. The Dutch and other

Europeans visited western and northern Australia for close to two centuries before 1788. There were plenty of reasons for 'traditional education' to adapt as external contact, trade and local circumstances changed and developed.

The education of Aboriginal children varied across Australia. We know there were close to three hundred major language groups. We also know that the histories, cultures and economies of these peoples varied, responsive as they were to local conditions—as well as their understandings of how they came to live in particular places. Each group of people had its ways of organising in order to survive and prosper in its own 'country'. Yet, if there were differences among Aboriginal peoples, there were similarities as well.

A child first needed to survive both birth and the dangerous period immediately following. Deliberate instruction of children necessarily occurred, usually in informal settings. It was more obvious for boys as they approached initiation, the crucial passage towards adulthood. Ronald and Catherine Berndt (1977, p. 167) tell us that had a boy not been wild, and instead had 'listened to his elders, shown willingness and ability to remember what he is told, and if his spear is straight and his skill as a hunter is developing, he may not have to wait long for the first rite'.

In some places, there is evidence of sex-specific songs and dances for young people. Pre-initiation instruction for boys came close to being formal. Other learning associated with language acquisition, food collecting, hunting, constructing shelters, and much ceremonial and sacred life, and the skills associated with making tools, weapons and clothing, were learned through opportunistic instruction. It is likely that girls remained closer to their mothers for longer than boys, and through assisting with tasks learned their duties early. There was also the complex business of learning about relationships, among kin and others: the persons who were safe to associate with, and those not; the question of whose authority was decisive and whose was not.

Puberty, menstruation, 'marriage'—each of these potentially involved the preparation and instruction of young people. Nor was such instruction always cerebral. Bodies could be scarred, groups of young people isolated from their usual social groups and teeth ceremonially knocked out as part of the process.

The learning associated with daily life was integrated with the broader cultural understanding that derived from Aboriginal 'dreamings'. These stories differed from country to country. They could inspire song, music and dance of great mythic and poetic statement. There were also great and long-lasting visual arts traditions. The topography of country itself, the form and activity of living creatures—these were all evidence of the mythic work of ancestral beings. The expression of dreamtime traditions changed over time, but their learning was an integral part of the lives of young Aboriginal people.

Access to different parts of the tradition was differentiated. In making the distinctions, as important as gender and age were family and 'totemic' or 'skin' associations. There were different kinds of 'custodianship' of the sacred and secret, of the different elements of the tradition.

We can draw some tentative conclusions about the educational experiences of Aboriginal children and youth, and speculate on the reasons for their resistance to early attempts to 'school' them. It is likely that most Aboriginal education was for immediate use in daily life. There was less of the disjunction between the 'learn this now' and 'it might be useful later on'. There was likely a stronger element of cooperative learning. Education was more closely integrated with the demands of the local environment, and the immediate pressure to secure food and shelter—though this was hardly absent from the education, if not schooling, of colonial children either.

It is likely that the moral and social education of Aboriginal children was performed with less stress than in the colonial society. 'Law'—and responses to its breaking—could be punitive in both societies, but there was likely less disjunction between 'authority' and 'people'. It was difficult to negotiate the distinctions of rank, caste and class in British-colonial society, and the privileges and oppressions that were intensified in its convict society form. This could lead to rather more alienation and resistance among those who felt hard done by than in Aboriginal societies.

The differences between Aboriginal and European society, including approaches to children and their education, were great. T.G. Strehlow (1947) reported the words of a 'ceremonial chief' of the Aranda people in central Australia. There is a sense of a different approach to the land and the lives of its people:

> Our fathers taught us to love our own country, and not to lust after the lands belonging to other men. They told us that *Ilbalintja* was the greatest bandicoot (*gurra*) totemic centre amongst the Aranda people, and that, in the beginning, bandicoot ancestors had come from every part of the tribe to *Ilbalintja* alone and had stayed there forever: so pleasing was our home to them.

The great traditions of the group (*tjuruna*) were to be learned slowly: 'An overpowering interest in the sacred traditions must be stimulated, but not satisfied.' If members of the group showed themselves worthy, then their curiosity could be satisfied later.

The educational traditions of Aboriginal peoples across Australia differed according to their language, spiritual and material cultures. The means of managing the land affected education. There might be the learning of tidal fish-trapping in the south, and the management of hunting on open plains through the burning of scrub elsewhere. The mining and use of minerals such as different ochres used for ceremonial purposes, and their trade, as well as the making and exchange of specialised tools, woven bags and ritual objects—all these were to be learned.

In the countries of each Aboriginal people were places for meeting, residing and the harvesting of certain foods—usually on a seasonal basis. There were also places of spiritual power, perhaps dangerous or forbidden to different persons within the group. These geographies of association and spirit were linked to the totemic and spiritual significance of certain animals and other beings—all of this was to be learned. Without such knowledge, Aboriginal peoples were unlikely to prosper. Education was essential for life. The schooling brought by the British to late eighteenth-century Australia must have appeared a mean affair. The literacies essential to social life were to be replaced by the mean literacies of the slate and book, and initially to Aboriginal people at least, were characterised by a powerful irrelevance to the conditions of daily life.

Ideas about children and schooling brought to New South Wales

Early in the eighteenth century in England, the Church of England had victories over Congregationalists, Baptists and other dissenters and non-conformists, and Roman Catholics in religion. Laws excluded dissenters from the universities, and in some cases the right to teach in schools. By the end of the century, as the French Revolution proceeded and Napoleonic aggression followed, an association was often made between dissent in religion, disloyalty to the nation and social unrest.

The exclusions directed against Protestant dissenters and Roman Catholics led to the establishment of schools other than those of the Church of England. Many of the dissenting academies for boys were interested in curricula that went beyond the classics-based grammar school subjects. There was often an interest in applied science and mathematical studies that supported engineering and navigation, and 'English' subjects such as bookkeeping that supported commerce. Such academies were almost always middle-class schools. The education of 'gentlemen' through the Church of England-endowed grammar schools was concentrated on the classics and supported entrance to the universities of Oxford and Cambridge.

There was often resistance to any kind of school education being provided for the labouring classes—especially late in the eighteenth century, when a literate labouring class was seen as potentially dangerous. Nevertheless, throughout the eighteenth century, agencies associated with the Church of England founded charity schools for girls and boys. The Society for the Promotion of Christian Knowledge (SPCK) was the most active of these. With the King James Bible and the catechism at the heart of the curriculum, many hundreds of schools were founded or reorganised during the century. Curricula of charity schools often included practical subjects along with the elementary reading, writing and religion. The schools were funded haphazardly. The funding of schools in New South Wales would be similarly haphazard. Early governors contributed direct grants, subsidies and redirections of fines and duties alongside private donations.

By the early nineteenth century, there was a Church of England 'National Society' that promoted national schools in England, though the establishment of such schools usually depended on local initiatives. There were problems for these schools, as the rise of child labour associated with the mines and factories of the Industrial Revolution meant less time for schooling. It was the rare industrialist who imagined a schooling regime during the working week for his child labourers—Robert Owen was exceptional in this regard. In part, the Sunday school was invented to compensate. Sunday schools were often associated with dissenters, and were therefore deemed suspect by the established Church of England and its supporters. For example, the Wesleyans—the 'Methodists'—advocated an approach to lived religion that included intensive Bible study. Reading and writing were central to the Wesleyan vision of self and social discipline, and spiritual and worldly improvement.

The two most influential chaplains appointed by the British government to New South Wales were influenced by such approaches. Their church was Anglican, but they were moved by the idea of personally lived religion. Richard Johnson and Samuel Marsden both organised schooling for convict and emancipist children in the early years of the colony. As it happened, they were often forced to appoint Wesleyans and other dissenters as schoolmasters—they had little choice.

Conservative approaches to education travelled with governors and chaplains to the colony. The context was the difficulty of survival so far from Britain and the overwhelming fact of the penal colony. Many convicts were reluctant to work, and maintenance of law and order was often a brutal process. It followed that officially supported schools would resemble the charity and national schools of England. They were typified by a narrow curriculum and an approach to the child that insisted on order and 'control'. Dissenter schoolmasters—usually convict or emancipist—were often in agreement. John Wesley himself had argued that the salvation of the child was dependent on the breaking of the child's will. No parent, no person in authority, could responsibly countenance a lax approach to the raising of children in a society such as New South Wales.

This approach contrasted with new ideas about the child and education that had appeared in Europe by the late eighteenth century. In France, Rousseau's *Emile* had advocated an education arising from the natural curiosity of children, unforced by the discipline of the schoolroom. The Swiss reformer Pestalozzi had also begun his projects, which became central to progressive schooling in the next century. In England, there were educators responsive to 'continental' ideas such as these, but in Australia there would be few glimpses of such influences for several decades. Government-sponsored schools would concentrate on the control and reform of the 'criminal' classes brought to the new colony. They would also support old and new hierarchies of social rank and class.

Through the eighteenth century in Britain, a great variety of schools existed. Few of them attracted the direct interest of government, and none had enrolments compelled by law. Britain stood apart from developments in Prussia, Sweden and Massachusetts for example, that pioneered the compulsory schooling of children.

Private schools, endowed grammar schools, dissenting and other academies, Church of England charity and national schools, among others, constituted the schooling landscape of Britain. There were also vocational and industrial schools. Dame schools flourished in villages and the poorer parts of cities and towns. These were the schools favoured by the labouring classes. They were likely run by a neighbour—maybe a woman who had lost her husband. There was flexibility over attendance and fees. Infants could attend in the care of older brothers and sisters, and children were easily withdrawn when parents required their labour. Such schools would also be formed in the Australian colonies. They constitute the kind of school we know least about—they rarely show up in surviving records.

Schools were responsive to social class and rank in Britain. Private schools, academies and grammar schools, greater and lesser, existed separately for boys and sometimes girls of the aristocracy, landed gentry, the rising bourgeoisie and lesser middle classes, poorer farmers and the great numbers of the labouring classes. This understanding of schools and schooling divided by rank and class arrived in New South Wales. Religion also divided education.

Such tensions were often exacerbated in the colony by its unusual rank, class and religious configurations. The new colony barely registered inhabitants from the upper ranks and classes of Britain. A new ruling or upper class would be created from those associated with the military and governing elite, and the slow trickle of wealthier free settlers. Later, there would be entrepreneurial emancipists who accumulated wealth from various sources, but whose status as former convicts excluded them from 'respectable society' for a long time. Substantial numbers of Irish Roman Catholic convicts also led to challenges. And then there was 'race'. Aboriginal people might on occasion be conceived as objects of charity, but almost never as persons equal to whites. Schooling arrangements in New South Wales would be shaped by these divisions.

The distinctive British communities that were established in New South Wales and Van Diemen's Land in the late eighteenth century inherited ideas about schooling that came from 'home'—but they were also adapted to the new circumstances.

Beginning schools in Australia

Isabella Rosson's school is the first we know of in the colony, likely conducted outdoors in a tent or rough hut. Though sponsored by the first colonial chaplain, it was likely a dame school of sorts. It was in existence in 1789. Rosson had been convicted for the theft of a waistcoat and bed curtains in 1787. She would marry another convict teacher, thereby forming one of the first 'teaching families' in the colony. She eventually earned her freedom and returned to England. Her few pupils in 1789 were probably the children of convicts.

It can be argued that the first governors of New South Wales gave the establishment of small schools greater priority than they did places of worship. This was a reflection on the pragmatic outlook of the founders, who sought to maintain social order through gathering the children of convicts together and teaching them the basics, including how to sign their names. There was concern for the 'rising generation' and the future. Here, the thinking was influenced by the Enlightenment and Lockean thought which asserted the power of education to mould lives for the better.

The colonial chaplains were usually in charge of schools. In this period, the most significant were Richard Johnson, Samuel Marsden and Henry Fulton. They were not independent, being accountable to the governors of the colony and their instructions about schooling. At the same time, the chaplains were expected to take their own initiatives. Government could assist these with buildings and the provision of convict labour. Government stores could provide rations and other goods. However, none of this assistance, including wages for teachers, was very dependable.

In giving evidence to a parliamentary committee in London, ex-Governor Hunter stated that the best he had been able to do was 'to give a particular artificer the charge of a boy to teach him his profession, and make him answerable for his conduct' (Select Committee on Transportation, 1812: Appendix, p. 22). This was about apprenticeship, not schooling. Hunter did meet children in schools once each year to examine them. He expected to see specimens of their work, and evidence of improvement. Ex-Governor Bligh said that during his time as governor (1805–09), he had required the chaplains, Marsden and Fulton, to attend all the 'private' schools to see that they were well regulated. He thought that in his period as governor some 400 children had had some schooling (Appendix, pp. 33–40). This was a small number. In 1810, the number of children—British and Irish, of course—in the colony was reported as 2721.

Government assistance for schools was less contested than it was in England, and the reason is easy to discern. As a penal colony, nearly all the British/Irish population was dependent on government, with neither the church nor chaplains independent of government. Government involvement in schooling was accepted as legitimate and necessary—although this did not mean an absence of disagreement about the involvement. The issues were remarkably long-lived. They

Responsible to the Governor for schooling in New South Wales was colonial chaplain Richard Johnson. He was active in the colony from 1788–1798. Through religion, the Church of England variety, the gifts of education, social order, civilisation and even salvation, could be brought to all. (Dixson Galleries, State Library of NSW, P1/854)

included the respective responsibilities of chaplains (churches) and government, the kinds of schools and curriculum thought appropriate to different sections of the population and the levels of direct control over schools. They also included disagreement about who might be acceptable as school teachers, what remuneration they should receive and their social status.

Government support of schools was dependent on cooperation from the Colonial Office and various church organisations in England. The Colonial Office usually supported colonial initiatives, but there were occasional directives that expenses be curtailed. For example, if there were to be schools for orphans, only the most destitute children should be enrolled. Church societies in England, such as the Society for the Propagation of the Gospel (SPG), the Society for the Propagation of Christian Knowledge (SPCK) or the London Missionary Society (LMS), were engaged in the struggle to provide suitable teaching texts and teachers. The LMS was a joint effort by evangelical Anglicans and members of dissenting churches.

Support from Britain was spasmodic. The delays in communication meant that one or two years could pass before requests were dealt with—or judgements passed on the initiatives of colonial authorities. Nevertheless, when the Colonial Office or missionary societies eventually spoke, policies changed as a result.

Two inquiries into the Australian settlements were initiated by the British government in the first 35 years. Both had something to say about education. The 1812 report of the Select Committee on Transportation and the Bigge Inquiry, conducted in 1819–21, remarked on the progress of schooling in the colonies. By the 1820s, there were settlements in Van Diemen's Land as well as New South Wales. The Bigge report and evidence alert us to the bitter politics of the main colony. Bigge was antagonistic towards Governor Macquarie's policies that hastened the entry of emancipists (ex-convicts) into 'society'. Schools were affected. There was a problem—especially for the emergent free settler and 'exclusivist' (non-convict, well-off, 'respectable') families—in allowing their children to be taught by convicts and emancipists, and also allowing their children to mix in the same schools with the children of convicts and emancipists.

In 1795, Elizabeth Macarthur, one of the wealthiest exclusivists, reflected on the favourable conditions in the colony as they affected her family. But there was

> the difficulty of educating our children, & were it otherwise it would be unjust towards them to confine them to so narrow a society. My

> desire is that they may see a little more of the world, & better learn to appreciate this retirement. Such as it is the little creatures all speak of going home to England with rapture—My dear Edward almost quitted me without a tear. (Quoted in Niall and Britain, 1997, p. 1)

There have always been difficulties in categorising Australian schools. The words 'public' and 'private' developed contrary meanings from the way they were used in Britain. In this book, the 'private' school is a school that is owned by individuals or families, a school that rarely received government assistance. Early in the colony, many schools were resourced at least partly by the colonial government. We tend to talk about them as 'government-assisted' rather than 'private' schools. An example of the difficulty occurs when ex-Governor Bligh in 1812 talked of schools in colonial Sydney and nearby districts. There was only one 'public school' in the colony—the orphan school for girls—but it was the government that identified locations for the several 'private' schools and not only remunerated their teachers but provided other forms of support. The 'private' schools were often supervised by government officials—the colonial chaplains.

Therefore, the earliest Australian schools were mainly government assisted. Richard Johnson took his responsibilities seriously. He sought to establish schools with reliable convicts as teachers. He brought with him tracts that would be used to moralise the convict population. They included 100 copies each of *Exhortations of Chastity* and *Dissuasions from Stealing*, and 200 of *Exercises Against Lying*, among others. He also brought two primers for teaching reading and spelling to children. Despairing that no church had been built in the early days of the colony, he caused a large, mainly timber building to be erected in Sydney in 1793. It was used as both church and school. Both Parramatta and Sydney had schools with convict mistresses and masters before the turn of the century. Not much later, there were government-assisted schools in different parts of the Sydney hinterland, including Toongabbie, Kissing Point and the Hawkesbury area. At least from Governor Macquarie's time, there were schools associated with the newly established villages at Liverpool and along the Hawkesbury River, at Windsor, Wilberforce and Richmond.

Attendance at such schools was usually considered disappointing. Teachers were often in the job for too short a time. Some were condemned as drunkards or considered unsatisfactory in other ways. A convict as teacher was always a pragmatic solution to the shortage of 'fit' persons. In 1798, a group of missionaries—free men—arrived from Tahiti and, despite their dissenting background, were immediately seen as potential non-convict teachers. In the main, they also turned out to be 'unreliable'.

One missionary did have an impact on schooling. William Crook was accepted as a missionary by the London Missionary Society (LMS), sailing for the south-west Pacific in 1796 and again in 1803. These ventures were mainly unsuccessful for him personally. By 1804 he was in Sydney, and engaged by Marsden to teach school in Parramatta. He reported to the LMS that two convicts had been assigned him to assist with the teaching, and that missionaries had a bad reputation in the colony. Crook said he would have been more effective had he been a free settler. Assuming the role of a Congregationalist minister, he conducted church services in and beyond Parramatta as well as conducting school. Later, after the deposing of Governor Bligh, he ran a boys' school that included boarders in Sydney. He also organised evening classes. Crook ran into trouble in 1810 through accepting an appointment from the conspirators against Governor Bligh. Marsden also made difficulties for him: Crook was apparently running Congregationalist church services, though he was not ordained as a minister. He left the colony briefly, but in 1811 his Sydney school was reopened, this time following the monitorial plan developed by Joseph Lancaster in England. We shall discuss the new monitorial approaches to schooling in their dissenting (Lancastrian) and Church of England (national, Bell or Madras) forms later. In 1813, Crook resumed evening classes for apprentices, and in 1814 employed a teacher, freeing himself for more preaching. At the end of that year he again left for missionary work in Tahiti, returning in 1830, when he founded yet another school in Sydney.

Crook's story underlines the difficulties for teachers negotiating around the colonial chaplains and the unstable politics surrounding governors. Schools were vulnerable not only to the variable enthusiasms of powerful individuals, but to those of teachers themselves. At the same time, in Crook's case at least, there was both market awareness (a demand for boarding schools, evening classes and instruction for apprentices) and an interest in pedagogic reform—in this case, monitorialism. The story also reminds us that the colony was part of other European efforts in the south-west Pacific. In 1815, for example, Marsden proposed and later established a school for Maori in Sydney.

In 1804, the *Sydney Gazette* announced the opening of two new boys' private schools. Parnell's academy offered the common English subjects, while Mitchell's academy offered the French language and mathematics as well—Mitchell's previous work had been satisfactory to 'many respectable gentlemen' in the colony. In 1806 and 1807, there were advertisements for private girls' schools. Mrs Williams offered training in morals and deportment, then reading, writing and arithmetic, plain and fine needlework and tambour work. Mrs Merchant asserted her respectability by promising attention to the morals and manners of her charges. Two years later, Mrs Hodges offered tuition to young 'ladies'.

Throughout the nineteenth century, 'respectability' was prime currency in the education of girls, especially for the growing middle classes. Credibility required that schoolmasters and mistresses needed to establish their own. Respectability was a rare commodity among the colonists of New South Wales and Van Diemen's Land. It was something for colonial families on the make to acquire—but that might be a long-term project. The right school could help. By 1820, W.C. Wentworth thought there were several 'exclusive' private girls' academies in existence, but in a society riven by controversies over rank and respectability, Wentworth himself hardly passed muster in some circles.

There are inaccuracies in the reports and evidence of Commissioner Bigge's inquiry. Nevertheless, they give us insight into the condition of schooling by 1820. The 1810–20 period saw substantial developments in economy and society, with a stronger civil society emerging—one that bore hope for emancipist families that they had a future in the colony. Bigge tells us that the dissenters—Wesleyan Methodists in particular—had three meeting places in the area around Sydney. At

Windsor, he observed a very well-run and attended Sunday school. There were two schools in Sydney 'under the immediate protection of the government', which were conducted by teachers recruited from England. One of them was reorganised on the 'national system', so reading, writing and cyphering (arithmetic) were taught as Bell's (Church of England) monitorial system required. Nevertheless, both attendance and progress of pupils were generally faulty.

At Parramatta, there was a school for children of the 'middle classes'. Though families paid fees, the school was still government assisted, with both the school teacher's house and the school itself being the property of the government. Teachers in other schools received government rations and limited payment from parents. By 1821, according to Bigge, there were eleven schools that were not supported by government. There was also a regimental school for children of the military. Bigge estimated that some 990 children attended school, if irregularly, but the 'muster' of 1821 suggested there were 7568 children—of European origin—in the colony. In country districts, the distance between home and school was usually an insuperable barrier to attendance.

Bigge reported the belief by Robert Cartwright, Church of England chaplain, that 'there was no want of inclination in the parents, generally, to educate their children, whatever might be the irregularity of their own lives'. In such a statement we dare to hear some labouring-class voices. Cartwright went on to argue that the challenge was 'to extend the system of education in the districts, and even in the towns of New South Wales'. He also argued the dominant view of the ruling caste that, despite any enthusiasm for schooling, what was provided should give 'as little control as possible . . . to the parents over the time, the habits, or disposition of their children' (Bigge, 1823, p. 74).

Bigge reported that Sunday schools were not being established quickly enough, although Marsden feared them as sites for proselytisation by dissenters and negative comment on the Church of England. Bigge argued that schooling effort in the colony had been reasonably vigorous. He argued for more and better teachers, and more admissions of children into schools. Only with such an effort could 'the influence of the bad habits of the parents . . . be successfully resisted' (Bigge, 1823, p. 78).

Bigge had also reported on the situation in Van Diemen's Land. Schools there had similar problems to those in the pre-Macquarie period in New South Wales. Convicts were considered unsatisfactory as teachers, but there were few alternatives. By 1821, the Hobart school was run by a free man, but convicts on rations, supplemented by parent contributions, taught reading and writing in small schools elsewhere. The number of children under instruction in schools was 193 from a muster count of 1021.

In 1818, colonial chaplain William Cowper composed rules for the government-assisted schools in New South Wales. They tell us something of the desired spirit of the schools, but there were likely practical difficulties that interfered with their full observance:

1. The object of these schools is to afford useful and religious instruction to the children of the poor in general.
2. Children shall be admitted from five to twelve years of age.
3. The children's attendance at school, during five days in the week, shall be from nine o'clock in the morning til twelve, and in the afternoon from two til five. NB—No attendance on Saturday.
4. The master shall be particularly mindful of the children's moral behaviour, cleanliness and regular attendance.
5. The children, according to their ages and improvements, shall be taught reading, English, writing, arithmetic; and the catechism of the Church of England.
6. The school-business of every day shall be commenced with singing part of a psalm or hymn and a short prayer.
7. A muster book shall be kept by the Master shewing the attendance of each scholar, both morning and afternoon; and a monthly report of the numbers, progress, changes etc., shall be made to the Resident Chaplain, who will frequently visit and inspect the schools.
8. The children who are admitted to the great privilege of being taught in these schools on the five days, shall be required also to attend on the Sunday, both morning and afternoon, before the hours of divine service; and on this day, they may bring with them any other

> children, who shall be disposed to come and receive instruction. After commencing, as in rule 6th, all present shall be variously exercised in lessons of piety, scripture reading, or in learning to read, until they shall proceed to the church for public worship, under the care of the Master. NB. The necessity of this rule arises from the impiety, the ignorance, or the negligence of the parents, through whose carelessness and disregard it is well known that, if children be not assembled for some good and useful purpose, they will assemble themselves for mischief and disorder. (*Historical Records of Australia*, Ser. 3, vol. 2, 1921, p. 358.)

These rules expanded an earlier set composed by the first chaplain, Richard Johnson, in 1798.

Schools for 'orphans' and 'natives'

The leaders of the civil and military establishment in the colonies had few illusions and many prejudices concerning the people they were required to control, organise and discipline. Condemnation of most convicts and colonists as unruly at best, and vicious at worst, was common. If adults were beyond redemption, there was often the hope that something must be done with the children. There was the prediction that cycles of criminality, viciousness and immorality would continue into the future unless there were interventions; unless at the very least, the most destitute of the children, the least likely to have parents who could raise them properly, and the most in danger of becoming criminals, were removed from the likely sources of 'contagion'.

As a consequence, the boarding out of boys and their apprenticing were to be supplemented by the establishment of confining institutions. Girls were the first targeted. They, it was argued, had the potential through ungoverned sexual activity to reproduce cycles of viciousness indefinitely. Jeremy Bentham in England was a strong advocate of the redemptive potential of well-conducted confinement. If panopticon buildings were beyond the resources of the colony, then barracks and orphan schools were not. However, the institutionalisation of the desperate went back much further than the eighteenth century. Workhouses had a history from Tudor times, though the attachment of an educational mission came later. Samuel Marsden put the case in the colony:

> Remote, helpless, distressed, and young, these are truly the children of the State, and though at present very low in the ranks of society, their future numerous progeny, if care is not taken of the parent stock, may by their preponderancy over balance and root out the vile depravities bequeath'd by their vicious progenitors. (*Historical Records of New South Wales*, 1892– , vol. 6, pp. 381–2)

It was an argument for breaking the link between parent and child. Gendered assumptions about unsatisfactory mothers and the differing vulnerabilities of girls and boys would help determine the character of the institutions provided.

Philip Gidley King ruled a subordinate convict settlement on Norfolk Island from late 1789. By 1796, he was sufficiently moved by the circumstances of the girls in particular to establish an orphan school. Charitable sentiment coexisted with the discourse of discipline and control. In 1801, he was governor of New South Wales, and in Sydney moved a second time, establishing another orphan school for girls. This school had many difficulties: trustworthy staff were difficult to find, and illnesses and deaths of inmates regularly occurred. Many of its girls appeared little 'reformed' on departure—prostitution was the great threat. Nevertheless, there was some separation of girls from the rest of society, and some attempt to provide a useful curriculum, often based around the skills of the seamstress, as well as reading and writing. Not all the inmates were actual orphans. Many mothers and sometimes fathers voluntarily surrendered their children as their circumstances sank low. The female orphan school survived into the middle of the nineteenth century.

Governance of this school, and of the male orphan school that opened in 1819, varied across the years. There was the expected participation of the colonial chaplains, but also the appointment of supervisory committees of respectable persons. They could include the wives of governors and other officials. As official 'visitors', they often

Without sufficient protection or encouragement towards useful lives, girls were at risk, and a danger. Girls were to be saved from immorality and disorder in the Female Orphan School, Parramatta. This building housed the school from 1818. Artist: Joseph Lycett. (National Gallery of Australia, 84.125.13)

had a beneficial influence in modifying harsh institutional regimes. Elizabeth Paterson, wife of the lieutenant governor in King's time, wrote of her hopes for orphan institutions. The children would be 'entirely secluded from . . . other people', and there would be a time 'when the young men will become useful members of society, and the women faithful and industrious wives' (in Bubacz, 2007). This was language familiar in the charity and national schools in England. Before the end of its first year, Governor King was cheerfully writing back to England that deserted female orphans had been 'rescued from the scenes of prostitution and iniquity, that disgraces the major part of the inhabitants of this colony' (*Historical Records of Australia*, 1914– , vol. 3, p. 123). The school at various periods would become a 'showpiece' for the colonial administration. By 1806, Marsden was reporting successes: six orphans between 1801 and 1806 had been married and a further eleven apprenticed to officers' wives. The relationship between the schooling of destitute girls and training for domestic service was begun early.

The orphan schools were conceived as 'total' institutions. The detailed rules that Governor Macquarie composed in 1818 organised each day by the minute, and laid down uniform clothing ('suitable to their condition in life'), what children were to be fed and the curriculum.

In some respects, the official approach towards the educational needs of destitute white children resembled thinking about Aboriginal children. They should be separated from probably irredeemable parents and communities; and they should be 'moralised', and turned into dutiful servants and labourers who might even become respectable through Christian conversion and marriage. Richard Johnson and Samuel Marsden, colonial chaplains, each took Aboriginal children into their homes—with manifest insensitivity towards the consequences of separation. Attempts to make the children grateful for kindnesses, and the opportunity to participate in their households as domestic servants in training, were unsuccessful. These failed experiments with Aboriginal children continued well into the nineteenth and twentieth centuries. Early attempts to re-socialise—to 'civilise'—Aboriginal children involved re-education, and schooling itself came soon enough. Children would be taken at a young age, to maximise the chance of breaking community bonds.

William Shelley, a Methodist-leaning Congregationalist with a London Missionary Society background, persuaded Governor Macquarie towards a school—a Native Institution—for Aboriginal children. Shelley had already started a private 'native' school before the 1815 official school starting date. The government sponsored a meeting at Parramatta in 1814, attended by some 60 Aboriginal people, many of whom were suspicious. By the end of the day there were a mere four children volunteered for the institution, adding to the four associated with Shelley's previous efforts. The numbers in the Native Institution were always small. Some of the children escaped and returned to their communities; parents also liberated their children from time to time.

The violence of colonialism was real as Indigenous children were brought to colonial schooling, despite the charitable sentiments expressed by the initiators. They argued that 'opportunity' was being delivered, and occasionally that such schooling provided some recompense for the clear damage done to the Aboriginal peoples by British settlement.

At the end of 1819, there were French visitors to the Native Institution. Rose Marie de Freycinet wrote that she had met some of its 30 children:

> The boys cultivate the garden . . . The girls are taught the tasks suitable to their sex . . . We saw the house where these little savages are kept: the advances they have already made are truly astonishing, and think how valuable a work! These children thus taught, will carry to the homes of their families the germs of civilisation, which cannot fail to produce good results: to appreciate this benefit it is only necessary to look at the present state, the miserable air, of the natives one sees in the streets of Sydney. (Quoted in Brook and Kohen, 1991, p. 79)

By 1820, of the 37 children enrolled, ten had either died or returned to their communities. Elizabeth Shelley, the director after the death of her husband, wrote in 1838 that the project was a failure. The girls who married black men returned to their old ways, and boys who went to sea were not heard of again. When she talked religion with old girls, they laughed, saying 'they had forgotten all about it'. At least there was the fleeting triumph at an Anniversary School Examination in Parramatta in 1819, where Aboriginal and European children demonstrated their proficiencies. The main prize was taken, to the disapproval of many, by an Aboriginal girl.

Pedagogy and curriculum

We have already mentioned one of the earliest academies, that of William Crook. His school had offered an English curriculum—reading, speaking and writing the English language, and instruction in bookkeeping, geometry, trigonometry and mensuration, with applications to navigation, surveying and 'gauging'. In 1810, Thomas Macqueen's school added 'knowledge of the Latin classics' to a similar list. Study of the classics was the curriculum of boys from the upper ranks of society, the staple of grammar schools in England. The classical rather than English curriculum would exist precariously in the colony for some time. It was an aspirational curriculum, for those seeking to climb socially, or to defend hard-won social rank.

Curriculum for the convict and labouring classes was determinedly moralistic and utilitarian. Much of it appeared to be about social control. The curriculum included reading and writing, and perhaps basic arithmetic, often with a parallel 'work skills' element, and moralisation through religion—preferably of the Church of England kind. Catechisms often provided the texts, the content of the literacy curriculum. Isaac Watts' catechisms were brought to the colony. Extracts from the second catechism for children follow. Reading, memorisation and religious duty are the skills to be acquired.

8. *What is God in relation to us, who are his creatures?* A. As the great God is our Maker, who gave us our being, so he continually preserves us, and does us good: He is our Lord and Ruler now, and he will be our Judge at last.
9. *And how do the scriptures teach you to serve God?* A. I must serve God, by keeping all his commandments; that is, by doing every thing, that he requires of me, and avoiding every thing, that he forbids me.
10. *What commandments has God given to men?* A. He gave the law of ten commandments to the Jews in the Old Testament; and they are summed up in two commandments for us in the New Testament . . .
21. *What is the sum of these ten commandments, which is given us in the New Testament?* A. The sum of the ten commandments is: Thou shalt love the Lord thy God with all thy heart; and thou shalt love thy neighbour, as thyself. (Watts, 1815, pp. 8–10)

For girls, the work skills were usually those of plain sewing, the work of the seamstress and sometimes hat-making, as well as the attitudes and accomplishments that would make them useful as domestic servants or as married women raising families. For boys, gardening, shoemaking and the like, sometimes associated with early apprenticeship on the docks, workshops or on farms, also supplemented the reading and writing. Both girls and boys were taught on the assumption that they would be domestic and farm servants, or wage labourers, or perhaps small landholders and renters. It was not a curriculum that encouraged much aspiration beyond their 'natural' place in society. Nevertheless, the intentions of pupils and their families were not necessarily the same as those of the school controllers. There were disturbing cases of the bottom ranks in society 'rising'. Schooling could help with this.

There is some evidence of how teachers taught. The place of catechisms in the curriculum points to the significance of memorised, rote responses to questioning. Popular literacy was often dependent on primers and related texts—religious and moralising tracts produced by the Society for the Promotion of Christian Knowledge. With the rarity of texts and paper, the mind was the place for imprinting the lessons of literacy. The 'individual method' of teaching was dominant. Children were taught, were given texts to learn and were required individually to demonstrate mastery of their lessons. Some students were slow, and drill and corporal punishment were part of the experience. There was a limited sense that groups of children should move forward at the same rate. Learning to read and write depended first on learning the alphabet, then syllables from which words could be constructed, and then words and eventually sentences. In 1810 there was what may have been the first school text printed in Australia—it was a spelling book adapted from an English source. It was distributed to the orphan school, the main Parramatta school and Crook's academy.

A report of the achievements of Aboriginal children from the Native Institution reveals a little of the teaching approach. Many were reading, spelling and writing with some proficiency. 'Maria', age 13, could 'spell four syllables in the Bible and reads', while 'Wallis', 'Jimmy', 'Henry' and 'Maria' could 'repeat the alphabet'. It was the kind of approach to literacy that demanded leaps of faith in the child: a belief that, after all the memorisation and recitation of unconnected series of letters, syllables and words, they might eventually be able to read and write something that made sense.

These first decades in the schools of New South Wales and Van Diemen's Land coincided with a significant pedagogic reform.

Monitorialism offered an approach to teaching and learning that was peculiarly modern. There was an attempt to apply science and system to teaching. Teachers would be trained systematically, though primarily in the apprenticeship mode. The pace and content of instruction would be regularised, and teaching aids would be specified. There would be a regulated labour process for pupils and teachers, and a new school architecture. In some parts of Europe, monitorialism was seen as progressive, as the men of the Enlightenment sought to bring literacy to large numbers of young people, breaking dull subservience to feudalism and the traditionalism of the Roman Catholic Church. In England and New South Wales, the stronger view was to see monitorialism as a means of education that upheld strong discipline. It would concentrate on the basic literacy required for young people's expected working lives.

Monitorialism was complicated by religious rivalry. The Lancastrian version was favoured by the Wesleyans and other dissenters. Its object was often literacy in terms of active Bible reading. The pupil might turn out 'non-conformist' in religious terms. The alternative 'national system', inspired by the writing of Andrew Bell in England, was securely tied to the texts and conformities of the Church of England.

In order to establish the Bell system in the Male Orphan School, Macquarie requested from the Colonial Office in 1821 not only a large supply of Bibles and 'Testaments', but '1,000 small slates, 2,000 slate pencils, 50 doz. black lead pencils, 1,000 complete sets of books, including the cards used in the system, 1,000 stereotyped cards of monosyllables, 100 do. of written characters, 100 do. of figures, 28 Bell's instructions to be given to the masters and mistresses, 200 prayer books, books for rewards and encouragement, a supply of paper and quills' (quoted in Griffiths, 1957, p. 25). This was schooling that was dependent on systematic instructions, practices and apparatus.

The debate over the preferred monitorial system of instruction was an issue for the colonies because many of the early schoolmasters were dissenters, and they favoured the Quaker—Lancaster's version, while Commissioner Bigge recommended the 'national' system. In 1820, Thomas Reddall arrived in the colony. He had attended the Central National School in London to gain proficiency in the Bell system. On arrival in Sydney as chaplain and schoolmaster, he went to work in the Male Orphan School, introducing the system and attracting praise from both Governor Macquarie and Bigge. The Church of England had won a victory.

Ideally, monitorial instruction required a large schoolroom—in some cases, sitting many more than a hundred children at different levels of attainment. There was a single schoolmaster who communicated the lessons through proficient older pupils, the monitors. There were 'stations' around the room set up for the teaching of particular content—whether it be spelling, reading or arithmetic. The monitors assisted pupils through the lock-step curriculum. There was little room for a 'liberal' education. Later critics alluded to similarities with the organisation of factories of the Industrial Revolution. The learning process was broken into specific skills and content that accumulated in an orderly fashion. The literacy curriculum remained based on religion. Learning aids included charts, slates and sometimes sand boxes, in which pupils could trace their letters and calculations. There was an educational psychology, too: cheap cumulative rewards were awarded for achievement—though Bell had less of this than Lancaster. Motivation was encouraged through the application of rewards—and punishments, including the corporal kind.

With so many students in the one schoolroom (there is no such thing as a 'classroom' under monitorialism), the school had to be rigidly controlled. Bells, hand signals, flags and whistles regulated the movement of children. The timetable, the movement of children in and out of the schoolroom, their learning groups (usually rows) all worked like clockwork. Almost a century later, hostile representations of monitorialism by progressive educators helped inspire the 'New Education'.

It is easy to see why monitorialism initially was considered an ideal system of schooling for Australian colonies. It seemed obvious that ill-discipline among the lowest ranks and classes demanded an education based on order and control. The external discipline of schoolmasters helped, but the religiously based monitorial approach apparently internalised 'self-discipline'. There was the possibility of a reformed colonial subject. Lord Bathurst, the Colonial Secretary, expressed it nicely in 1820 when he said that Bell's system would bring youth up 'in the habits of industry and regularity', also implanting in their minds 'the principles of the established church' (quoted in Griffiths, 1957, p. 24).

It was expected that schools would be examined regularly. This often meant the inspection of written work, the hearing of recitations and the answering of questions by colonial chaplains and others from the respectable ranks. Sometimes governors of the colonies would make it their business to undertake this task. Examination of pupils was public business.

•

At the end of this period, the great number of Australian children and youth were still being educated in Aboriginal lands according to long-standing practices. But disruptions were already occurring through Van Diemen's Land and eastern New South Wales. A trail across the Blue Mountains had allowed Bathurst, the first of the inland towns, to be established in 1815. In advance of such settlements came the stories, the fears, the diseases of European settlement. Resistance, the disruptions to traditional education and society and deaths of Aboriginal peoples soon followed.

In Sydney, Parramatta, Hobart and Launceston by 1820, there were schools that were roughly approximate to a restricted range of institutions found in Britain. They were often founded by men, and less often women, who believed that the different ranks of society required different kinds of schooling. The conflicts between dissenters and Church of England conformity were brought to the colony. They also affected schools as institutions.

Something else brought by the ruling group was discrimination against the Roman Catholic Church—a special problem in the colonies, considering the high proportion of Irish in the convict and emancipist population. It was not until 1820 that Catholics had regular access to their own chaplains and the mass. Between 1803 and 1806, a school for Catholic children was founded under Governor King's protection, but suspicion was high. Priests who had arrived in the colony were not allowed to be schoolmasters. According to

King in 1803, priests were likely to install 'improper ideas' in youth, and 'no description of people are so bigoted to their religion and priests as the lower order of the Irish; and such is their credulous ignorance that an artful priest may lead them to every action that is either good or bad' (quoted in Fogarty, 1959, p. 17). A breakthrough appeared with the arrival of the priest Jeremiah O'Flynn in 1817, but Colonial Office permission for him to operate in the colony was not forthcoming. O'Flynn was expelled. If Catholic children were to be educated in government-assisted schools, they would be supervised by Church of England chaplains. In 1810, Marsden had written to William Wilberforce: 'Roman Catholics, Jews, and persons of all persuasions, send their children to the public schools where they are all instructed in the principles of our established religion.' (quoted in Cleverley, 1971, p. 41) Uneasy relations between churches and government over schooling would grow during the nineteenth century.

There was also debate over the populations in which the state as educator should take most interest. The early answer was those children and youth who were considered most vulnerable—or the same thing, the most likely to be the source of future criminality and ill-discipline. There was fair agreement that government and established church needed to be active in correcting and subsuming the rights of unsatisfactory parents when it came to organising the education of their children. The Australian colonies were founded in an age of revolution in Europe. There was reason for engaging schools in the governing of potentially fractious populations—especially in colonies where most inhabitants were or had been criminals.

There were growing possibilities for middle-class schools, but very few for academies and grammar schools that made the classical languages the core of their curricula. The main effort was in elementary education, including the teaching of practical work skills to the children of the labouring class. Where there was advanced education, its core was the English subjects that met the need for bookkeeping, surveying, navigating and the like. Only a minority of young people had even a limited time in schools. This included not only the children of poorer and isolated families, but some from wealthier families, where a home education delivered by mothers or governesses or tutors was probable. Such families often sent boys back to England for schooling. Samuel Marsden sent his daughter, Anne, back in 1800; she remained there until 1810.

Genuine private schools had started up in New South Wales by 1820, with some aiming to enrol the children of wealthier families. Others—such as dame schools—concentrated on poorer children. Government-assisted schools, usually supervised by colonial chaplains, did most of the work.

In practice, the period of childhood dependency, including time that may have been spent in schools, varied among different social groups, as did the amount and difficulty of labour that was demanded of young people. Childhood in the colony was experienced differently according to social class and gender—and race. Child labour of various kinds—paid or unpaid—could start early, as boys and girls contributed to household economies. This might mean staying in the family household or relieving parents of their care by moving elsewhere. Their contributions were often (though not always) demarcated by gender. Girls might be involved in the care of younger siblings or perhaps hired out as housekeepers or nurses for other families. Boys might work on farms, in family businesses or elsewhere for wages. One of the key differences between childhood in Britain and Australia was that the lack of large-scale manufacturing or mining meant that the larger economy did not rely to the same extent on the massed labour of children.

Further reading

On pre-contact Aboriginal childhood and youth, see Mulvaney and White (1987), Berndt and Berndt (1977), King-Boyes (1977) and Paulson (1996). On British childhood, schooling and society before 1820, see Silver and Silver (1974) and Cunningham (1991, 2005). Cleverley (1971) provides the most comprehensive portrait of schools and society in the early years of British settlement. Austin (1972) concentrates on church and state. Ramsland (1986), Kociumbas (1992, 1997) and Windschuttle (1980) are more oriented to social history. Add Bubacz (2007) for the orphan schools. On the Native Institution, see Brook and Kohen (1991). See Mooney

(1997) and Sherington, Petersen and Brice (1987) on early attempts to establish post-elementary schools and academies. See Fogarty (1959) and O'Farrell (1992) for Catholic schooling. For Tasmania, see Reeves (1935) and Phillips (1985). On European educational efforts across the south-west Pacific, see Campbell and Sherington (2007). On monitorialism in the colonies and beyond, see Fletcher (1968) and Kaestle (1973).

CHAPTER

2

School entrepreneurs 1821–1860

This period was marked by the enterprise of owners and teachers of private venture schools. There was a developing market for schools, and astute entrepreneurs—women and men—could make money. A few churches developed more exclusive schools, which would have the primary responsibility for educating boys from the families of the wealthier classes. For girls from the same families, the demand for schooling was not as strong, and where there was demand, private ladies' schools—or, in the Catholic sector, convent schools—could meet the demand.

The argument that children needed more and better schooling—perhaps even in regulated *systems*—became more persuasive from the 1820s. Growing tensions between churches and colonial governments concerning how this might occur ensured that its achievement would be a project marked by setbacks as much as progress.

This was also a period during which different schools were established for different parts of the population. For those Aboriginal children who lived in the occupied lands, schooling—if organised at all—was usually treated as a different kind of endeavour. The main ethno-national divisions within the mainly British/Irish population usually coincided with religious division. The number of Catholic schools grew in this period, and children of Irish origins were the main attendees. There were a small number of Presbyterian schools, mainly for families of Scottish origin, and Lutheran schools for German colonists.

In this period, the idea that girls and boys should be schooled separately was strongest for the wealthier classes. In the government-assisted schools for the poorer classes, separation would only occur if enrolments were substantial. Nevertheless, whether male or female, schooling for prolonged periods was most unlikely for children of the poorest classes. The idea that schooling should be compulsory and free had very few supporters. Compulsion only applied to children institutionalised as orphans, or made the subjects of missionary effort.

From 1820 to 1860, the number of British colonies in Australia grew from two to six. Responsible parliamentary government was established from the mid-1850s in every colony but Western Australia, the only colony in which the convict era continued. The number of free settlers rapidly increased, and the production of copper, wheat, gold and wool contributed to the wealth of individual colonies. The population grew from some 30 000 people of European stock, to 1.152 million. Indigenous people were not often counted by the census-takers. Inland settlement had advanced with pastoral and agricultural expansion, and sometimes schooling developed along with it. Adelaide, Brisbane and Melbourne did not exist in 1820, and nor did major inland towns such as Goulburn and Ballarat. By 1860, they each had a substantial population, a few impressive civic buildings and civic cultures. Schools proliferated—and in Sydney and Melbourne there were universities that sought to spread higher learning and British culture, 'under different skies'.

We begin with a study of the school history of the inland town of Goulburn in New South Wales. It illustrates much about the haphazard development of schools in the mid-century education market.

A developing school market in Goulburn

The settlement of the Goulburn district by British colonists followed rapidly from its exploration and naming about 1820. In 1833, the growing town received official recognition. The census of 1841 counted 655 persons—444 male and 211 female. Of the males, 305 were free and 139 were convicts. Of the females, 200 were free and eleven convicts. Many of the convicts held tickets of leave, enabling them to work and live in relative freedom. In terms of religion, 51 per cent were Church of England, 23 per cent Catholic and 20 per cent Presbyterian. Wesleyans and other dissenters accounted for just over 2 per cent. There were 22 Jews and three 'Muslims/Pagans'. Schooling such a population would be complicated, as there would be resistance to an Anglican monopoly. The families of free settlers would likely not approve the mixing of their children with those of convict origins. The smaller religious denominations would also have difficulty in establishing schools.

There were dame schools in Goulburn in the 1830s. These were usually ephemeral, with the teachers often widowed or separated women. Nevertheless—they gave some instruction to children from poorer circumstances and of all ages, including infants. Churches often opposed them, as their religious instruction—if existing at all—was considered haphazard. At the same time, where a church could not establish its own school, an informally affiliated woman running a small school may have been better than no school at all. More positively, such schools represented a positive choice by labouring class families to have their children educated in basic literacy and sometimes more.

In 1839, the Church of England established boys' and girls' schools, though they soon became one with separate girls' and boys' departments. This school was organised according to Bell's system of monitorialism. The school ran both as a day and Sunday school. The new Anglican bishop of New South Wales, William Broughton, reported in 1840 that the boys' school was promising. Under instruction were 'about sixteen of the sons of highly respectable families' (quoted in Wyatt, 1941, p. 359). In 1850, the school was enlarged, and grants were secured from Anglican societies—both the Society for the Propagation of the Gospel and the Society for Promoting Christian Knowledge. With the assistance of government subsidies, the school lasted until 1876. It allowed a Presbyterian Sunday school on its premises—and if the first master was Anglican, the first mistress was not. It had been the complaint of Church of England chaplains from earliest times that they had been forced to employ too many Wesleyans as teachers.

The first Catholic school did not appear until the 1850s. It was also subsidised by the colonial government. By 1859, the Catholics of New South Wales had an Archbishop, John Bede Polding, who was in Goulburn in late 1859. Not only was he welcomed by the faithful, but also by five newly arrived Irish Sisters of Mercy. They opened schools in three cottages, one each for girls, boys and boarders. The boarders came from a failed private school in Yass.

With fewer families to support it, a Presbyterian school begun in 1839 faltered. A second attempt, and a boarding school, also failed in the 1840s. Support from the Denominational Schools Board, the conduit through which the colonial government assisted such schools, allowed a further attempt in the late 1840s. This Presbyterian school sought the distinction of being a normal school—that is, having as part of its task the training of teachers. It continued through the 1860s. A Methodist denominational school existed for a while, and several ephemeral Baptist schools met in Goulburn's Baptist chapel. At least one was a private school, but supported by Baptist families.

Other private venture schools offering a 'superior' education were established. Edward Sanden was active from the early 1840s, taking boarding and day students. Church of England clergy often ran tiny establishments to increase their incomes. Mrs Sigmont ran one of Goulburn's early ladies' schools from the late 1840s. Albermarle Layard established, and then decided to sell, his Goulburn Academy in 1848, with 30 students included as goodwill. Layard confessed that as a bachelor he had found it too much to both manage his domestic affairs and run the school. Two of his visiting teachers in French and Music added to his woes by suing for unpaid wages.

David Patterson, formerly a classics master of Sydney College, turned up in 1849 or 1850 to open a boys' grammar school, promising a 'mild' system of discipline. One pupil remembered Patterson hoisting delinquents 'on the back of a big lad during flagellation' (Wyatt, 1941, p. 367). A second grammar school from the late 1850s was a proprietary school—that is, a company school with investors.

It eventually boasted old scholars prominent in business and the professions. There was another ephemeral 'Classical and Mathematical School' advertised in 1853, with its principal being an Anglican clergyman and Oxford graduate.

Another Anglican clergyman, D. Hulbert, opened a school for day boys and boarders in 1855. He included mercantile subjects in his curriculum. Desperate for customers, he condescended to teach young women, putting to rights 'the defects of earlier education'. He differentiated the curriculum according to religious affiliation. Unbaptised students would be prohibited from reading the Bible, while circumcised (Jewish) boys would be restricted to the Old Testament. Hulbert found that an English curriculum brought him more students than a classical one. He would teach modern rather than classical languages, and useful subjects that would assist with his boys' future employment in business. Subjects included arithmetic, bookkeeping and modern geography.

There were other boarding schools in the 1850s. Given the dispersion of pastoral and farming families, they served a need. Mrs John Martyr opened a boarding school for young ladies in 1850, assisted by a governess and a master for drawing and dancing. This school expanded into a second cottage. The wealth generated by Goulburn's proximity to an 1851 gold discovery helped both the town and its school proprietors.

From 1850, there were schools—'preparatory' and 'young ladies'—run by members of the Shrubsole family. This was an age when teaching families pooled their resources. They had advantages that bachelors such as Layard could not match, and were shrewd players in the emerging school market. Wives, mothers and daughters in various combinations could run boarding establishments as well as teach, depending on their skills and education. In general, women were likely to teach girls and younger boys, and men to instruct older boys. Sometimes a master was brought in to teach girls in special or extra subjects. The Shrubsoles promised strict attention not only to the intellect, but also to moral and religious instruction.

The first 'National' (non-church-controlled, government-assisted) school opened in 1858. Despite being the centre of an administrative district for the National Schools Board, enrolments were limited. The school appears to have closed just over three years later. It was not until 1868 that a school of this type, the Goulburn Public School, was firmly established.

This brief history of schooling in Goulburn testifies to the diversity and energy of the effort. It also points to the problem of too many small schools finding it difficult to survive. Children from Goulburn's labouring classes had very little sustained schooling. However, boys and girls from better-off professional, farming, pastoral and merchant families had more opportunities. There is no record of Aboriginal school attendances. One Wesleyan missionary despaired in 1842 that local Aboriginal people were not responding to the gospel, the cause being 'so powerful their superstitions, and so frequent their quarrels', and 'their connection with the worst class of Europeans' (Wyatt, 1941, p. 110).

School markets in towns like Bathurst in New South Wales, Ballarat and Bendigo in Victoria or Launceston in Tasmania were not dissimilar to that of Goulburn. They also resembled—albeit on a smaller scale—the school markets of the growing capital cities in each colony.

Who would run the public schools of the Australian colonies?

The answer to this question was different in the various colonies. In this section, we look briefly at what occurred in each.

New South Wales

In 1820, the British government and the governor of New South Wales continued to believe that government-subsidised schooling—sometimes discussed as public schooling—should be supervised and developed by colonial chaplains, and then churches—in fact, by the Church of England.

Following the creation of an archdeaconry for New South Wales, Thomas Hobbes Scott became the first appointee. Scott would not only assume responsibility for the Church of England in New

South Wales, but also public schooling through the newly created Church and School Corporation. It was the first attempt to create a school system in Australia. From 1826, it was to assume ownership of one-seventh of lands in the colony, revenue from which was to support its enterprises.

Most historians consider that the corporation was doomed from the beginning. More than one newspaper raged against it because it would extend the power of the Church of England in the colony. William Charles Wentworth's *Australian* newspaper told its readers in 1826 that New South Wales was in danger of becoming 'priest-ridden'. Nor would John Dunmore Lang, leader of the Presbyterians, accept the subordination of his Scottish church to that of England. Both colonial office and governor were appalled by Lang's assertion that the corporation sowed the 'seeds of future rebellion' in the colony. Lang also argued that the corporation would cause economic regression (by alienating so much land), lower moral standards and diminish respect for religion in general. Nor did John Joseph Therry, on behalf of his church, accept the subordination of Catholics in the colony.

Nevertheless, Scott increased the number of corporation schools, including a school for infants. As King's Visitor, he supervised and appointed teachers, and also developed the idea of a schools' inspectorate. He maintained the ruling caste's discourse on the necessity of schools: they would correct the dissolute habits and viciousness of much of the population.

The Church and School Corporation argued that not only were local elementary schools required, but so were infants, grammar and collegiate schools. Male and female orphan schools should continue, and evening schools for young men, mechanics institutes and native schools for Aborigines should also be established. Reflecting the disillusionment with previous attempts to educate older children, Scott argued that Indigenous children should enter new institutions before they turned five, in order to most effectively separate them from the influence of their kin and community.

In 1826, William Cape, who was headmaster of the largest corporation school, Sydney Public, reported that 320 pupils had been taught to read, write and cipher according to Dr Bell's system. In 1827, Scott reported that there were 28 parochial schools under his control. With 1220 children enrolled, the average attendance was 804, consisting of 462 boys and 342 girls. Fees were only insisted upon after children reached the age of 10.

Opposition to the corporation was assisted by the difficulties in surveying proposed corporation lands. Estates granted to the Church of England produced little income, so the government-assisted schools of the colony, now owned and run by the corporation, remained uncomfortably dependent on grants from the colonial treasury. Under these circumstances Scott could not rely upon consistency of purpose from the British government. He departed the colony in despair in 1829, and in 1833 the corporation was wound up.

The collapse of the corporation renewed the determination of many that there would be no privileged or established church in New South Wales. Public or 'national' schooling in Australia would be organised differently from that in Britain. William Broughton, Scott's replacement, and later the first Anglican bishop in Australia, was a great advocate for the Church of England, but its struggle for hegemony was defeated.

Other events assisted the end of the corporation. In Britain, Acts of Parliament reduced discrimination against non-conformists and even Catholics. By the early 1830s, Edward Gibbon Wakefield's ideas about colonial policy became influential. Colonisation should not depend on large land grants to the few, including churches; rather, land should be sold at a price sufficient to create a yeomanry of small farmers—and the older inefficient estates, dependent on unfree labour, should be broken up.

Governor Darling had endured the period of the corporation, but it was a new Governor, Richard Bourke (1831–37) who was faced with constructing a post-corporation future for colonial schooling. His work in this area is usually praised, especially by those who read the colony's educational history as progress towards establishing a non-denominational public school system.

Through the nineteenth century, Ireland—with its mainly Catholic population—presented the British government with difficulties. Finding a form of schooling that might arrest the tendency towards

A major attempt to rationalise schools and curricula. Governor Richard Bourke believed that the Irish National system would work for New South Wales. The Church of England disagreed, and the scheme failed. Artist unknown, Sydney, between 1831 and 1837. (Mitchell Library, State Library of NSW, ML 125)

rebellion was a challenge. In 1831, 'National' schools were introduced, governed initially by a board containing representatives of the major denominations, including the Catholic. Its innovation was a curriculum that attempted to separate denominational religious instruction from other instruction that could combine both secular and 'common Christianity' elements. One result was a new series of textbooks, mainly readers. The success of the system's introduction, which included initial Catholic Church cooperation, gave hope to Governor Bourke. He proposed the Irish National system for New South Wales, a move that displeased the Anglican bishop. Bourke had already offended by daring to fund all denominational schools equitably, in proportion to their adherents in the population. Bishop Broughton saw both equitable funding, and now the Irish National system, as challenges to the primacy of the Church of England.

Given Catholic support for Bourke, Broughton worked instead on the leaders of the other Protestant denominations. How could a form of schooling be tolerated that disallowed access to the Bible? He made allies of the Presbyterians and Wesleyans. A petition presented to the governor by the Protestant combination argued that the Irish National system, 'in the vain endeavour to unite light and darkness, truth with error, interdicts (in the ordinary business of the schools) the use of the holy Scriptures in their entire unbroken form, as a *complete* revelation of the Divine will' (quoted in Griffiths, 1957, p. 57). The Reformation itself was under threat! Bourke retreated.

In 1838 in greater New South Wales (including the future colonies of Queensland and Victoria), the following schools were supported by government subsidy: 33 Church of England, thirteen Presbyterian and thirteen Catholic, and then the male, female and Catholic orphan schools.

Governor Gipps succeeded Bourke. In 1839, he argued that to allow every denomination its separate subsidised schools was to accept that 'a large proportion of the population shall remain uneducated' (quoted in Griffiths, 1957, p. 63). The result was wastage of public funds and the impossibility of establishing much-needed 'normal' schools providing for the training of teachers. Discontent was rife in all sectors. Bishop Broughton was disturbed that funding for Church of England schools was reduced as Catholic funding increased. Catholic Archbishop Polding thought Broughton's views fanatical, arguing that the grants—however distributed—were too low to employ competent teachers. He thought that children were being taught little more than the catechism, and the mere basics of reading, writing and arithmetic (Griffiths, 1957, p. 68).

Gipps built a national school in Wollongong—but the events that followed illustrated the sorry politics of colonial schooling. The rules meant that Gipps was then obliged to fund a planned rival, a Church of England school, rendering 'useless' the new National school. Other denominations, seeing the Church of England activity, also began planning. A Catholic school was soon built. Gipps and others argued that one well-run National school could have served the small community; instead, there would soon be five struggling

The first Church of England bishop in Australia, William Broughton, originally believed that all government-assisted schools should be Anglican. His opposition to the development of National schools based on 'common Christianity' was successful through the 1830s and 1840s. (Mitchell Library, State Library of NSW, ML P2/346)

schools, each with likely undistinguished enrolments, curricula and teachers. Newly appointed denominational school inspectors, however competent, would not make much difference. The churches, not inspectors, retained control over teachers and curriculum.

In 1843, Governor Gipps nominated a recent immigrant, Oxford graduate and lawyer, Robert Lowe, to the Legislative Council. Lowe chaired an inquiry into schooling, and its report in 1844 enabled a breakthrough for publicly funded education in the colony.

By the mid-nineteenth century, the fact that many (non-Aboriginal) children were not schooled at all became a significant public issue. Lowe put forward a conservative argument for increased schooling. With the pressure for democracy, British civilisation (and property) was threatened if coming voters—the 'mob'—were not schooled: 'We must educate our masters.' There was also a fear of falling behind Prussia, with its comprehensive school system, together with a growing belief that national strength was linked to economic advance, and that associated technical skills and science could only be supported by reformed educational effort.

In 1844, Lowe reported that of 25 676 colonial children between the ages of 4 and 14, some 17 000 were receiving no education at all. Of 12 507 children in school, 7642 were in public (government-assisted denominational) schools and 4865 in completely private schools. He argued that public education was over-expensive because of its denominational character: 'Wherever one school is founded, two or three others will arise, not because they are wanted, but because it is feared that proselytes will be made . . .' (quoted in Griffiths, 1957, p. 74). Lowe reasserted the rationality of the Irish National system. Schools were required that could offer a common curriculum, with perhaps one day a week set aside for specific denominational instruction. Such schools would increase the numbers being instructed while preserving the right of British subjects to decide whether their children should be schooled at all.

Predictably, Bishop Broughton opposed the proposal, but his coalition of Protestants fell apart. J.D. Lang threw his support behind Lowe: it was ridiculous, argued Lang, that in one small village 'there were three petty schools, and three scarecrows of teachers, where one good one would have performed the duty with the most perfect ease' (quoted in Griffiths, 1957, p. 78).

In 1848, New South Wales established two boards, National and Denominational, to organise and fund publicly assisted schools. The Denominational Schools Board was the weaker authority, and the churches themselves would retain primary control over their schools. In 1851, the Denominational Schools Board distributed funds according to the numbers of church affiliations reported in the census: Church of England £4364; Presbyterian £851; Wesleyan £464; and Catholic £2666.

The National Schools Board was better funded. It made three significant moves: it imported Irish National readers as the basis of the new common curriculum; it appointed George Rusden—ironically the son of one of Bishop Broughton's more aggressive supporters—as one of two agents in the establishment of National schools; and it employed William Wilkins as its principal teacher, and then administrator of the incipient National system.

Rusden visited settlements across the colony, convening meetings in cooperation with local landholders and asking the question: 'Does your community wish to establish a National school?' Despite the predictable hostility of the local Anglican clergy, the answer was commonly 'Yes'. Rusden rode hundreds of miles across rugged country, from Sydney to Albury, then on to Melbourne and through to Portland in the south-west of the colony. He worked the Hunter Valley, and then further north through New England to Moreton Bay.

At the local meetings, Rusden displayed the textbooks and regulations of the board. If the meeting voted for school establishment, he assisted the preparation of an application and, following acceptance, made sure building contracts were let. After two years of such work (1849–51) a system of 22 National schools was in operation, and applications from a further nineteen districts were under consideration. The goodwill of the local squattocracy was essential in this enterprise. While middle-class families predictably supported proposals, there was often labouring-class support as well. Rusden became a great promoter of non-denominational government schools, publishing a significant polemic on the subject in 1853.

William Wilkins had been educated at London's Battersea Training School, a pioneering institution for new methods of teacher training. There he had discovered the enlightened educational thinking of Pestalozzi, among others. One consequence was the displacement of monitorialism in National schools; however, it would linger in the denominational schools. At the newly established Fort Street Model School (1850–), Wilkins classified students by age, ability and sex, grouping them in *classrooms* rather than whole of school *schoolrooms*. Infants, boys and girls would constitute three departments. The aim was a 'great machine' for National schooling, to be run by detailed regulation. Teacher promotion and salary would depend on conformity with the regulations. Pupil teachers, rather than monitors, would be the new apprentice teachers. Teaching was to be professionalised, rescued from the untrained and importunate.

All this required a powerful inspectorate, and Wilkins was himself the first inspector, appointed in 1854.

In 1855, the Legislative Council reported on the provision of education in the colony. Wilkins, the primary author, wrote that of the 202 schools reviewed, the National schools were in poor enough condition, but the denominational schools were worse. A Catholic school at Charcoal Creek, with accommodation for 29 pupils, was attended by 98. Schools like this in slab huts with dried mud floors and bark roofs resembled the 'miserable homes of the lower classes', so any potential of the school to counter the raising of 'children in habits of dirtiness and indelicacy' was unlikely. Indelicacy arose from boys and girls sharing toilets, for example. Too many families avoided fees—and there remained too many schools in sparsely populated areas—leading to insufficient fees being collected, and the subsequent impoverishment of teachers. Wilkins argued that most local boards

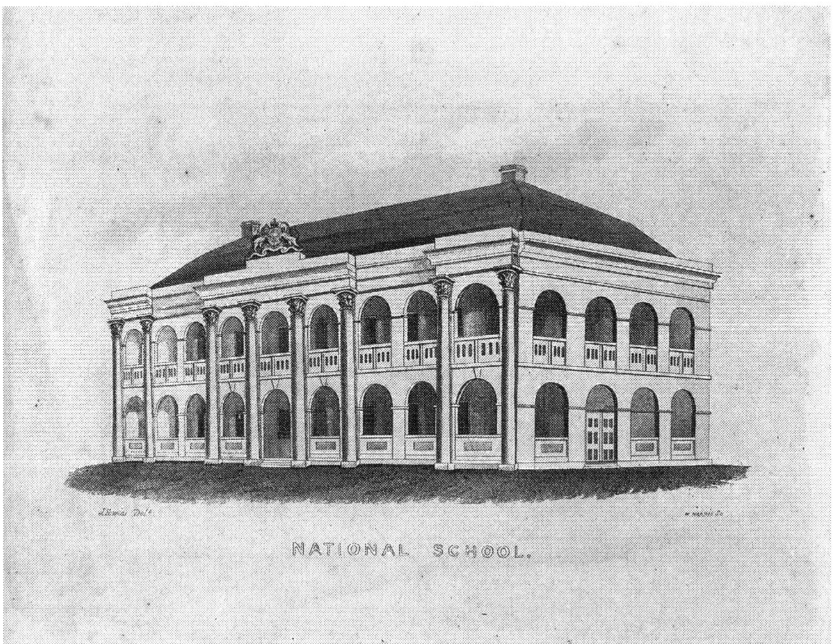

The beginnings of a National system of schools. The Fort Street National School in the Rocks area of Sydney in 1848. It was the founding institution of the public school empire to come. (National Library of Australia, vn5754287)

supervising schools had 'utterly failed'. Local clergy, among others, were too busy to do the job. In denominational schools, too many incompetent and untrained teachers were appointed. Such arguments became standard for school systematisers over the next half-century.

Table 2.1 shows that over 90 per cent of the National school teachers were trained, and only 38 of the denominational. Bear in mind that what 'training' meant in 1855 is variable, and doubtless many untrained teachers were at least as effective as the trained. Nevertheless, for colonial policy-makers, the capacity of the National system to produce trained teachers added to the argument against denominational schools. Later in the 1850s, Wilkins allied with the rising politician Henry Parkes. Their relationship helped produce new schooling settlements in the 1860s and 1870s, when the National schools would become the only public, or government, schools.

TABLE 2.1
Trained teachers in the publicly funded schools of New South Wales

	National schools	Church of England	Catholic	Presbyterian	Wesleyan	Total
Trained in the colony	30	24	14	4	0	72
Trained in Britain	7	6	11	1	2	27
Not trained	4	53	33	10	5	105

Source: Reproduced from Commission of 1854–55 in Griffiths (1957, p. 97).

Western Australia

Western Australia was settled as a separate colony in 1829. Early school foundations were fleeting. Late in the 1840s, however, there was increased population and a new capacity for school development. Private, denominational and non-denominational 'colonial' schools each came into existence. Though the Catholic population was small, the leadership of its vicar-general, John Brady, was effective. In 1845 he returned from Europe with a diverse group of French, Spanish and Irish missionaries, priests, nuns and brothers. Consequently

Spanish Benedictines established a mission for Aboriginal conversion at New Norcia in 1847. By 1848, Catholic schools were organised and educating numbers well above their population share. Some of these schools attracted Protestant families. The attractions of a safe female environment in convent schools for girls outweighed fears of proselytisation. In 1849, a dual system of publicly funded schools was adopted. There would be colonial schools, with a non-denominational curriculum. A separate grant was made to the best organised of the other denominations, the Catholics, whom Governor Charles FitzGerald was under instruction not to alienate. The want of an Anglican bishop in Western Australia assisted such an outcome.

In 1850, convicts were introduced to Western Australia. Governor Kennedy insisted that under the circumstances any publicly funded school need only offer a 'plain and practical' curriculum. Kennedy cancelled the grant to Catholic schools in 1856, hoping to substitute Irish National texts in all publicly funded schools. The decision was resisted. By the 1850s, across all colonies, Catholic opposition to the Irish National system had become firmer as the church itself consolidated its opposition to secularism and other modernities. According to Western Australia's Board of Education in 1864, public schools were only for children of 'small tradesmen, mechanics and labourers'. Families who sought superior, religious or exclusive education would have to go elsewhere.

South Australia

Founded in 1836, South Australia's large numbers of dissenters were resistant to any hegemonic pretensions of the Church of England. Planned by enthusiasts for Wakefield's colonising ideas, a school society for the colony was founded well before actual settlement. A system including infants, agricultural and trade, as well as elementary and grammar, schools was imagined, but the difficulties of the early years of colonisation saw the plan collapse. Nevertheless, there were schools established from 1836. They included private ventures—amongst them dame schools. Congregationalist minister Thomas Stowe even founded a short-lived Classical Academy. Without the support of endowments and land grants, ministers of religion often looked to developing schools and the enrolment of fee-paying pupils.

From 1846, Governor Robe subsidised churches to provide schools through a Board of Education. Opposition saw that decision overturned five years later. From 1851, South Australia would license and help pay teachers in non-denominational schools only. It would subsidise local effort in the erection of buildings and provide some supervision of publicly assisted schools. South Australia was the first colony to strip government subsidies from denominational schools.

The schools supported by the Board of Education were a version of the Irish National schools. William Wyatt, the inspector, had recommended this, though the term 'National school' was not much used in South Australia. With smaller Church of England and Catholic populations, dissenters had the influence to enforce a separation of churches and state. Colonists were alert to dangers to non-conformity in religion—the reason so many colonists had left England in the first place.

This acceptance of religious freedom, and churches separate from the state, suited the newly arrived German Lutherans, who had resisted the reorganisation of their church by the Prussian government from 1817. Leaders of the migrants, August Kavel and Gotthard Fritzsche, had successes from the 1840s in encouraging their community's farming villages to support elementary schools. They were among the first denominational schools in Australia with a principal language of instruction that was not English.

Elsewhere in 1838, newspaper advertisements began to appear promising the teaching of accomplishments to girls. By 1850, Mrs Hugh Snell Chauncy's Ladies' Educational Establishment offered piano, dancing, calisthenic exercise, guitar, harp, singing, drawing and painting, the modern languages—French, Italian and German—as well as the basics.

As in Goulburn, dame schools were popular with poor families, despite the deficiencies with which they were charged, including failure to secure regular attendance or deliver an ordered curriculum. Their popularity was based on their acceptance of the rhythms of labouring-class life. Children could be absent as their families needed them, since family economies through the nineteenth century often required the labour of children. Fees in these schools were low. An 1855 newspaper advertisement demonstrated their utility to the women who ran them: 'A Widow, with a small family, in a healthy situation, close to Adelaide, would be happy to take charge of three children of similar ages to her own, from three to seven years, and daily instruct them in the rudiments of education' (quoted in Hyams, 1988, p. 17).

As early as 1839 there was public advocacy for a grammar school. Families with property and rank required advanced education—at least for their boys. The existence of Sydney colleges was acknowledged, but the problem was that colony's convict population, 'a moral barrier against the voluntary approach of those whose chief concern is the instruction of the young' (quoted in Hyams, 1988, p. 23). In 1847, the Collegiate School of St Peter for boys was founded. There was support from the Society for Promoting Christian Knowledge and a private endowment. The school was a Church of England establishment. The first headmaster, the Rev. Theodore Wilson, MA (Oxon.), was to develop St Peter's as a 'public school' in the tradition of the greater public schools of England.

Therefore, despite the want of state subsidy, church schools were founded in South Australia. Some board-licensed schools, as a result of the affiliations of their principals, were reckoned by the market to be denominationally associated.

For large numbers of children, Sunday schools were the only source of literacy instruction. In 1857 in South Australia, there were 192 Sunday schools with 10 586 pupils, out-enrolling by far the 7480 pupils in board schools.

Tasmania

Tasmania was administratively separated from New South Wales in 1825. There, Governor George Arthur despaired of the Church of England as a competent organiser of schools, despite the achievement of orphan, infants and several elementary schools. He eventually decided in the late 1820s to support any denomination that would provide schools—despite the opposition of Archdeacon (then Bishop)

Broughton. Nevertheless, through the 1830s, most publicly assisted schools were Church of England. Governor Franklin (1837–43) established a Board of Education that recommended British and Foreign School Society texts. This caused trouble: these were the texts of Lancastrian (dissenter), not Bell's Church of England-approved monitorialism. A publicly subsidised grammar school, the Queen's School, was established in 1840, but it failed before Archdeacon Hutchins' determination to found a Church of England grammar school. The Hutchins School followed in 1846. By 1843, the Church of England in Tasmania had its own bishop, in opposition to the Board of Education. He declared that he would rather see his children dead than have them educated in board schools, sitting next to infidels (Austin, 1972, p. 80). In the 1840s, the position of the few non-denominational board schools weakened. Six married teacher couples sent out from England were 'starved out' of their situations.

One of the 'starved-out' imports was James Bonwick. Brought out to establish a normal school in Hobart, he survived by opening his own private-venture boarding school. Late in the 1840s, Bonwick began writing school texts that were more suitable for colonial circumstances than the usual Irish and English readers. This was an important effort for the beginnings of an Australian curriculum.

By 1849, there were 59 Church of England, four Catholic and eight surviving former board schools receiving state aid. In 1850, Thomas Arnold (son of the Rugby headmaster) inspected Tasmanian schools. He argued that the administration of the government subsidy—a penny a day for each attendance—led to the degradation of teachers and poor attendance. Denominational schools tended towards exclusiveness, while those small schools run by ex-convicts were 'inefficient in the extreme'. A new Central Board was established in 1852 with some support from the Catholic bishop. For once, expected Anglican opposition did not eventuate. The board established a system of National schools, with denominational instruction only being allowed for one hour each day. Churches could nominate their own instructors. This system seemed to work well enough, and by 1856, denominational strife was greatly reduced in Tasmania.

Victoria

Victoria inherited the dual-boards system when it separated from New South Wales in 1851. The churches campaigned against the National schools from the beginning, but school reorganisation was disrupted as Victoria was swept into the gold rushes. Victoria's National schools survived for two main reasons. The unruly populations chasing gold from field to field inspired new warnings that, without schools, the population would be even more difficult to control. Also, among the gold-diggers were radicals, veterans of Chartism in England and even the revolutions of 1848 in Europe. There was new pressure for secular or non-denominational public education. Early leaders of responsible government in Victoria, Anglican William Haines, and Catholic John O'Shanassy, starved the National schools of funds. George Rusden for the National Board was their defender, until better times—which began from 1857 when a Bill proposing the abolition of government subsidies to church schools was introduced into the legislature.

Denominational (church) schools continued with government assistance, usually into the 1870s. This is the Anglican St Mary's school, manse and church with children playing in the schoolyard, North Melbourne, Victoria, 1850s. (National Library of Australia, an8860724)

As in the other colonies, by 1860 Victoria had a great range of private-venture, as well as church/denominational and National schools. The University of Melbourne, founded in 1853, sought grammar school educations for the boys it hoped to enrol, and such schools were founded. They included Scotch College (Presbyterian, 1851), and Geelong and Melbourne Grammars (both Church of England, 1855 and 1858 respectively). As yet, there were no corporate schools for girls but there were new private colleges for each sex. For girls, there was the Ladies' College in East Melbourne, owned by the artist Julie Vieusseux and her husband Lewis and opened in 1857. Private ladies colleges of this period have been dismissed in the historiography as being class-ridden and superficial, teaching nothing but an 'accomplishments' curriculum for manners and marriageability, but the Vieusseux school pioneered not only arts education, but also the academic subjects more likely to be associated with the education of middle- and ruling-class boys (Theobald, 1991). When the Australian universities opened enrolments to women later in the century, many of the pioneering women attending lectures were from such schools.

Queensland

Queensland's schooling history only became separate from that of New South Wales from 1859. There had been an early school under the authority of the Church and School Corporation, supervised by the Moreton Bay commandant and taught by Esther Roberts. Evidence of her work includes religious as well as elementary literacy instruction. A statement from 1827 identified the school texts used as Church of England meditations, exhortations, psalters, prayer books and catechisms. A convict outpost from 1825 under military control, the Moreton Bay settlement barely registered a free settler population apart from military and convict inhabitants. Sometimes soldiers were even appointed to teach school, while girls were more likely taught at home. Though school enrolments were small, Bell monitorialism was in evidence in 1828.

In 1838, German missionaries arrived to begin a mission and school for Aboriginal people. This was an inter-denominational

Lutheran, Presbyterian and Pietist effort with Moravian inspiration. In 1841, the school was operating for five hours a day. The curriculum included the alphabet, numbers, spelling and singing—including the learning of the Lord's prayer:

> The children were by no means docile. They were apt to refuse to do school work, and gave the impression that they attended as a special favour to the teacher who in their opinion did no work. One group of them surprised the mission by going from house to house reciting the Lord's prayer and demanding payment. (Wyeth, 1955, p. 45)

From 1842, Moreton Bay was opened to free settlers. Private and denominational schools educated the majority of pupils. The first denominational schools were Catholic—with Brisbane commencing in 1845 and Ipswich in 1847. The Church of England awaited grants from the Denominational Schools Board. Private schools opened in the Darling Downs agricultural district as well as in Brisbane.

The story of the opening of the first National school in what became Queensland illuminates the process not only there but elsewhere. George Leslie occupied land in the Warwick district, south-west of Brisbane. To educate his children and those of his neighbours, he hired a tutor and provided a building for the purpose. When Leslie heard about the National Schools Board, he petitioned for a district school. A building grant of £140, along with a teacher salary of £40 per year, was sought. The school building, with teacher accommodation, was to house 50 children. There would be three school rooms, one each for boys, girls and religious instruction. A school patron who provided a necessary local contribution was found, and Leslie recommended a husband and wife teacher team, the Abbotts. They were readily appointed, but not so readily dismissed when Mr Abbott was charged with frequent drunkenness. The board, having accepted the local recommendation, insisted that the local school committee take some responsibility for the problem. The Abbotts were given some training at William Wilkins' newly opened Fort Street training school.

By the time George Rusden, agent of the board, arrived in Warwick, matters were so well in hand that all he needed to do was arrange for a consignment of textbooks to be sent to the school. In 1853 Abbott died, and was replaced by a teacher from a local private school. The National school at Warwick evolved into a public Education Department school later in the century.

Brisbane and Ipswich were different matters. No National school opened in Brisbane before 1859, despite the advocacy of Catholic journalist and customs official, William Duncan. His *Lecture on National Education* advocating National schools was delivered and published in 1850.

Queensland's separation from New South Wales occurred at the end of the period discussed in this chapter. Unlike the position in Victoria at separation, there existed effective champions of the National schools. Charles Nicholson, a founder of the University of Sydney and a National Board commissioner, argued in Queensland's new Legislative Council that National schools were the obvious solution to colonial needs for schooling. The newly appointed Anglican bishop, Edward Tufnell, arrived too late to affect the debate. Schools that were owned by the denominations, if they were to receive any government subsidy, had to agree to inspection by a new single board, and the assistance would be in terms of salaries and textbooks only.

Schooling Aboriginal children

There are similarities between what happened in the first decades in New South Wales and the later colonies with regard to the schooling of Aboriginal children. We have already noted the Catholic activity in Western Australia, and Lutheran efforts in South Australia and Queensland. Governments tended to retreat from school provision, but not always. Though missionaries grew in importance, older approaches towards Aboriginal schooling tended not to change. Separating children from their families, communities and culture remained an objective. Aboriginal children were to be remade as 'civilised' and orderly Christian subjects, and prepared to be agricultural labourers and domestic servants. British colonial society remained unsympathetic at best towards Indigenous people and cultures.

In South Australia, a Protector of Aborigines arrived in 1839, soon after the establishment of the colony. Under his supervision, the education of Aboriginal children was placed first in the hands of missionaries from the Evangelical Lutheran Missionary Society based in Dresden. Their educational approach soon conflicted with that of the governor and influential colonists. Clamor Schürman and fellow missionaries believed that Christianisation was the main goal, and they sought to transform the 'hearts' of their students. Access to the 'heart' required instruction not in English (or German), but in the Indigenous language Kaurna, of the Adelaide Plains people. Nor were outward appearances, clothing, polite behaviour and so on of initial concern. Governor Grey opposed the approach, and in succeeding government-controlled native schools of the 1840s, 'civilisation' displaced 'Christianisation' as the correct approach to the school curriculum. Teaching English, English as the language of instruction, attention to respectable dress and behaviour, and training for domestic and agricultural labour took first place.

In 1837 Governor Gipps encouraged missionaries prepared to work with Aboriginal peoples. Christianisation and absorption into colonial society had been policy since the 1820s. The original Native Institution, now at Blacktown, finally closed in 1833. Its three remaining children, Agatha, Polly and Martha, were transferred to an Anglican mission at Wellington hundreds of miles away in the central west of New South Wales. Christian missions established in the 1830s and 1840s included Wellington and the inter-denominational effort at Moreton Bay. The Catholics also operated in the Moreton Bay area and Western Australia, as did Wesleyans at Port Phillip.

Teachers at the Wellington school believed that infant teaching methods were best for Aboriginal children of all ages. 'The clapping of hands, marching, etc. falls in so much with their native habits of corrobborring that the Black Children are quite delighted with it' (Fletcher, 1989a, p. 25). There were successes with reading and writing, but the school lost parental support when it began to forcibly separate children from their parents to increase school attendance.

An Aboriginal father in South Australia whose children had been taken, and then rejoined him by running away, insisted that if his children were

> taken any more he would steal some European children instead, and take them into the bush to teach them; he said he could learn them something useful, to make weapons and nets, to hunt, or to fish, but what good did the Europeans communicate to his children? (quoted in Hyams, 1988, p. 86)

Missionaries themselves in the 1830s often thought of their efforts as ineffective.

One consequence of the anti-slavery movements in Britain was new policies of 'protection' towards Aboriginal peoples. A protectorate was established in Victoria, but the schooling of Aboriginal children was not a high priority. In 1848 there was a policy change, and religious instruction would be downplayed in favour of work education. Aboriginal families might be kept together in reserves. Any changes to the education of the small number of Aboriginal children in schools as a result of such policy changes were probably minor. The Merri Creek School (1845–51) near Melbourne had a chequered history. The Assistant Protector made sporadic efforts to school children on the Merri Creek Station, with the assistance of the Baptist church in Melbourne. The teacher from 1848 to 1851 was accused of neglecting reading and writing in favour of constant sermonising. Governor La Trobe was unimpressed with the results.

The National and Denominational Boards of Education appointed from 1848 were disinclined to intervene in Aboriginal education. The opinion of William Duncan, liberal in other respects, was to oppose National schools taking any interest in Aboriginal children. The board agreed in 1853, deciding that even attendance at National schools would not be encouraged. By mid-century, the British government was losing interest in Indigenous policy, and without external stimulation, colonial governments did little.

In Victoria, a new Church of England mission was started in Mildura in 1853, while the Moravians established a mission in the Wimmera. In Adelaide, there were small residential schools run from 1839 to 1853, with the Poonindie Anglican Mission on the Eyre Peninsula beginning in 1850.

In the 1850s, there was a less obvious presence of Aboriginal peoples in the cities. School readers began arguing that the Aborigines of Australia were beginning to 'die out'. European forms of schooling remained largely irrelevant to the lives of Aboriginal children. Children continued to be caught up in terrible circumstances as their communities lost lands when the settlement frontiers moved inland. Children died from the effects of introduced diseases and malnutrition, and from violent confrontations. Many were orphaned and left to survive on the fringes of colonial society; some were taken from their families. Survivors were often forced into servitude with neglectful, uncaring and sometimes brutal white employers (Haebich, 2000).

The work of the school

By the 1850s, much of the enthusiasm for monitorialism had dissipated. Most colonial schools had always been too small for its systematic implementation, and new ideas about teaching were becoming influential. Despite his monitorial training in the Borough Road School in London, James Bonwick—like William Wilkins—was interested in 'continental' educational ideas. Each advocated alternatives to the rigidities of monitorialism. In South Australia, Inspector Wyatt felt that the best teachers implemented the 'mixed method' of teaching, where they took an interest in individuals and their progress but also instructed whole classes. He believed in grouping students into classes, allowing students with similar levels of attainment to be taught efficiently. One name for this was 'simultaneous teaching'. Wyatt knew about 'model instruction', a variation of monitorialism, but he preferred mixed individual and class teaching. He also believed that teachers should use the method of instruction they felt best suited their circumstances.

Wyatt argued that student progress was more dependent on regular attendance than teaching method. What was the point of teaching new skills and knowledge, dependent on what had been learned before, if half the class had barely attended previously? He explained that there was more than rote learning going on in board schools, and that teachers did attempt to explain the principles behind English grammar and arithmetic, but poor attendance and early school leaving meant success was limited. In the larger schools, there were prizes for good students. Wyatt thought that corporal punishment should be used minimally (quoted in Hyams et al., 1988, pp. 49ff). Wyatt was only one side of the issue, however. One of Catherine Helen Spence's fictional characters asked another why her children were not at school. She replied, 'I did send them a bit, but Fanny got scolded, and Bob got thrashed; and the little ones were kept in and got no dinner at all one day; so they just hate the school, and won't go to it no more.' (quoted in Hyams, 1988, p. 88). In 1856, the *South Australian Government Gazette* summarised the problems, with irregularity of attendance and absence causing mischief:

> Pupils are seen dropping in to school at all hours . . . Children are . . . kept at home to assist in the accumulation of wealth; or, for the sake of a trifling saving, are sent to schools of the lowest description . . . under the charge of persons whom poverty, misfortune, or extravagance, has forced into the ranks of teachers, and who tempt the niggardly parent by the smallest of the weekly fee . . . (quoted in Hyams, 1988, p. 85)

This is an example of an educational discourse that became prevalent as school systems became better organised: the virtuous school in opposition to reprehensible, irresponsible parents.

Monitorialism left a legacy of teaching aids. In the 1840s, missionary teachers of Aboriginal children in South Australia cut out cardboard letters then pasted them on blocks of wood. Spelling and vocabulary building were taught with their help. Reformed teaching required more teachers, smaller classes and better record-keeping. Standards of attainment were set and pursued. The range of measures encouraging school efficiency, by which teachers and pupils could be judged, began to increase. These approaches developed fitfully across each colony.

Progress was rarely fast enough for the reformers. If model and normal schools were established, they were usually too few in number, and teachers in training spent too little time in them. Wyatt believed that it was only in large schools that systematic approaches could occur. 'Individual teaching' was inefficient, with the further burden of 'much additional labour to the master or mistress' (quoted in Hyams, 1988, p. 49).

Teachers from this period rarely portrayed their work as pleasurable. Georgina Cawthorne and her son, William, decided to open a school in Adelaide. Georgina taught the girls while William attended to the boys. In his diary, William complained that its writing was too often interrupted by his pupils. He was responsible for fifteen of the 'rising generation', having to 'hear them calling b's for p's and m's for n's and d's for b's or to see them subtract instead of multiply; to add instead of dividing or to hear them read or spell or write . . .' He needed to 'exhort, entreat, command, forbid, permit, & beat those blessings of marriage, & for what? Why to make them mark, learn, read & inwardly digest all that they do learn.' (quoted in Brice, 1997, p. 83). The word 'digest' in the diary suggests 'forced feeding'.

William had been teaching since the age of 11. His income was low, so when the school closed for Christmas and fees stopped, he took up farm labouring. He complained about his students' parents. Some would not accept that their children were dull; others complained about the pace of his teaching. If he gave a boy a deserved 'sound thrashing—You would lose your school'. Having to assume a schoolmaster role at an early age deprived him of the amusements that his peers enjoyed.

He noted the arrest of an older male teacher who had interfered with a 9-year-old girl, and prayed that he would be spared similar 'temptations of the world'. In 1843 there was an allegation that he was interested in kissing girls at the school. Such charges could close a school. Georgina dealt with the parents, and the matter was dropped. Eventually the Cawthorne school grew, receiving favourable attention from the governor, but William's older pupils were catching up with him. He struggled to stay a lesson ahead in geography, geometry and arithmetic. An offer in 1847 by the Protector of Aborigines to superintend the Aboriginal school at Walkerville was rejected, despite its sure salary of £50 a year, because insistence on autonomy within the school was not granted. Nevertheless, by 1851 Cawthorne was recognised as a leading teacher in the colony, being appointed to the Central Board of Education.

William Cawthorne's story tells us much about the era. Teaching was often a family enterprise. Small schools were common, but their preponderance caused problems. There was over-reliance on the inefficient individual method of teaching if students of different ages and attainments were to be kept occupied. There was also the respectability question: the parents of girls from families aspiring to the middle class feared the moral dangers that schools might harbour. (On the Cawthornes, see Whitehead, 2003 and Brice, 1997.)

Corporal and other punishments were little regulated in this era. If Cawthorne watched his step for fear of losing enrolments, the government orphan schools were a different matter. In 1830 in Sydney, girls who transgressed were issued with demeaning clothing, and placards proclaiming their offences were attached to their backs. They were given 'laborious and degrading work according to their ages and strength'. Dark cells isolated older girls. In the boys' school, Archdeacon Scott had protested against boys being chained to logs which they dragged while doing their daily work. Children were sometimes deprived of food. In 1850, the government orphan schools of New South Wales were partly disestablished. A Protestant Orphan School took over the main work, while the Catholic school continued from its 1837 foundation.

For isolated families, schooling was hardly an option. Parents of wealthier girls often preferred a governess to a school—even if governesses were hard to keep, especially if 'pretty or young'. In 1848, Hannah Villiers Boyd wrote a manual advising colonial mothers about teaching their own children. A 'useful' and literary curriculum was outlined. Boyd encouraged mothers to relate lessons to the child's experience, warning against extremes in teaching accomplishments to girls.

The graded Irish National readers were useful in non-denominational schools. The denominational schools favoured alternatives produced by their own church educational societies. The Irish National readers included Bible and animal stories, which explored the virtues of kindness, cheerfulness, honesty and selflessness. If the

Irishness of the flora and fauna in the readers produced criticism soon enough, nevertheless they were written with the conscious purpose of gaining the interest and sympathy of children. When the time came for colonial readers to be produced, the Irish National would be the model to be both imitated and improved upon.

•

By 1860, schools and schooling were an increasingly common part of colonial life. Even if the relationship between public schooling and churches was not yet settled, at least it was clear that the Church of England would not control all government-assisted schools. Colonial governments had begun to detach themselves from churches as primary agents in the education and moralisation of children.

The character of schooling in different places and for different populations varied dramatically. Schools followed the shifting frontier of white settlement. During the gold rushes, sometimes there would be tent schools; at other times, there would be none. Denominational rivalry could cause over-supply in some areas, and neglect in others. School teaching itself was a difficult profession, and the conditions that might affect the collection of fees and enrolments varied. School foundations were numerous, but in the private sector school closures were also numerous.

Nevertheless, there were the beginnings of substantial institutions. Some denominational schools established in this period continue through to the present day. They include The King's School at Parramatta (Anglican, 1831) and St Catherine's, a school intended for daughters of the clergy in Sydney (Anglican, 1856). There was also the deliberately secular Sydney Grammar School (1854), intended to provide students for the new University of Sydney. This last school was founded by Act of Parliament, giving Henry Parkes experience in arguing the case for non-denominational public schooling. The diffusion of gold-rush wealth supported numerous 'corporate' school foundations in Victoria. In Tasmania, the successors of Catholic boys' and girls' schools under the name of St Joseph also exist through to the present day. These schools were founded by the Sisters of Charity, an Irish order invited to Australia in the 1830s. Launceston Grammar (1846) and The Hutchins

School (1846) were Anglican foundations. In South Australia, there was St Peter's College (Anglican, 1849). We have already noted the activity of the Catholic church in Western Australia. Mercedes College was founded by the Irish Sisters of Mercy there in 1849.

Despite these early *corporate* school foundations by churches and state, *private venture* schools dominated the market for 'superior' education. At the other end of the market were dame and other tiny private schools for poorer families in urban and rural districts of the Australian colonies. This period also saw the growth of National and other government-assisted schools, supervised by boards of education. School provision and access was unstable and patchy despite all the growth.

Schools in the colonies were marked by their diversity of purpose, enrolment and governance. There were pressures towards a 'common school'—that is, National schools for colonial children—from the governorship of Richard Bourke, but at the end of the 1850s they were hardly in the ascendant (see Table 2.1). Nevertheless, schools had expanded beyond their early aims. More was expected of public schools than the mere production of orderly and useful subjects from an unruly population tainted by convictism. Some schools now worked on producing middle and ruling classes. Nevertheless, resolving differences arising from religious conflict remained significant for many communities and colonial governments for the entire period.

Social class, gender, religion and race were strong predictors of school enrolment. There was charitable provision in church and non-denominational schools, but fees were required in most. For some schools, including private ones, fees supported social exclusivity, but finding the right level was difficult. Fees also had to be low enough to fight off rival schools. However, very low fees and too few enrolments failed to provide teachers with an adequate living. The National schools could be attractive to teachers, promising more secure employment, particularly as National school boards were more likely to support some kind of teacher training. Their employment of inspectors could be a mixed blessing however. Scathing criticisms of teachers might be counter-balanced by local support for local schools and teachers.

TABLE 2.2

Schools and enrolments in three colonies, 1861

	Public/ National	Public/ denominational	Private
Number of schools by sector			
Victoria	181	484	211
New South Wales	178	278	387
South Australia	219	0	*na*
Enrolments			
Victoria*	9 713	24 224	5 128
New South Wales	11 400	16 562	9 087
South Australia	5 861	0	*na*

Note: For other colonies, statistics for 1861 are not available. These statistics are as accurate as government agencies could manage at the time. Private school enrolments are likely under-counted.

* For enrolments, there is a significant mismatch in that 'average attendances', not enrolments, were counted for the public schools of Victoria.

Source: Tables ES 1–6, 22–29, 57–64 in Vamplew (1986, pp. 330–2).

It is difficult to determine much about the effectiveness of schooling, especially in relation to literacy levels in this period. Much of the population consisted of immigrants, and levels of literacy owed as much to experiences, usually in Britain and Ireland—and informal and family efforts, as they did to schooling. By 1838, about two-thirds of the men and about half the women across the four colonies could write and read. Those who were highly literate were fewer. Although a school education was not yet necessary for most male employment, for middle-class women, in the absence of marriage, an education could lead to teaching and perhaps a small school. It was almost the only respectable occupation for such women.

Many children continued to experience no schooling at all. There were no laws providing for compulsory attendance, and the colonies naturally followed England in this matter. The labour of children remained valuable, not only domestically but for the variety of farms and businesses that constituted the colonial economy. The value of child labour is reflected in part by the 6.8 average number of live births per (non-Indigenous) woman in the period 1841–46. Family and household economies usually depended on the joint efforts of all their members.

Convict transportation—mainly men—continued to parts of eastern Australia until 1852. Stable family formation remained problematic, and the gold rushes gave new life to the problem. Children often suffered in these circumstances. The voices of children themselves are rarely heard, although there is one recorded incident from early in the period. In 1822, a group of boys at the Male Orphan School gathered the courage to complain that food was too often withheld as a form of punishment for minor offences. They were only ever well fed prior to the arrival of official visitors, and they were worked far too hard (Bubacz, 2007).

Wealthier families usually had a much stronger attachment to schooling—for boys at least—than the labouring classes. Schooling brought knowledge and skills, but the right kind could bring cultural capital—even respectability sometimes. Upward social mobility was a common pursuit in the Australian colonies, and increasingly the right kind of schooling could assist.

Further reading

On Aboriginal children and schooling, see Haebich (2000), Scrimgeour (2006), Fletcher (1989a, 1989b), Clark and Heydon (2004), and Brook and Kohen (1991). Along with the *Australian Dictionary of Biography* (<www.adb.anu.edu.au>), the following biographies are useful: Richard Bourke (Waugh, 2005), Bishop Broughton (Shaw, 1978), J.D. Lang (Baker, 1998), Robert Lowe (Knight, 1966), Thomas Arnold (Bergonzi, 2003), William Wilkins (Turney, 1992) and George Rusden (Austin, 1958). On corporate schools, see Sherington, Petersen and Brice (1987), but also individual histories such as those of Sydney Grammar (Turney, 1989) and St Peter's College (Tregenza, 1996; Thornton, 2010). On private venture schools with a classical bent, see Mooney (1996). For orphan schools in Sydney, see Bubacz (2007). On girls' education generally, see Windschuttle (1980), Theobald (1996) and Kyle (1986). On schools in the Victorian gold rush, see Moore (2004). On the problem of local school board control, see Vick (1994). Essays in Theobald and Selleck (1990) analyse relationships between families, teachers, schools and the colonial state. On children, see Kociumbas (1997), as well as Mossenson (1972) for Western Australia, Phillips (1985) for Tasmania and Hyams (1988) for South Australia. See Austin (1972) for church–state relations in education.

CHAPTER

3

Inventing public school systems 1861–1900

Between 1860 and 1900, there was a demographic transition underway in Australia. Families became smaller, and the growing withdrawal of child labour from family enterprises meant that children increasingly became a drain on, rather than a benefit to, household economies. Longer stretches of childhood were likely to be spent at school. By the end of the period, there was a prolongation of childhood for many in the form of 'adolescence', where older youth, as well as children, were separated from the paid workforce. This growing separation continued through the twentieth century.

Different social groups experienced these changes at different times. Working-class and farming families stayed larger for longer than those of the urban middle class, as did Irish-Catholic and German Lutheran families in comparison with Anglo-Protestant ones. The changes saw the average age of the urban population increase by ten years between 1861 and 1901, and the number of live births per (non-Indigenous) woman decrease from 5.1 to 2.8 (McDonald, Ruzicka and Pyne, 1987, p. 55).

As schooling grew more central in the lives of children, the arrangements made to deliver it became more systematic. The universalisation of elementary schooling—for that is what the colonial state attempted in this period—demanded not only new institutions, but new pedagogies and new kinds of teachers as well. In fact, the origins of childhood as we know it today were largely founded in this period.

The colonial state and its intrusions into the lives of families expanded substantially. The effort to educate, regulate, supervise, moralise and even *create* more satisfactory populations saw not only an expansion of state agencies, but also the use of new managerial technologies to implement these ambitions.

The universalisation and systematisation of government schools meant a decrease in the proportion of young people in private and church schools. As Education Departments were founded, they were headed by inspectors-general or directors, responsible to Ministers of Education. The very meaning of *public* schooling changed. By the end of the nineteenth century, no denominational school could consider itself a public school unless it sought to imitate the elite grammar schools of England. A *public* school in Australia became an ordinary, mainly secular, government school.

In these new schools, the work and careers of teachers were transformed. There was movement away from apprenticeship models of teacher training. Where teaching itself had once mainly been a family enterprise, by 1900, teachers were more clearly engaged as individual employees. The greatest number—young women—became salaried servants of the state. Men and long-term unmarried women had careers. New gender regimes organised the teaching workforce.

Regulations, mandated curricula and standard school timetables proliferated. Education Department gazettes made known the new regulations and helped secure compliance with them. They spread news of recommended teaching practices and could promote imperial loyalty. The Departments of Education, initially the cramped offices of a few school inspectors with too few clerks, began their evolution into substantial bureaucracies.

The social significance of schooling grew. Public examinations organised by the new universities provided valuable credentials—especially important to the rising new middle class. Prolonged schooling became an investment in children's futures as white-collar work was sought in expanding businesses and government. Girls as well as boys became more likely to receive a prolonged education. The school began to assume an historically unprecedented centrality in the lives of Australian young people—but there were exceptions.

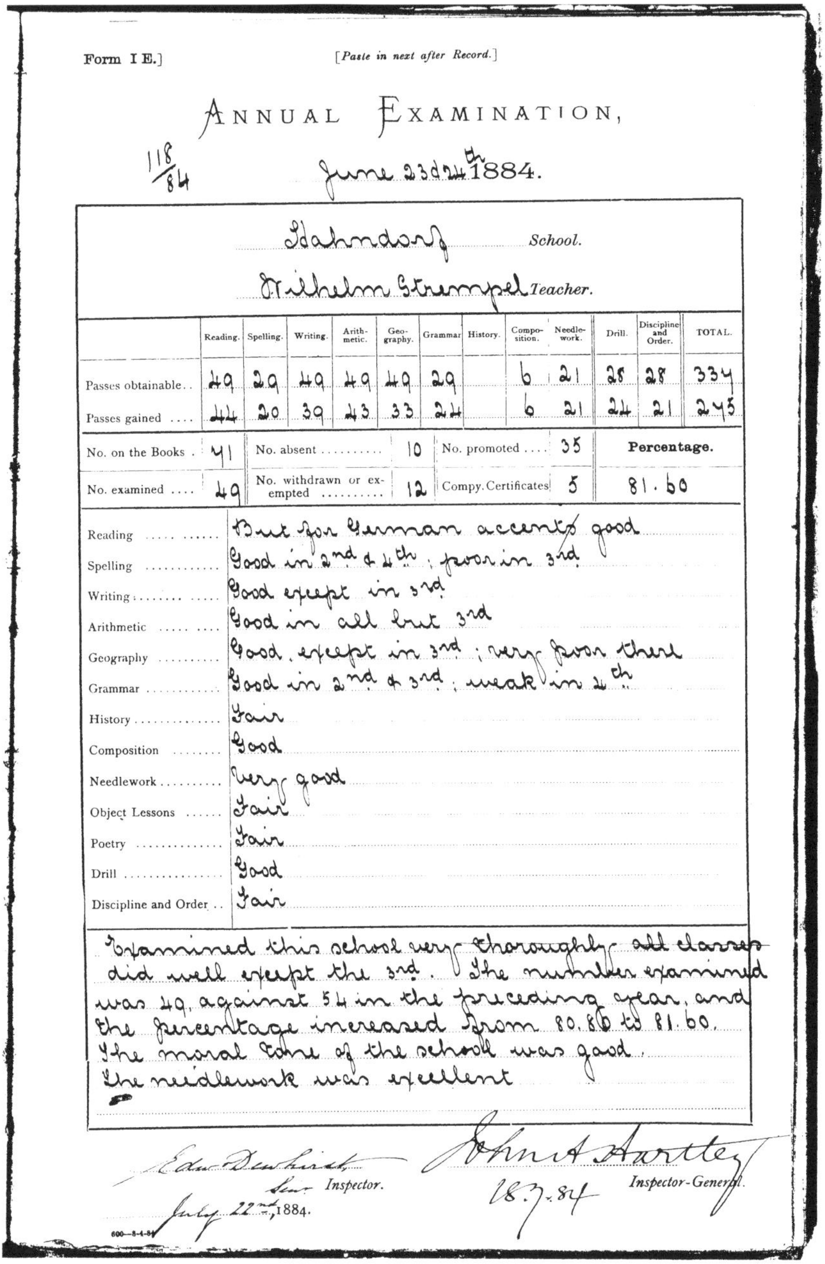

Form I E.] [*Paste in next after Record.*]

ANNUAL EXAMINATION,

118/84

June 23d 24th 1884.

Hahndorf School.

Wilhelm Strempel Teacher.

	Reading.	Spelling.	Writing.	Arithmetic.	Geography.	Grammar	History.	Composition.	Needlework.	Drill.	Discipline and Order.	TOTAL.
Passes obtainable..	49	29	49	49	49	29		6	21	28	28	334
Passes gained	44	20	39	43	33	24		6	21	24	21	275

No. on the Books .	41	No. absent	10	No. promoted	35	Percentage.
No. examined	49	No. withdrawn or exempted	12	Compy. Certificates	5	81.60

Reading	But for German accent good
Spelling	Good in 2nd & 4th; poor in 3rd
Writing	Good except in 3rd
Arithmetic	Good in all but 3rd
Geography	Good, except in 3rd; very poor there
Grammar	Good in 2nd & 3rd; weak in 4th
History	Fair
Composition	Good
Needlework	Very good
Object Lessons	Fair
Poetry	Fair
Drill	Good
Discipline and Order ..	Fair

Examined this school very thoroughly. All classes did well except the 3rd. The number examined was 49, against 54 in the preceding year, and the percentage increased from 80.86 to 81.60. The moral tone of the school was good. The needlework was excellent

Edw. Dewhirst, Senr Inspector. July 22nd, 1884.

John A Hartley Inspector-General. 18.7.84

600—8-4-84

An annual school report of an Education Department inspector. Quality control by means of highly intrusive supervision and regulation marked the new public education systems. Standard English pronunciation and high moral tone required. Hahndorf Primary School, South Australia, 1884. (Butler, 1979, p. 34)

Among them were infant children, less readily accepted into the new public schools than the older private schools.

Schooling Torres Strait Islander and Aboriginal children

Separate schooling for Indigenous children was justified on several grounds. In the late nineteenth century, there were new theories about racial difference, with Social Darwinism impacting on Indigenous peoples. The idea of caste—whether Indigenous persons were 'full blood', half or quarter-caste, and so on—could lead to different treatment. A select committee of the South Australian parliament in 1860, for example, pronounced that half-castes were more educable than full-blood Aborigines. Caste determination became a new reason for separating children from their families. The isolation of Indigenous peoples from the rest of society also developed new force, and schools potentially were powerful instruments in such policies. Church involvement continued despite a lessening influence over schooling more generally.

There was also a popular belief that Indigenous populations were 'dying out'. Protection, reserves, separations and confinements might be justified as kindnesses under the circumstances. Such attitudes were incorporated into more explicit racist discourses and actions. Despite the new requirements from the 1870s that all children attend schools, which we discuss later in this chapter, exceptions were made. Local white prejudices were often effective in barring Indigenous children from local schools. Some Aboriginal communities continued to resist schooling altogether, but there was also accommodation towards colonial society. Many Aboriginal families sought schooling for their children; they were not always successful in achieving it.

The story of Torres Strait Islanders and their schooling demonstrates the unique circumstances applying in different places. Despite their remoteness on many measures, the Torres Strait Islands were at the centre of an industry: the harvesting and trading of *bech-de-mer*. This gave Islanders a rare economic strength in comparison with other Indigenous peoples. The London Missionary Society (LMS) took an interest in the islands. They could constitute a step in taking

Christianity from LMS strongholds in the south-west Pacific to New Guinea.

The Islands were claimed by Queensland in 1872. The LMS opened a school on Murray Island a year later. Active in the Pacific from the late eighteenth century, the society's model of proselytisation was for white missionaries to translate the Bible into Indigenous languages, and to train promising Indigenous men as teachers and evangelists.

Unlike mainland Aborigines, the Torres Strait Islanders mainly held on to their land. This was not only economically significant, but enhanced local power to sustain culture. Nevertheless, Christianity was generally adopted and, despite resistance on some of the smaller islands, schools were developed. But their influence was limited. 'Childhood learning and traditional education underwent little change as a result of European contact because the primary place of the community and kinship group in Islander society had not been disturbed. This was particularly so in the LMS period.' (Williamson, 1994, p. 23)

School photo, Murray Island, Torres Strait, Queensland, c. 1895. (Fryer Library, University of Queensland, Hume Family Photograph Collection, UQFL10/634)

LMS schools commonly operated with Indigenous languages, with early teachers from the Loyalty Islands. The Papuan Gulf Native College was founded to train evangelists and teachers,

> to assemble promising young men and boys from different points of the mission, speaking different languages, at a central station; and there, removed from their evil surroundings and family influences, teach them, making the English language and an industrial school prominent features in the course of instruction. (Williamson, 1994, p. 41)

By 1889, when the college closed, 26 Indigenous students had graduated.

In the 1890s the Queensland government became suspicious of the LMS, especially of some of its Samoan teachers. They were accused of trying to gain control of Island communities. Nevertheless, the Thursday Island-based resident administrator (1885–1904), John Douglas, sought special status for the Islanders, maintaining that they should be accepted as British citizens. He also argued for joint efforts in education with the LMS—but he believed that English language instruction and the use of the Queensland state school syllabus were essential for the shaping of a useful and compliant workforce.

In 1900, the Queensland government took full control of Torres Strait schools. White teachers were favoured over Pacific Indigenous and a 'civilising' mission replaced the evangelical mission. The Islanders were included in the disabling Aboriginal protection legislation that applied on the mainland. Because school enrolments were small, most schools were classified as non-vested and provisional. This meant that communities had to provide school buildings. The teachers were 'provisional' teachers, less well trained than those in full public schools. As a result, these schools were poorer than those in much of Queensland.

This brief discussion has shown the continuing influence of churches on Indigenous education. It has also shown the eventual determination of the colonial state to organise a standard form of schooling across the colony, regardless of local circumstances. Lack of regard for Indigenous culture, the intention to replace Indigenous languages with English, and the desire to create a compliant labour

Few, if any concessions to Indigenous culture. For more on Yarrabah Mission in North Queensland see Haebich (2000). Aboriginal schooling on an Anglican mission, North Queensland, 1893.(Mitchell Library, State Library of NSW, SPF/1237)

force were ambitions common to the administrators of Indigenous schooling across Australia.

The stories of the schools that educated Aboriginal children vary from colony to colony. In this period there was pressure to 'unlock' lands suitable for agriculture. The ensuing *Selection Acts* often added to the pressures on Aboriginal communities seen to occupy promising agricultural lands. On Eyre Peninsula in South Australia, the Poonindie Aboriginal reserve was dismantled in 1894 to provide more land for white farmers.

In 1875, the Victorian Aborigines Protection Board had attempted to close the reasonably successful settlement, including a school, at Coranderrk. When these efforts failed, 'the Board's coercive and petty control of Coranderrk remained to undermine the independence of the people' (Broome, 2010, p. 93). By the end of the century, Aboriginal communities and schooling would be impacted by a growing number of competing government agencies. Boards of Protection, Education Departments, the police and emergent welfare organisations all sought to manage Aboriginal families and communities.

Maloga Mission was a settlement on the New South Wales side of the Murray River, and its history displays the paradoxes in policy that existed during this period. Daniel Matthews was an activist in the 1870s, seeking a better deal for the Aboriginal people along the Murray. Matthews was 'so shocked by the poverty and demoralisation of Aborigines that he and his wife Janet, after praying for guidance, became convinced that they should devote their lives to work amongst Aborigines' (Fletcher, 1989a, p. 42). Impressed by Coranderrk, Matthews sought New South Wales Council of Education assistance to educate Aboriginal children at Maloga; unfortunately, it was not forthcoming.

Matthews believed that Aboriginal people were 'childlike', requiring strong supervision. Such patriarchal attitudes by the governing classes towards the less powerful were common and, combined with the new management of caste, such an approach meant that distressing family expulsions became part of life at Maloga Mission. In 1879, Matthews' school was inspected by the Council of Education. Attendance rates were found to be poor as were the reading and writing achievements of the children tested. The council's inspector reported that the curriculum consisted largely of repeating and singing hymns and psalms. It failed, he said, to prepare Aboriginal boys for low-level agricultural labouring jobs. Nor was there sufficient training of girls in domestic work. He argued against assisting such a school.

From 1880, the date of the ambitious *Public Instruction Act* in New South Wales, Maloga was caught up in the general history of public schooling in that colony. Aboriginal children were not excluded from the requirement of compulsory attendance from 1880, yet there was little effort made to provide public schools where Aboriginal families lived. As part of the new public school regime, all children were required to meet standards of cleanliness, acceptable clothing and behaviour—clauses that were soon used to exclude Aboriginal children from schools. Fifteen Aboriginal children were expelled in Yass in

1883. The local Catholic convent offered to enrol them, seeking government assistance to do so. This provided a fine problem: having withdrawn funding for church schools from 1880, the government found that the only school open to meeting the public responsibility of educating Aboriginal children was denominational.

From the mid-1880s, small schools were increasingly founded to educate Aboriginal children separately as the removal of Aboriginal children from mixed public schools continued. At the Gulargamborne Public School in New South Wales, white parents—unable to achieve the exclusion of Aboriginal pupils—withdrew their own children. A local grazier promised to provide a school for the Aboriginal children. The white families returned to the school, but the grazier's promise was empty and the schooling of local Aboriginal children ceased. There are many similar stories of exclusion during this period.

An 1882 census in the colony found that of 1500 school-aged Aboriginal children, fewer than 200 were at school. Of them, 170 had made it into public schools, but these included thirteen segregated schools. By the end of the century, the old test for exclusion—that children be 'clean, clad and courteous'—had been supplemented by a policy that further empowered white parents. Petitions for the exclusion of Aboriginal children were allowed, and often succeeded.

The significance of the missions declined. At Point McLeay in South Australia, the Education Department sought to implement its curriculum. This was despite Point McLeay's 'successes' in the 1880s with attendance, comparable 'results' to children in white schools and the children being neatly presented. The mission even boasted the waning use of the local Aboriginal language. The South Australian Education Department took over in the 1890s, classifying the school as 'provisional'.

The Northern Territory, still part of South Australia, saw new missionary activity. Lutherans established the Hermannsburg mission west of Alice Springs in 1876. The Arrente people were offered work, food and protection in return for attending church—and for rejecting much of their traditional life. The school house was built in 1896. Reading, writing and arithmetic were taught, as were—on a gendered basis—gardening, carpentry and needlework.

One historian has argued that in the late nineteenth century, relationships between the state and those families and children 'on the margins' were duplicitous (Theobald, 1996, p. 223). Apparent intentions to provide schooling for all were actually marked by combinations of neglect and new racialised patterns of administration. Universal schooling was not quite yet on offer, despite the apparent intentions of new colonial *Education Acts*.

Rise of the new government systems of public education

From 1852 through to 1908 in the Australian colonies, then states, there were laws passed that introduced often free and mainly secular public schools, with some compulsory attendance required. They became the foundation of modern *primary* education. The colonies looked to each other for inspiration on how to construct systems of public schooling, but they also looked to England where, in 1870, an *Education Act* was passed. Yet, except for Western Australia, the terms of the English Act were already considered unacceptable by colonial governments—state-supported denominational schools were rejected in the colonies.

At the beginning of the twentieth century, there were sufficient similarities among the new laws across the colonies to suggest that public schools in Australia were developing common characteristics. Table 3.1 summarises progress towards this commonality.

Western Australia provides a narrative of public school system foundation that illuminates the experiences of the other colonies. This is the kind of argument that valorised improvement and progress: 'By the turn of the century Western Australia had acquired a centralised and efficient system of public instruction' (Mossenson, 1972, p. 105). According to this argument, before the new centralised systems there was inefficiency, patchy coverage and schooling held hostage to religious interests. Opposing ideas—that local control over public schooling was valuable; that more concessions to the Catholics may have allayed sectarian bitterness; that the new systems imposed authoritarian forms of schooling on labouring class and rural populations, oppressing pupils and teachers alike—were rejected.

TABLE 3.1

Education laws systematising colonial and state systems of public education

Establishment of Departments of Education under ministerial control—that is, centralised, bureaucratic control	
Victoria	1872
South Australia	1875
Queensland	1875
New South Wales	1880
Tasmania	1885
Western Australia	1893
Compulsory school attendance of children, with generous allowances for non-attendance	
Tasmania	1868
Western Australia	1871
Victoria	1872
South Australia	1875
New South Wales	1880
Queensland	1900*
Abolition of school fees for the years of compulsion	
Queensland	1870*
Victoria	1872
South Australia	1892
Western Australia	1901
New South Wales	1906
Tasmania	1908
Withdrawal of state funding from church-controlled (denominational) schools	
South Australia	1851
Tasmania	1854
Victoria	1873
Queensland	1880
New South Wales	1882
Western Australia	1895
Establishment of a secular curriculum in government schools, with or without compensatory rights of access for denominational teaching or non-denominational scripture instruction	
South Australia	1852
Tasmania	1854
Victoria	1872
Queensland	1875
New South Wales	1880
Western Australia	1895

* Apparent contradiction explained by gap between legislation and implementation.

In the 1860s in Western Australia, those government schools that existed were basically for the children of the lower classes. Instruction was 'plain and practical'. In a few schools, teachers taught 'higher subjects' by private arrangement with families. Buildings and rooms were often rented, and teacher quality and supply were issues. From 1861 monitors were replaced by pupil-teacher indenture, but generally the status of the government schools remained low.

The alternative private schools were often ephemeral, and there were few denominational schools other than Catholic schools. Differing social class expectations of schools may be seen in the petition of a group of parents in the township of York for an *increase* in national school fees, to 'rescue parents from the shame of accepting charity' (Mossenson, 1972, p. 25). Higher fees could convert a common school into a more exclusive academy. Kiama Public School in New South Wales and the Grote Street Model School in South Australia provide examples of public schools accommodating children from better-off families. In Victoria, the argument entered Henry Handel Richardson's *The Getting of Wisdom*. As her daughter left home for boarding school, Laura's mother declared, 'Yet what else could I do? To a State School, I've always said it, my children shall never go—not if I have to beg the money to send them elsewhere!'

Inspector William Adkinson reported on Western Australian National schools in 1868. School attendances, facilities and instruction were all weak, signified by the continued presence of now 'antiquated' Irish National readers in schools. The report helped provide a path to reform, including the recommendation that teachers should be paid in accordance with the 'results' achieved by their pupils.

The politics preceding the *Elementary Education Act* of 1871 were similar to those elsewhere. The Catholic Church demanded state aid for its schools, but the presence of a Catholic governor who supported aid to denominational schools led to a different outcome from that in other colonies. Governor Weld, using the example of the English *Education Act* of 1870, secured some funding for voluntary or assisted (actually denominational) schools as well as the National schools.

Western Australia was also an outlier by establishing potentially powerful district boards to manage the appointment and dismissal of teachers. The discovery of gold in that colony brought new migrants from eastern Australia, prepared to argue for replicating the systems of public education established there. David Shearer, a Presbyterian minister, argued that government schools continued to be held back by poor curriculum, obsolete readers and now payment by results—and, significantly, by the diversion of funds to denominational schools.

In 1893, a new administration under a constitution that finally instituted responsible government decided to abolished state aid to church schools—the last of the colonies to do so. This was implemented in 1895. An Education Department was also established, under ministerial control.

The number of children in schools was increased substantially, and new schools were built. School curricula were reformed to include subjects such as singing, history and object lessons. Kindergarten work was introduced for infants, and advice to teachers on good pedagogy regularly occurred. An education gazette was published. Teachers were given more protection against salary docking for uncollected fees, and schools and teachers were classified, enabling an orderly promotion and transfer system. Patronage declined as a factor in teachers' careers. Savings were made by discriminating against the employment of married women, and fixing the wage of unmarried women teachers at 80 per cent of that of men. District board powers were reduced. Regular inspection of teachers and schools ensured that the policy of the department was implemented in even the most remote of schools.

By the end of the nineteenth century, the word 'efficient' was increasingly being used to describe the centrally controlled school. Western Australian public schools were widely assumed to have reached this standard.

Through one Act of Parliament, Victoria appeared to come closest to what was eventually thought of as the Australian settlement in public education. The *Education Act* of 1872 established compulsory attendance, and also made attendance at public schools free. The Act stated that, 'In every state school secular instruction only shall be given and no teacher shall give any other than secular instruction in

The last decade for government-assisted elementary denominational schools. Church of England school, Dunolly, west of Bendigo, Victoria, c. 1861 (State Library of Victoria, b36129)

any state school building . . .' The Act also established an Education Department and withdrew state aid to denominational schools.

To reach a point such as this, there needed to be advances in secular and liberal conceptions of the state and modern citizenship. It actually helped that the Catholic Church intensified its hostility towards science, liberalism, nationalism and other perceived modernist threats to its authority. The church could be sidelined as 'extreme'. In the 1870s, supporters of public schools rarely argued against a role for Christianity in family life. School secularists usually believed that moral instruction could proceed from common Christian values. In that way, public schools would not be the home of godlessness—the charge brought by Bishop Goold of Melbourne and other Catholic bishops.

This coincidence of rising secular liberalism and Catholic reaction caused bitter struggles in each colony as discussed below.

Victoria

In Victoria the lead-up to the 1872 Act was protracted. George Higinbotham, sometime Attorney-General, initially had supported religious instruction in public schools, but there were difficulties with both Catholic and Anglican churches. Often opposed to each other's policies, both the *Age* and the *Argus* newspapers agreed for once. There was no solution other than a fully secular school system. Higinbotham was frustrated by the 'unpatriotic policy pursued by the leading Christian sects' (quoted in Austin, 1972, p. 196).

As in other colonies, there were arguments that democracies required educated citizens, and that good public education would lead to national prosperity. Pressure groups, Leagues of Public Education and others helped win the argument—not only in Victoria but also in New South Wales and South Australia—that governments were the only reliable organisers of public education.

In Victoria, then, a mere ten years had seen a reversal of the fortunes of national/public schools. In 1862, the Victorian government under John O'Shanassy (Catholic) and William Haines (Anglican) had cut the funding of National schools so ruthlessly that their survival was doubtful. The 1872 Act led to nearly all religious denominations except the Lutherans and Catholics withdrawing from elementary school provision. The achievements of the new Department of Education in providing school buildings and teachers were impressive.

New South Wales

In New South Wales through the 1860s, William Wilkins—first as chief inspector and then secretary of the Council of Education—led the building of a system of national education. In 1865 he summarised progress. The assessment of teachers' work had been regularised and 'the machinery of the system was slowly completed', only requiring more in the way of 'facilities and opportunities' (quoted in Griffiths, 1957, p. 103). Phrases such as the 'machinery of the system' typified the reforms in progress. Efficient bureaucratic machinery would replace the 'inefficiencies' associated with many denominational and private schools.

The number of government schools in New South Wales grew from 144 with just over 9000 pupils in 1860 to 263 in 1865, approaching 17 500 pupils. Sometimes there were National schools with high numbers of Catholic pupils, over which the Catholic Church sought control. This kind of pressure, along with continuing negative assessments of ill-attended denominational schools, led to the 1866 *Public Schools Act*, sponsored by leading politician, Henry Parkes. He argued that some 100 000 children under the age of 14 in New South Wales were still not being educated. The system of dual boards—National and Denominational—was not doing the job, especially for 'destitute and neglected' children. The system was expensive, leading to inferior schools, and it fostered social conflict. Parkes believed that parents had no 'serious objection to sending their children to good schools, though these schools may not be of denominational character' (quoted in Griffiths, 1957, p. 119).

The 1866 Act replaced the dual boards with a Council of Education, providing for more intrusive inspection and regulation of all public and government-assisted denominational schools. In public schools there would be four hours of secular instruction daily, with an hour each day set aside for religious instruction by church-provided teachers.

This approach lasted fourteen years. Council of Education inspectors regularly criticised denominational schools for their inefficiencies. New provisional and half-time public schools were praised for increasing educational access in poorly populated rural areas—though not always for Aboriginal children. The new public school effort could be turned to a variety of purposes. In the Braidwood area, notorious for its bushrangers, the schooling of children in bushranger-friendly families was meant to assist in dealing with the threat (Freeman, 2009).

Parkes later justified his 1880 *Public Instruction Act* as having been brought on by the libels of Catholic bishops against public schools, but there were reasons beyond the sectarian. The 1880 Act established a public school system that might include 'superior' schools, enabling the 'higher branches' (secondary curriculum) to be taught. Evening schools were to be provided for those with little education. Teaching was to be 'non-sectarian', but could include non-dogmatic religious teaching. The 'common Christianity' idea endured, despite its rejection by the Catholic Church. School fee exemptions for the poor were allowed, and only 70 days' attendance in 140 school days each year was required. Clergy would be allowed into public schools under similar circumstances to those detailed in the 1866 Act.

The 1880 Act ended the dual system of denominational and National schools. Henceforth, there would be a government department, led by a public servant—the director—who would be responsible to a minister of the Crown; he in turn was responsible to the parliament.

The 1880 Act is a good example of the reality behind most of the so-called 'free, compulsory and secular' *Education Acts*. It did not provide free education, its compulsory clauses were timorous and, with potentially one-fifth of each school day given over to denominational instruction, it was hardly secular. Nevertheless, state aid to denominational schools was abolished. As in other parts of the country, resistance by Wesleyans, Baptists, Congregationalists and Presbyterians to the claims of the Catholic and Anglican churches made those groups favourable to public education. Splits among Anglicans helped as well.

Tasmania

In 1868 there was a *Public Schools Act* in Tasmania. In that colony there was an exceptionally generous approach to compulsory school attendance. Allowable exemptions included evidence of private education in reading and writing, ill-health or inability to safely attend school. Another was parents not being able to do without the labour of their children. Nor did Tasmania provide penalties for non-attendance. Some rural districts were exempted altogether, and Tasmanian school attendances remained low. The 1885 *Education Act* was tougher, and was the real equivalent of those laws on education that the other colonies had passed in the 1870s.

South Australia

Arguments for an educated workforce supporting economic development underlay the passing of the South Australian *Education Act* of 1875. Within the labour movement, there was discussion about the impact of education on social class. Was education about social betterment, people leaving the working class—or was it really about creating a stronger, more capable working class? The *Weekly Herald*, a labour newspaper, looked to a decline of the ill-educated rabble-rousing elements of the movement. The paternalist social control and improvement argument was also present. Inspector Jung (no exemplar of respectability, as it turned out) believed that the moral training of children was the priority of the public schools. As in the other colonies, the compulsory clauses were weak. Some parents chose to pay the fines rather than lose essential labour (Hyams, 1988).

The struggle to achieve *free* public schooling was complicated by the parental neglect argument. Would free education encourage irresponsible parents? In 1891 in South Australia, fees were abolished, but it was a fraught question. As in the other colonies, the 1890s depression saw reduced revenue for government, yet the argument that the universal male franchise demanded universal free education won the day.

The 1875 Act in South Australia concentrated power over public education in the hands of the new Inspector-General, John Hartley. As in other colonies, rigidity, hierarchy, efficiency and paternalism became features of the emerging system.

Queensland

In Queensland, Charles Nicholson had become increasingly frustrated by the charges of 'godlessness' against National schools. The *Primary Education Act* of 1860 transferred all the denominational schools to non-vested status. *The Grammar Schools Act* of the same year was also interpreted as a blow to the churches. The grammar schools would be non-denominational. Bishop Tufnell for the Anglicans had victories and defeats during the 1860s, but—as in Victoria, and for the future in Western Australia—gold mining, and the migration it attracted helped defeat the denominationalists. In 1870, fees for National schools were abolished. Such schools increasingly were considered the only viable source of schooling in remote areas. Compulsory attendance was accepted in 1875. Aid to denominational schools ceased in 1880 and public school curricula would be secular. A Department of Education was established.

Significance of the *Education Acts*

There has been some debate about how to interpret the rise of compulsory schooling. Some have argued that a crisis in patriarchy provides a broad explanation. New means of governing the young, women and the dangerously mobile labouring classes were required as older forms of patriarchal authority—monarchic, aristocratic, church, community and familial—broke down. Strengthening capitalist relations and new alienations associated with the conditions of labour weakened traditional social bonds. The 'fatherhood' powers and responsibilities of post-feudal authority retreated in the age of fraternal revolutions marked by liberalism, democracy, and even socialism in some places. New patriarchal institutions were required, and schools requiring compulsory attendance would be one of them (see Miller and Davey, 1990; Miller, 1998).

Nevertheless, the strengthening of the school among and over populations was measured. Weak compulsory clauses in the *Education Acts* were in fact politically astute. They established the principle of compulsion, but avoided the damaging opposition that they would have faced had they been too thoroughgoing. Many family economies—rural and urban—continued to depend on children making a contribution with their labour. There were other factors as well. The depredations wrought by disease and epidemics alone—whooping cough, scarlet fever, influenza, scarlatina, mumps and so on—were reason enough for a cautious approach to compulsion.

Late in this period, enthusiastic public school system promoters began to redefine irregular school attendance as *truancy* caused by parental irresponsibility. Intolerance towards child labour developed. Children and youth on the streets of cities and towns were increasingly defined as a social problem. This, as well as an anticipated growth in national productivity and prosperity arising from a better educated population, was the context of pressure towards making schooling compulsory.

Many parents resisted the new public schooling. In New South Wales, a teacher in 1871 collected parents' reasons for withdrawing their children from a public school (see Griffiths, 1957, p. 140). They included:

> You are being far too hard, and keep them too close at work, and give too many home lessons, and make too much fuss about nothing, if they do not prepare them, or if they happen to be late in the morning.
>
> I have decided and [sic.] insuperable objection to my children, who have noble blood in their veins, mixing with the common throng. I was never teached [sic.] at a public school, and I will not allow my children to be so, if I can help it.
>
> Well, you see [the private school teacher] owes me an account for the last three months, and I will never get it unless I take it out this way.
>
> The poor [private teacher] asked me to give him a turn, and my children are so young that it does not matter much where they go for a year or two.
>
> My children were getting too impudent at the public school; they came home and bounced me about not having the house clean, and I could not stand it.

The opposition of the Catholic bishops to Catholic children attending mainly secular public schools became an Australia-wide campaign in the 1860s and 1870s. The language grew more vigorous:

> this expenditure on godless education, this studding the colony with schools which the church knows from experience will, in course of time, fill the country with indifferentists, not to speak of absolute infidels; this use of Catholic funds—of taxes paid out of Catholic pockets . . . is an act so galling to every feeling of fair play . . . (quoted in Griffiths, 1957, p. 154)

Protestant versus Catholic sectarian strife developed as an enduring feature of Australian life. It was often played out as schools emptied each day, when children from public and Catholic schools hurled insults and more at one another.

By the end of the century, a transformation in the character of public schooling had occurred. The victories of those believing in secularisation, compulsion and even free education were significant, but not without consequences. The construction of intrusive, centralised and bureaucratising Departments of Education in the name of efficiency would soon attract critics beyond the denominationalists.

Denominational and private elementary schools

The schools of the Catholic Church, progressively deprived of state funding, continued under difficult circumstances. Signs of hostility had been everywhere. At one point, the New South Wales Council of Education had rejected Christian Brothers textbooks. Bishop Geoghegan in Adelaide was an advocate of a complete break with public education. He was granted 30 000 francs by the Society for the Propagation of the Faith to assist in the founding of separate Catholic schools.

Within the church, an argument developed as to whether its schools needed to be systematised. Leakage of enrolments to secular schools occurred because Catholic families saw them as better schools. In 1868, at the Fort Street Public School in Sydney, of 1900 pupils, 455 were Catholic. This was no isolated example. One of the advocates of Catholic systematisation was a priest, Julian Tenison-Woods. As Director-General of Catholic schools in South Australia from 1867, he dismissed unsatisfactory teachers. A new religious order, the Sisters of St Joseph, led by Mary MacKillop, was given the task of founding schools in poorer districts of the colony. The sisters also began a pupil-teacher training system on behalf of the church, though monitorialism survived where simultaneous classroom instruction could not be afforded.

Catholic schools were classified. Attention was paid to the production of standard school timetables and the distribution of new textbooks. Uniform curricula were developed, as were uniform standards of achievement across schools. As would be the case in the new public schools, the representative teacher would be an unmarried woman, in this case a nun. Tenison-Woods, like many of the leaders of public school systems, believed women would be better teachers, and that they were more likely to be hard-working, devoted, honest and amenable to discipline.

In South Australia, the Catholic schools were systematised faster than the secular board schools. With the withdrawal of state aid, lay Catholic teacher salaries could no longer be afforded. Bishops across the colonies sought Irish, English and European orders of sisters, priests and brothers to staff schools. The South Australian approach was adopted in Queensland, and then elsewhere. From the mid-1860s through the 1880s, the number of lay Catholic teachers plummeted. The proportion of Catholic children in public schools also declined.

The orders that taught in Catholic schools had different histories. The Irish Christian Brothers were initially less welcome in New South Wales, given Bishop Polding's English Benedictine affiliation. The Sisters of Mercy, active early in Western Australia, established schools across the colonies. A French order, the Marist Brothers, originally devoted to elementary schooling in rural France, established both elementary and superior schools in Australia. Higher fees could be charged in superior schools. In Adelaide by 1900, the Dominican sisters' School of St Mary was running a dual system. Upstairs was a middle-class or superior school for girls, offering the 'higher branches' and accomplishments. The fees paid subsidised the downstairs school for children of poor families in Adelaide's West End. The children from the two schools were not to consort (Northey, 1992).

Small private schools—some of them 'dame schools'—continued through this period, especially in the colonies where 'free' elementary schooling was yet to be won. They were attractive to many working-class and poorer rural communities in comparison with the intrusively 'efficient' public schools. Private schools were criticised by Education Department officials. Somewhat typical was the problem they caused the Hindmarsh Public School in Adelaide in the 1880s. The private schools, necessarily sensitive to the exigencies of working-class family lives, simply could not afford to 'care' as much about attendance and punctuality. They undercut the fees of the public school. The public school headmaster complained that the privately schooled children

A private dame school in rural New South Wales in the 1870s. Children and parents from poorer circumstances often felt more comfortable in these than the denominational and public schools. Possibly Miss Mayes' school at Fighting Gully in rural New South Wales. (Mitchell Library, State Library of NSW, ON 4 Box 8/18784))

were not encouraged to adopt habits of cleanliness, let alone propriety of conduct.

Older approaches to schooling died hard. The new public schools had to persuade as well as compel families into them, and new government regulations began to harass 'inefficient' private schools out of existence. Nevertheless, populations on the borders of the new educational state remained resistant. In Adelaide, there was a school for Chinese children supported by a mission. Hiring a governess remained popular in some families, and this practice provided an occupation for the novelist Miles Franklin. In *My Brilliant Career*, Sybilla attempts to teach the uncouth M'Swat children: 'One Monday morning I marshalled my five scholars . . . in a little black skillion, which was set apart as a schoolroom and store for flour and rock-salt.' The M'Swat children, abetted by their parents in slovenliness and defiance, were perfect fictional examples of what was wrong with inefficient schools, and Sybilla made little difference—until she soundly thrashed the prime rebel, Jimmy.

As most Protestant churches departed from elementary schooling, more effort was required in the Sunday schools. The Methodists were particularly active, imitating the public schools in standardising instruction—though monitorial methods survived within them.

Superior schools

If private elementary schools were running into difficulties by the end of the century, private schools that taught the 'higher branches'—those that called themselves 'high' schools, colleges and academies—were more resilient. Some, like the new Abbotsleigh school in Sydney, were shocked by the impact of the new public examinations, an enterprise of the new universities. A student remembered that in 1886 she and all her classmates failed the Junior Public Examination:

> I shall never forget the morning the results came out . . . Miss Clarke . . . was terribly disappointed. She gave us all a holiday . . . and she sent us round to 'Branthwaite', my home . . . We were given strawberries and cream to cheer us up. The following year, after much work, we entered again and all passed. (Emilsen, 2000, p. 2)

Marian Clarke, the founder of Abbotsleigh, had some education in Germany, and when at the University College in Bristol she passed the Cambridge higher local examination with honours. She taught for four years at Manchester's High School for Girls, one of the English schools that took the education of girls 'seriously'—meaning that girls were taught subjects that hitherto had belonged to boys' grammar and 'English' curriculum schools.

The education of middle-class girls was reformed in this period. The older accomplishments curriculum that had put the arts—including music, ornamental needlework and drawing or painting—and modern languages and the social graces at the heart of the curriculum was criticised, not always in well-informed ways. These accomplishment studies became more peripheral, sometimes becoming 'extras' that were paid for separately. Sometimes there was conflict between parents and school proprietors. Some parents wanted the safe and homely environment, and a degree of 'finishing' with the accomplishments, rather than concentration on publicly examinable subjects. In the 1890s, a student at Mrs Kelsey's private school for girls in South Australia remembered being taught that they were ladies, and should sit with their knees together and keep their voices low. She learned reading, writing and arithmetic, but behaviour was the thing: 'It was a snobby age. You were taught to always remember your manners . . .' (G. Lock, quoted in Hyams, 1988, p. 171).

Private-venture schools for both boys and girls laboured under old difficulties. The health and respectability of school principals and their families were crucial in maintaining enrolments. An eye had to be kept on changing demands in the market. 'The city' began to demand the new credentials that university public examination boards offered. There were even intimations that middle-class girls might enter an expanded labour market offering more than teaching. Growing operations such as the railways and public service began running their own entrance examinations to determine the suitability of boys for employment. Parents expected schools to help boys prepare for them.

In South Australia, one private school, credited with the education of many boys from well-off families was John Lorenzo Young's Adelaide Educational Institution. From an engineering background, and after returning from the Victorian goldfields, Young founded his school. It became the largest private school in South Australia, taking boarders and day students. Young's curriculum concentrated less on the classics and more on the 'English' commercial subjects. Young offered moral philosophy, technical drawing and physiology. He refused to teach religion. The school closed in 1880, and—unusually for a private school—at a time of the proprietor-principal's choosing.

By the end of the century, private superior/secondary schools remained numerous but problems loomed. Their main competitors were the church corporate schools. Invariably, they were more stable than the private schools. They could survive a scandal and were more likely to have the resources to meet the demands of the university public examinations syllabuses. They could also provide

Small private schools were market aware, sensitive to the social class and respectability aspirations of their client families. Samuel Belcher's school catered for the sons of 'gentlemen'. These are the day boys. Garroorigang, near Goulburn, New South Wales, c. 1875. (National Library of Australia, vn4979993)

expensive sports fields. Many proprietors of private schools could see the end coming, and a commonly sought solution was selling a school to a church. This occurred in all colonies, though many of the transfers were only completed in the twentieth century. Marian Clarke's Abbotsleigh School was sold first to another proprietor-principal, but in 1924 Sydney's Anglican diocese bought it.

Table 3.2 shows the significance of the period 1861–1900 for the foundation of the corporate, mainly church schools. The Protestant churches concentrated on the school market, serving the families of their wealthier members once their elementary schools closed. They eclipsed the private schools as the most significant providers of post-elementary education. In 1900, there were only five government-controlled public high schools in Australia. By far the greatest number of corporate schools belonged to churches.

TABLE 3.2

Foundations of corporate schools, mainly church owned, that continued to exist in 1985

	1821–1860	1861–1900	1901–1940
Victoria	5	28	23
New South Wales	3	28	17
South Australia	2	8	7
Queensland	0	13	17
Western Australia	1	5	9
Tasmania	3	3	2
Total	*14*	*85*	*75*

Source: Sherington, Petersen and Brice (1987, pp. 183–5).

There were corporate schools other than the church colleges. Sydney Grammar had been founded by Act of Parliament in 1854. Queensland followed with its state grammar schools, with enrolments supported by government scholarships. The first was in Ipswich. After fighting off an attempt by the Catholic Church to orient the grammar school as a publicly funded denominational school, Governor Bowen opened it in 1863. He remarked that classical languages remained relevant, providing a practical and liberal education, significant in social intercourse. Great wisdom was to be found in the literature of Greek and Roman antiquity (Turney, 1975, p. 299).

Ten non-denominational grammar schools eventually were founded in Queensland, four of them for girls. Their students sat the University of Sydney public examinations from the mid-1870s. A similar pattern emerged in Western Australia, as students worked towards the examinations of the University of Adelaide. The secular Perth High School in Western Australia was also founded by Act of Parliament in 1876, but it was later taken over as the Anglican boys' Hale School.

The female principal of one of Queensland's secular grammar schools, Brisbane Girls' Grammar, had her difficulties. The male head was unsympathetic to the problems arising from men coming from the boys' school to teach girls the classics and mathematics.

Janet O'Connor resigned, taking 30 girls with her, to establish her own private school. Such fluidity between corporate, private and government sectors was not uncommon. O'Connor, however, saw that the future lay with corporate and public schools: 'no private school can do what a government school can do, for the public is rich and never dies' (quoted in Theobald, 1996, p. 100). There were other struggles. Should the school concentrate on the academic—as one of its trustees and sometime Queensland premier, Samuel Griffith, believed—or focus on a female-oriented curriculum organised around generalist rather than subject-specialist teachers? Eliza Fewings was eventually sacked, in part for advocating a curriculum that would include cooking, music, dance, millinery and sport. The academic curriculum triumphed under her replacement.

A Melbourne school, Presbyterian Ladies College, founded in 1875, is often credited with being the first 'modern' corporate school for girls. It entered girls for public examinations; it taught them classical languages and mathematics. Its founding principal, Charles Henry Pearson, believed in educating for 'the higher culture of women', yet the school continued to offer accomplishments as well, and certainly held to the belief that it was producing 'ladies' rather than academic swats. The school was simultaneously advanced and traditional. Nevertheless, it contributed to first-wave feminism, as many of its students pioneered female graduation from the university. Some developed careers like the novelist 'Henry Handel Richardson'. *The Getting of Wisdom* is a revealing portrait of teachers and girls, the culture of the school, and its teaching and curriculum. All colonial capitals soon boasted similar schools. There were several Presbyterian and Methodist ladies' colleges, and the Anglicans began producing Church of England Girls' Grammar Schools.

In this period, boys' corporate schools responded to the reform of 'greater public' schools in England. 'Arnoldianism'—named after Thomas Arnold, the head of Rugby School in the 1840s—entered the colonies, often via headmasters with prior English careers. There would be prefects, school magazines, old scholars' associations, school songs, school colours and a new role for 'games'. Cricket, rowing and Rugby (and Australian Rules football in the southern and western

Presbyterian Ladies College, Melbourne. Reputedly the first church collegiate school offering a serious education for middle- and ruling-class girls, 1875-1890. (State Library of Victoria, 1978795)

colonies) could do things for a boy that Latin, chapel and classroom could not. Through games, boys learnt about leadership, rules, fair play and teamwork. They learned that good manners were appropriate in victory—and defeat. At least, that was the theory.

There was some resistance to these reforms. Too great an emphasis on sport became the problem of 'athleticism'. The only boys worth looking up to were the sporting heroes. Boys who avoided sport, or were too interested in reading, the arts, or religion, might have their masculinity questioned. One example of resistance occurred in a Marist Brothers school in Sydney. The headmaster of Saint Joseph's, Emilian, held that enthusiasm for sport among Australian boys was a threat to religious seriousness, encouraging barbaric behaviour. He resisted sports fields, the joining of inter-collegiate sports associations and the introduction of Saturday sports. There was an ethnic component to this. Emilian was French, and Basil, the sports master, was Irish. Most of the boys were Irish-Australian. With the departure of Emilian from the school, 'Joey's' rapidly developed its sport, and a ruthless Rugby culture. If the 'games' revolution began in the Protestant schools, the middle-class corporate Catholics were not far behind.

South Australia pioneered public high schools under the direct control of an Education Department. In 1879, Adelaide's Advanced School for Girls offered an academic curriculum. Like most public high schools of the era, it charged fees. It would meet the demand for modern schooling for girls where private girls' schools apparently had failed.

In New South Wales in 1883, eight public high schools were founded, with separate boys' and girls' schools in Sydney, Maitland, Bathurst and Goulburn. Of these, only the Sydney and Maitland schools survived the first few years. In Bathurst, the hostility of the Anglican school, All Saints, towards the public high schools was fierce. Its head, Edwin Bean, offered scholarships to clever boys bound for the high school, a practice that remains popular to the present day. There were confused purposes, especially in the girls' high schools. An early headmistress of Bathurst Girls apparently rejected the enrolment of a publican's daughter, a threat to the tone she hoped for in the school. Perhaps the concept of an enrolment based on merit rather than social background remained a little too innovative. One of the main problems for the early New South Wales schools was the competition for students from other Education Department schools. Pupils could get a low-fee secondary education at 'superior' public schools.

The idea that secondary education—whether public, private or corporate—was middle-class education persisted into the twentieth century. In Victoria, the private and corporate school lobbies successfully blocked Education Department schools from offering secondary subjects. In South Australia, Inspector-General John Hartley told a Royal Commission that the secondary curriculum was unsuitable for working-class children. Mixing children from the respectable classes with those from the working class was a problem. High fees could ensure a degree of exclusivity. Nevertheless, Hartley believed that a narrow path should be left open for the deserving and clever from the lower classes.

And then there were state high schools, in New South Wales from 1883. This is Ethel Turner, later a novelist, one of Sydney Girls High School's earliest students, 1885. (National Library of Australia, an10998777-332)

He supported a limited number of scholarships that might take boys to the better private and corporate colleges, and girls to his own Advanced School for Girls. In Queensland, Education Department director Ewart blocked the foundation of superior public schools in that colony.

Towards the end of the nineteenth century, there was a developing argument for specialised technical and agricultural education. New institutions were founded by the state: Roseworthy in South Australia in 1885, Dookie in Victoria in 1886 and the Hawkesbury Agricultural College in New South Wales in 1891. By the end of the century, there were also great technical colleges in capital cities and larger towns like Ballarat in Victoria.

In 1878 in Victoria, Charles Henry Pearson had argued for public high schools—'intermediate schools'—between the public elementary school and the university. Many families 'suffered severely by the want of middle-class schools' (quoted in Turney, 1975, p. 314). In South Australia, E.L. Batchelor, on behalf of the emerging Labor Party, also argued for accessible public high schools. Not only were fees, clothing and charges for 'extras' expensive, they were calculated to exclude working-class children from the better private and church schools. They saturated their pupils 'with class prejudice before they were out of their teens'. Many ended up as 'confirmed little snobs' (quoted in Hyams, 1988, p. 174). Though there were many schools teaching secondary subjects—some of them secondary schools—by 1900 they were inaccessible to most young people.

Education of infants and other special populations

That there should be separate arrangements for infants had been recognised for much of the nineteenth century, but the ideas of Pestalozzi, and later Froebel, took time to achieve institutional reality. Infants should not just be minded, but their education begun. Australian kindergartens and the introduction of Froebel's 'gifts' belong to this period. The gifts were designed to teach children important concepts through their manipulation. The first gift consisted of six soft coloured balls. The idea of the sphere, the identification of colours, and understanding movements such as rolling and bouncing could be learnt from the first gift. More gifts followed. There were also 'occupations': games, songs and movements. Through 'play' with a purpose, the child would learn naturalistically. Children were expected to make rapid progress when transferred into a regular school. There was even a vocational preparation argument behind the new infant curriculum.

Progressive infant education could help save children from the 'gutter', though better-off children were also catered for. In Victoria in 1899, Annie Westmoreland gave lectures on Froebel at the University of Melbourne. She opened her kindergarten within the private girls' school, Ruyton. It doubled as a training school for kindergarten teachers. Similarly, Margaret Windeyer in New South Wales worked for kindergartens. Maybanke College, among other girls' schools for better-off families, ran a kindergarten in the 1890s.

Some public schools introduced kindergarten classes, but parsimony saw the movement falter. Crown Street Public School had opened a kindergarten in 1882 with Froebel in mind, but closed it in 1884. In South Australia, Inspector Whitham complained in the mid-1890s that little to nothing was being done for infants, nor was there special training for infant teachers. Private philanthropists—especially women, child-savers of various kinds—were more likely than governments to establish nursery schools and kindergartens. One consequence of the 1890s depression was raising the age at which a child could attend school. The exclusion of infants saved money in a number of colonies.

Reformers of infant education demanded trained teachers who would pay attention to the special requirements of the very young. The old infants school architecture, the stepped gallery, gave way to spaces that accommodated the inquisitive, moving child, who was to learn through play rather than sitting passively in a row.

Progressive educators and philanthropists also paid attention to the 'plight' of 'deaf, dumb or blind' children. Special schools—often total institutions, since boarding was common—were established. New teaching methods competed as children apparently were saved from apathy and neglect. Sydney's Deaf and Dumb Institute, later the Royal Institute for Deaf and Blind Children, was founded in 1860. In 1872 it occupied a grand building across the road from the University of Sydney. Children were enrolled not only from New South Wales, but from Tasmania, Queensland and New Zealand. In 1870, the institution became 'public' in part, as the first government assistance was granted. Despite this, the 1880 New South Wales *Public Instruction Act* made no special provision for the compulsory schooling of such children, a responsibility not assumed until the 1940s.

Teachers and the rise of a modern teaching profession

The period 1860–1900 saw the emergence of a modern teaching profession, with most teachers becoming salaried employees of growing public education systems. The number of younger, unmarried women who became teachers increased dramatically:

> At mid-century, the calling of the elementary school teacher had still to be invented. By the end of the century, the hundreds of 'lady teachers' who staked a claim to this new professional space had been confined to the lower echelons of a hierarchy dominated by men, a position which they shared with women teaching for the state throughout the Western world. (Theobald, 1996, p. 130)

Teachers began making tentative, then strong steps to organise into professional associations and then unions. In the 1890s, their annual conferences often became forums for the promulgation of new educational ideas.

In the 1860s and 1870s, the new pupil-teacher had appeared as a progressive step towards better teacher training. Working in schools as apprentices, they were theoretically subject to wise supervision and instruction by school heads. The truth was more often exploitation and drudgery, as they took responsibility for large classes. They had little education beyond their own schooling, and little room for thinking about pedagogies other than those of their preceptors. They were also poorly paid. Critics of the system argued that the teachers produced by this system tended towards docility as they tried to measure up to the career-determining assessments of their superiors, but recent research has contradicted this view. The struggles between teachers and their superiors—whether school heads, inspectors or education department heads—are now well documented (see Whitehead, 1999, 2003, pp. 67–78; Theobald, 2006; 1996, pp. 163–91).

Following England's introduction of the payment of teachers by results in 1862, most Australian colonies followed suit. Some argued—in Western Australia, for example—that it initially improved the quality of instruction in national schools. Nevertheless, corruption and unfeeling administration eventually epitomised the system. Attendance rolls could be falsified, children's ages juggled, clever students who were ill forced into unwise school attendance, and students who were not so clever threatened if they dared attend. Teachers fresh from inspection warned nearby schools of what to expect. Those parts of the curriculum that would most affect teacher assessment were drilled. In Victoria, there was worse to come: 'When as a refinement of the whole evil system, it was determined that the headmaster's salary should depend in part upon his assistants' results a reign of terror in the colonial classroom was assured' (Austin, 1972, p. 252).

In South Australia in 1878, a schoolmaster reported the following classroom exchange to the Education Department, protesting his subsequent salary loss (in Hyams, 1988, p. 139):

> *Inspector:* Do you know how many shillings make a pound?
> *Child:* Twenty.
> *Inspector:* I did not ask you how many. Answer my question. Do you know how many shillings make a pound?
> *Child:* No.
> —So every child in the class said 'No'. Consequently my Junior Class, twenty two in number, had only three passes in Arithmetic.

Other problems affecting teacher salary included school classification and location. Especially if student fees supplemented salaries, teachers in large urban schools were better paid than rural teachers with fewer children and fees that were more difficult to collect.

Despite all the efficiency-based reforms, there was no immediate transition from older ways of doing things. Ministerial patronage over appointments persisted in Victoria, and teachers feared giving evidence against their superiors at Royal Commissions. The new Education Departments often looked less like Max Weber's rational bureaucracies than fiefdoms.

The early teaching career of the poet Mary Gilmore was not atypical. From 12 or 13 years of age, Mary became an 'unofficial' pupil teacher in three small country schools. At 16, she passed the entrance exam to become a probationary pupil teacher at Wagga Wagga Public. Failing her teacher's examination, she was employed in a provisional school. (Rural provisional schools usually got the unqualified teachers.) After sitting the IIIA teachers' exam in 1887, she was sent to a school near Broken Hill as a temporary assistant. In 1899, she transferred to Sydney, to teach at Neutral Bay Public, and then Stanmore Superior Public. After that, her career was less typical. Her socialist politics caused her to resign in 1895, to follow William Lane to 'New Australia' in Paraguay and to marry.

Teachers of the higher branches of the curriculum in the private and corporate schools developed different career trajectories. Very late in the period, they might benefit from access to university subjects and even degrees. A status gap was developing between the gentleman and lady teachers in these schools and the employees of the public schools. There was also a status gap developing between the young unmarried women from better-off families going into kindergartens and those enmeshed in the examination- and inspection-ridden public school system. Embryonic at the turn of the century, these movements intensified quickly in the next decades.

What to teach, and how to do it

In the early 1870s, F.J. Gladman was appointed to the model and practising school in London's Borough Road Training College. In 1877, Gladman accepted an appointment to Melbourne's new teacher training college. He was the author of manuals on how to teach and organise schools: *School Method* (1877) was followed with his comprehensive *School Work* (1886), a compendium of the 'best teaching practices' of his time:

> He was a rigorous thinker and well-read by any standards; by colonial standards his opinions were progressive . . . His great contribution was to bring to a narrow and parochial education system a generous view of the task of schooling, a stern moral and intellectual concern, a pride in the craftsmanship of teaching and a passionate conviction of its importance. (Selleck, 1972, p. 254)

School Work gave advice on corporal punishment and discussed the significance of different elements of the curriculum. Gladman advocated physical exercise for pupils as part of each school day, and stressed the importance of timetables. He advocated well-designed schoolrooms and classroom furniture. Though generally encouraging the simultaneous instruction of young people in classrooms, he warned that individual students were different, and it was too easy to neglect slower students. He argued the special role of head teachers: 'He has to loosen or tighten the screws of the machine, and to oil it on occasion, as well as to drive it' (Gladman, 1898, p. 413).

In the developing public education systems, it was often difficult to introduce new ideas in the face of the system's grind. Towards the end of the century, the criticisms grew, and the 'New Education' found support. Disenchantment with the pupil-teacher system and payment by results helped the process along. One much-read educational philosopher was Johan Freidrich Herbart. He argued for the 'unique potential' of each child, even if the means of his or her liberation was a rigorous, formalised education, and a strong framework for citizenship, moral and intellectual development. The writing of detailed lesson plans and the introduction of object lessons, with their practical outcomes, were part of his influence. The continuing inspiration of Pestalozzi, the post-monitorial ideas of Kay Shuttleworth and the influence of David Stow, as well as that of Froebel and Herbart, all looked to improved schooling.

Because the Irish National readers had been such an influence on curriculum, the development of new readers was a priority. The idea that Australian children should read something of their own geography, history and literature grew. In New South Wales, William Wilkins had written a geography of his colony for schools in 1863. In the 1870s, he assisted the preparation of *The Australian Reading Books*. In Victoria, *Nelson's Royal Readers* replaced the Irish Nationals by the 1870s. Nevertheless, the new readers invariably argued the superiority of the white race, of men, and of the world's northern temperate zone as the workshop of the world and the source of high civilisation. Most historical events worth noting also took place there. Pride in the achievements of the British Empire was a given (Theobald, 1996, p. 201).

In South Australia, the Education Department's *Children's Hour* began publication in 1889. Costing a halfpenny, this magazine written for children was published monthly. Its articles, stories and poems shared the ideological propensities of *Nelson's Royal Readers*, but by the end of the century it was also advocating a love of the Australian environment and Australian patriotism. It introduced a

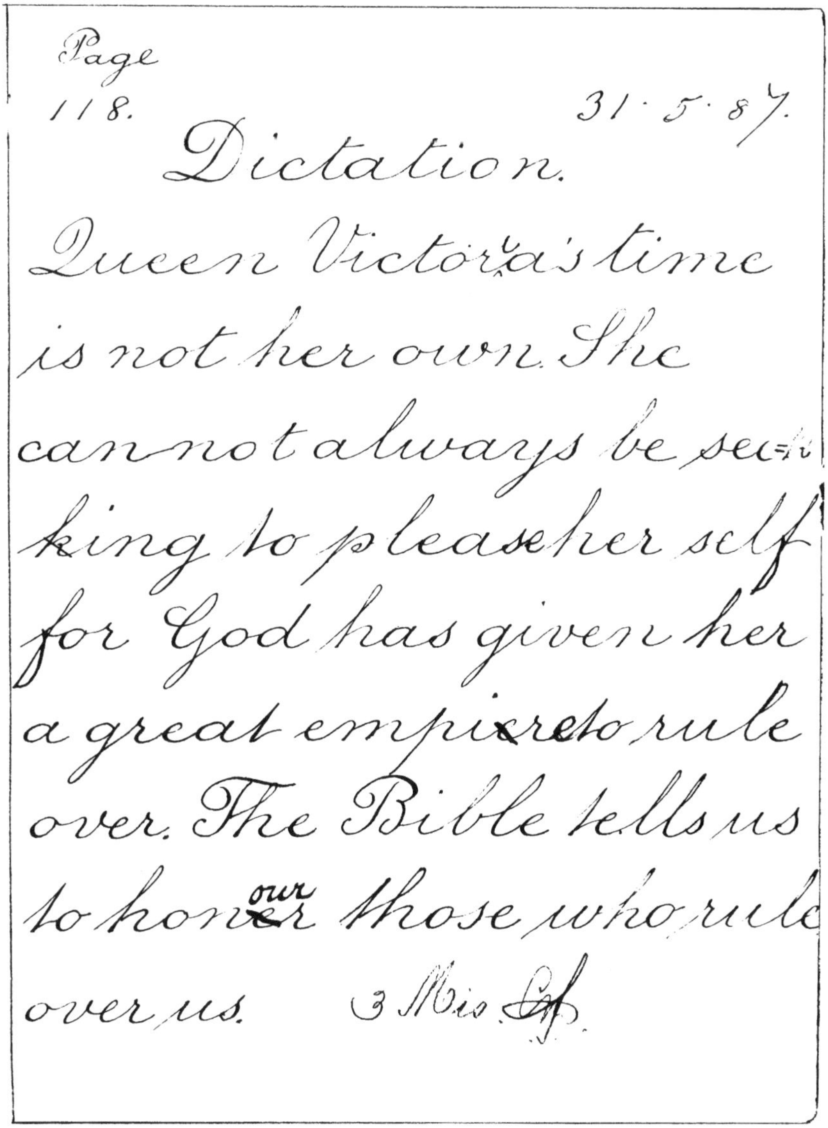

Page 118. 31·5·87.

Dictation.

Queen Victoria's time is not her own. She cannot always be seeking to please her self for God has given her a great empire to rule over. The Bible tells us to honour those who rule over us. 3 Mis [illegible]

Writing practice, taking dictation, common Christianity and British Empire loyalty and citizenship, all in one lesson. Hahndorf Primary School, South Australia, 1887. (Butler, 1979, p. 36)

lively set of readings into the school days of children and, if taken home, also provided reading for the family. In the other colonies, similar publications ensued. They contributed to the making of the new Australian subject-citizen. Also contributing were events such as Arbor Day, introduced in Queensland, for example, in 1891.

The new Departments of Education were well aware that the churches and community beyond would be interested in the moral training of young people in the public schools. Both the older boards and the new departments insisted that teachers model moral conduct. The South Australian Board of Education in 1860 had required training that repressed 'quarrelling, profanity, cruelty to animals, and every approach to vice'. Obedience to parents should be encouraged, as was the inculcation of truth, honesty, self-reliance, industry, temperance and other virtues. Punctuality was included. School and class timetables needed to be prominently displayed (Hyams, 1988). Clearly, the aim was self-regulation in an age where new industry and modern transport demanded the end of relaxed rural approaches to time. The clock in the classroom became more significant than the position of the sun.

The 1875 *Education Act* in Queensland listed the subjects of instruction: reading, writing, arithmetic, English grammar, geography, history, elementary mechanics, object lessons, drill and gymnastics, and vocal music. The list varied from colony to colony, but the first four subjects remained the same in each. With new forms of inspection, performance standards and payment by results, older forms of examination eventually disappeared. In public schools, pupil promotion was dependent on meeting published 'standards'. The written test replaced oral performance in front of local worthies and parents, though some of it survived in Sunday school events.

Gender differentiation in the elementary curriculum was not great, except for sewing for girls. From the 1870s, pressure on girls grew. Through an enhanced domestic curriculum, including skills such as sewing, cooking and laundry, social reformers argued the potential for improving unsatisfactory working-class families. The rise of domestic science/arts/economy as a special subject for girls had begun, though the domestic servant crisis meant pressure towards such a curriculum was not always altruistic. In some public schools, especially as colonial troops made their way to the Sudan, China and South Africa, military drill for boys was introduced into the curriculum.

The first really effective advocate of the New Education in the colonies was Cyril Jackson, appointed director in Western Australia in 1897. From an English background, he pursued school architecture reform. He denounced the pupil-teacher system of training, preparing the way for a new training college. He advocated the object lesson as a means of integrating children's senses, activity and learning. Compulsory attendance was tightened. Jackson wrote of the need for child self-education, leaving children intelligent and alert. Teaching should proceed from what the child knew, moving to the unknown. A practical and engaging course of instruction was required. But this was only the start: the New Education would be a work in progress, not of a few years but across much of the next century.

•

By 1900, public schooling had been redefined in all the Australian colonies. Economic, social and political changes were paralleled by changes in schooling. Melbourne in the 1880s, for example, grew faster than Sydney. Under protectionist tariff policies, manufacturing developed, and the emerging new middle and working classes made additional demands of schooling.

By 1900, the most common metaphor describing colonial educational arrangements was that of the 'ladder'. Through merit and hard work, anyone could rise to the universities, the pinnacles of the systems. This was wishful thinking, however. Secondary schooling continued as mainly middle-class education. Children from poor families—even in cities, let alone rural and remote areas—found it difficult to complete primary school. The head teacher at Sydney's Macdonaldtown Public School in the 1880s, Peter Board, was distressed by the conditions of local working-class families. Living in slum tenements, their struggle to produce school fees caused him to write multiple applications for fee waiver (Crane and Walker, 1957). Aboriginal families had uncertain rights to schooling of any kind. Poorer outback families—white, black, Chinese or Afghan—were usually on their own unless the colony attempted to hire itinerant teachers, or introduce half-time or some kind of provisional schooling.

A romantic image of rural school attendance New South Wales, c. 1895. Horses were a common means of transport for children. (Photographer, George Bell. Tyrell Collection, Powerhouse Museum, Sydney. 85/1284-227)

The provision of an academic education for middle-class girls remained controversial. Some critics linked the declining fertility of educated women to the dubious effects—physiological and psychological—of over-demanding school work. A letter to a South Australian newspaper in 1869 would have had a fair amount of support: 'I fancy their time would be much more profitably spent in learning to make a good wholesome pudding, or in stitching a gusset' (quoted in Hyams, 1988, p. 26). Nevertheless, by encouraging thousands of young women into teaching, the state itself encouraged transformational gender relations.

It would have surprised the makers of compulsory public school systems to be told that they had not always increased opportunity. Some of their arrangements institutionalised disadvantage among groups marked by racial and ethnic difference, social class, sex and religious affiliation.

There had never been much toleration by the respectable classes for unruly labouring-class populations. Colonial governments increased their power over such populations in this period. New public schools were only one of the new forms of intervention. Then again, the growing economy and the advent of nationhood each contributed new arguments for the schooling of the Australian population.

Further reading

Biographies of founders of schools and systems include Martin (1980) on Parkes, Turney (1992) on Wilkins, Tregenza (1968) on Pearson and Dow (1964) on Higinbotham. See Turney (1972) for Tenison Woods, Charles Liley, F.J. Gladman, Cyril Jackson and John Hartley, and Kociumbas (1997) and Grimshaw, McConville and McEwin (1985) for the social contexts of schooling. The essays in Theobald and Selleck (1990) provided new interpretations of the educational history of this era. See Theobald (1996) and Whitehead (2003) on women teachers. For secondary education, see Dunlop (1965), Goodman (1968), Sherington, Petersen and Brice (1987) and Campbell, Hooper and Fearnley-Sander (1999). On the reform of middle-class girls' education, Theobald (1991, 1996) are essential references. Aboriginal educational history is patchy, except for the reliable Fletcher (1989a, 1989b). The 1870s Education Acts are discussed in all the standard histories, but also see Grundy (1972). See Miller's (1986) revisionist study of South Australian schooling. On Tasmania, see Phillips (1985); for Queensland, see Wyeth (1955); for New South Wales, see Barcan (1988); and for Western Australia, see Mossenson (1972). See Freeman (2009) for rural schools and bushranger prevention. On Arnoldianism in Australia, see Turney (1966, 1967), but Crotty (2001) takes the argument into middle-class masculinity. See Brennan (1998) and Elliott (1982) on the rise of the kindergarten. On payment by results, see Pawsey (1994). The best study of the rise of new public examinations is Musgrave (1992).

CHAPTER

4

Towards universal provision 1901–1925

The beginning of the twentieth century saw a new idealism concerning schools. They could contribute to the making of better people, a better society and new citizen-subjects for the new Australian nation. Federation had been achieved in 1901. At the same time, the federal Constitution left responsibility for education as a residual power to the states. Coordinated national approaches would be some time coming.

The new idealism in education was attended by criticism of the public systems established 30 years earlier. Public schools 'trained' rather than educated; they closed off rather than enabled higher education; they failed to meet the demand for much-needed technical education—their conception of the child learner was narrow. Teachers were poorly paid labourers confined by harsh regimes that controlled and punished rather than encouraged. At least, that is how critics portrayed the systems. The standard narrative then continued in a positive vein. Under the influence of New Education ideas, public education systems were reformed by the new directors of education, most notably Cyril Jackson of Western Australia, Frank Tate of Victoria, Peter Board of New South Wales, Alfred Williams in South Australia and later William Neale and William McCoy in Tasmania and John Story and Reginald Roe in Queensland.

When reporting officially on Tasmanian public education in 1904, William Neale, a South Australian inspector, thought that the New Education would correct some obvious deficiencies. It represented a

> higher view of the aim and the method of education, and the influence of education on personal and national life . . . the result of the new appreciation of the marvellous possibilities of the human soul. The bases of this appreciation are the conceptions of human nature given by modern psychology and the related sciences. Each child is a germ of infinite potency, and 'Education' is the process and the total sum of all the forces that tend to complete self-realisation (quoted in Phillips, 1985, p. 87)

In the American historiography, a distinction is made between two kinds of educational progressivism. There is the philosophical, idealist kind, whose iconic representative is John Dewey, with his laboratory school, experimentalism, and democratic and communitarian approaches to the educational work of teacher and child. There were also the 'administrative' progressives, who concentrated on applying lessons from the social sciences to the management of schooling—the 'testers', 'sorters' and 'selectors'. Their aim was also to transform the work of children, teachers and the school in ways that would maximise personal and collective potentials, but it was perhaps less centred on individual soul-making, with social, economic and national development a higher priority.

The New Education mainly arrived in Australia from the United Kingdom. Nevertheless, American progressivism became influential. The two progressive tendencies—philosophical and administrative—often coexisted in the same persons with, over time, the administrative tending to come to the fore—though not in the female-dominated kindergartens and early childhood education. Another reform discourse, eugenics, also became important. The language of modern reform had moved on from cruder approaches to the controlling and disciplining of unruly populations. State instrumentalities would develop more sophisticated means of social administration enabling social improvement. The use of schools for mass medical inspections and health interventions is one example, as was the use of truancy rates to measure parental competence.

Children and youth, subject to psychological and intelligence-testing procedures, might be placed in special classes or schools appropriate to their varying aptitudes. The curricula for such classes and schools would be adapted to meet their scientifically determined 'needs'. Schooling, differentiated in this way, could advance national efficiency. That much of this activity probably increased some long-term discriminations against populations such as Aborigines and others, based on class, ethnicity and gender, is certainly true—but it could also produce some historically unique opportunities for other groups and individuals. Many white working-class children who tested as highly intelligent were a case in point.

In the first quarter of the twentieth century, the implementation of progressive ideas in education was slow. As Frank Tate liked to put it, this was a period in which 'school power' was only just being realised.

In 1912, there was a national survey of feeble-mindedness among children—a good example of psychology getting involved in social administration. Not all state Education Departments participated, but a problem was declared. In Tasmania, a quarter of the 2000 children surveyed were declared 'mentally feeble'! Such knowledge required a means to deal with it. So, where different forms of schooling had previously occurred as a result of families' social status, gender, race and religion, in the early twentieth century, fitness, ability, aptitude and intelligence were added to the mix. Where earlier understandings of difference were usually thought 'natural'—poor Irish-Australian Catholic girls, or Indigenous children *naturally* needed a different education from wealthy Anglo-Australian Protestant boys—new sources of difference would be identified from scientifically based medical and psychological testing and observation. New kinds of education and training in reformed institutions were the consequence, and new occupations were invented in the process. Female university graduates—especially in psychology and medicine—would work with the 'problem' populations as education, health and welfare bureaucracies expanded.

From late in the previous century, there had been a rethinking of the role of the state in economic and social life. Unlike the older *laissez-faire* kind, the new liberalism legitimised state intervention in new areas of social life. It criticised the harsh class politics that led to the 1890s strikes and social disorder in general, the worst consequences of which were proven in Russia in 1917. In Australia, several of the colonial, then state governments, and certainly from 1901 the new federal government, legislated to ameliorate the conditions of much social life. Educational progressivism, philosophical and administrative was connected to this. Most political parties—particularly the emerging Labor, Protectionist and then Liberal Parties—shared the approach. Educational reform could play its part in ordering society in more stable ways. There would be new opportunities for deserving, hard-working and intelligent youth. Reform was also a consequence of emerging demands by the upper working and new middle classes for the schooling that might lead to upward social mobility.

The impact of these movements was stronger later in the century, but in this 1901–25 period, the direction was set. World War I slowed the reform movement, but not completely. Reform did not just occur in public schools; there were changes in private and church and secular corporate schools as well. Some of the more radical educational experimentation occurred in the non-government sector—including private schools. Of all the policies formulated by governments, the idea that post-elementary—sometimes called 'secondary'—intermediate or continuation schooling should be as universally accessible as primary schooling was the most challenging. The attempt to provide for the newly discovered 'adolescent' in new institutions was responsible for some of the most significant changes in this era. At the other end of the school-age spectrum, governments deferred to the private sector in the provision of pre-school education.

The educational renaissance

In New South Wales, the significance for reform of Francis Anderson's speech to the Public School Teachers' Association in June 1901 cannot be ignored. He was Professor of Philosophy at the University of Sydney, and the husband of Maybanke Anderson, a feminist and effective advocate of free Kindergartens and public playgrounds for children. Francis Anderson

> smote the public school system hip and thigh. He castigated the pupil-teacher system of training and the role of the teachers' colleges, and alleged that too few future or present teachers attended the university, even part time. He complained about the over-scholastic and rigid curricula of the primary and of the emerging secondary schools and the relative absence of study of the natural, physical and social sciences; he criticized the predominance of 'drill' and 'cramming' in teaching and the absence of 'inquiry'. He deplored the role of the school inspectors who, instead of encouraging innovation, assessed teachers in terms of their conformity to established norms. (O'Neil, 1979, p. 54)

Anderson condemned rote learning with the image of hundreds of children learning their geography as secular catechism. They would chant: 'New Guinea—North of Australia—Birds of Paradise—Gold'. Anderson's audience was enraptured. Women stood on chairs waving their handkerchiefs and parasols. Men stamped and shouted, shaking hands with perfect strangers (O'Neil, 1979, p. 54). The speech was quickly published, and soon afterwards, George Knibbs and John Turner, senior public servant and principal of Fort Street Public School respectively, were commissioned to report on what apparently was *not* the best public education system in the world. Anderson, Knibbs and Turner established the argument for reform, but for actual reform, Peter Board was the more significant figure.

Board, a relatively junior inspector, aligned himself with the New Education at the right time. A consequence was his rapid promotion, replacing the retiring Director of Education in 1905. Before promotion, he had self-funded an educational tour of Europe and published a report in favour of public school reform. This and other of Board's writing were shorter, and more accessible, than the massive Knibbs and Turner reports. Board began his program, first producing a new primary syllabus that concentrated on connecting separate school subjects. It encouraged the 'interest' of the child.

The examination of pupils by inspectors was replaced with inspections of teachers. Board began recruiting university graduates like himself—'men of culture'—to the inspectorate. He worked on modifying the hold of the university on the secondary school curriculum, and in the process established new Intermediate and Leaving Certificates to replace the Junior and Senior Public. He defined the boundary between primary and secondary education, systemising post-primary schooling into at least three different kinds of schools other than the academic high. As a consequence, he hoped that the inclusion of young people in some form of post-primary school would help lead to universal access. The responsibility of schools to teach responsible citizenship and to prepare young people for employment was at the heart of his program.

A new qualifying certificate (QC) was introduced to help sort students into the high schools, the superior public and the evening continuation schools. The reformed superior publics would offer technical, commercial or domestic science curricula.

The growth in post-primary enrolments in New South Wales, as in other states, was rapid. Table 4.1 outlines the enrolment and institutional changes. Some of these figures are not quite as they seem. In 1925, many young people left school only a year later than their contemporaries may have in 1901, but by 1925 their last school was much less likely to have been a primary school.

The number of 'provisional' schools, too small to be fully fledged 'public' schools, suggests that many rural children experienced little more than an elementary education. For white children in the more

TABLE 4.1

Growth of different kinds of public schools and public school enrolments in New South Wales, 1901 and 1925

	1901	1925	Change (%)
Children in primary schools	208 868	278 477	+33
Youth in post-primary schools	521	40 169	+7610
Number of public schools	1 889	1 995	+6
Number of provisional schools	428	605	+41
Number of separate secondary schools	4	34	+750

Source: NSW DET (2003).

Most of the rural schools in tiny communities continued with primitive conditions. Often the teachers were minimally trained. This photograph records the work of an itinerant teacher, probably responsible for two half-time schools. Tambo-Adavale district, near Charleville, Queensland, c. 1912. (State Library of Queensland, 149763)

remote rural areas, there was one development, however. Provisional schools, and sometimes half-time schools kept by travelling teachers, were supplemented by correspondence lessons. By 1922, in New South Wales alone, some 1500 children were receiving lessons by mail.

Peter Board's reforms were not easily won. Curriculum reforms in primary schools were often resisted by teachers, school heads and even some inspectors. Influential members of the university resented changes to public examinations and associated credentials. The Leaving Certificate was eventually colonised to become the University of Sydney's new matriculation standard. In so doing, the university maintained fair control over the kinds of subjects accepted, their syllabuses and chief examiners. Board himself did not quite trust teachers to implement new department syllabuses in the correct spirit. Syllabuses tended towards the prescriptive, and the long-term influence of the Qualifying Certificate was to calcify primary curricula and pedagogy. By the 1920s, many teachers were again protesting against examination cram and an illiberal curriculum. Nevertheless, opportunity and access were improved. Fees were removed for public schooling in 1906—even for the high schools. But they came back again in 1922 with a Nationalist-Country Party government. Board retired in protest. Three years later, Jack Lang's incoming Labor government restored fee-free high school entry in New South Wales.

Cyril Jackson's efforts for the New Education in Western Australia were renewed in 1903 when Cecil Andrews succeeded him as Inspector-General of Education. During his 26 years in charge of public education, his greatest achievement was to 'complete' the public system. Perth Modern School was founded in 1911 with several teachers from Fort Street High in Sydney. Among Andrews' inspirations had been the Knibbs and Turner reports (1903–05) on educational reform in New South Wales. This was one of several Royal Commissions and inquiries that provided the arguments for reform before World War I. The Modern School, Western Australia's first Education Department high school, was 'modern' in terms of its curriculum, with classical languages giving ground to the sciences and modern languages. Government schools like the Modern School were expected to support Western Australia's agriculture and mining. Also developed were central, continuation and evening schools, which would collect qualified children from primaries, introducing them to appropriate post-primary curricula. Central schools would develop alternative courses: commercial for boys and girls, industrial for boys alone, and domestic science for girls.

In each of the states of the new Commonwealth of Australia, there were similar developments. There would be new secondary schools, differentiated by their courses of instruction. Economic progress and national development would surely follow.

The study of reform in Victoria has led to modifications of the reform narrative that had concentrated too much on the initiatives of the Directors of Education such as Peter Board and Frank Tate. Austin and Selleck (1975) pointed to the critical significance of their reform-minded predecessors. For example, industrialists were frustrated that the demand for skilled labour was well in advance of investment in technical education. There was also the significance of politicians who spoke for reform. In Victoria, Alfred Deakin—backed by the *Age* newspaper—played this role. Even though the official focus of the Fink Royal Commission (1899–1900) was technical education, it expanded to most aspects of public education. Frank Tate, an Education Department inspector, advocated reform. His judicious evidence to the Fink Commission helped with his appointment as Director of Education in 1902.

Tate, supported for the most part by Ministers of Education, attempted key elements in the New Education program and other reforms. Payment of teachers by student results was abolished and the pupil-teacher system modified. A new course of study for primary schools was introduced—according to its opponents, full of New Education's 'fads and frills'. The University of Melbourne was persuaded to introduce a Diploma of Education. The registration of non-government schools was expected to improve the 'efficiency' of both that sector and the public sector.

In 1907, travelling with the newly appointed Director of Education in South Australia, Alfred Williams, Tate studied public schooling in North America, Europe and Britain. Both men gathered arguments for government high schools. There had been public high schools in the north-east of the United States from the 1820s, which had been embraced by the urban middle class. Older town grammar schools and rural academies had declined as a result. In Victoria, however, there would be no easy establishment of public high schools. Earlier attempts to follow New South Wales in allowing larger public schools to add junior secondary 'tops' or establish full public high schools were defeated. New arguments about citizenship education for democracies, the necessity of new efforts to educate and socialise adolescents (potential larrikins) and the necessity for new technical and vocational training helped reduce the opposition. In 1910 in Victoria, an *Education Act* finally allowed the creation of state high schools. The approach of World War I had increased anxiety through the British Empire about German technological and industrial advance. The Empire had to keep up, and government-controlled secondary schools might assist in this.

If the argument seemed clear for new effort in post-primary education, then industrial, agricultural and perhaps commercial and domestic science education were the most likely justifiable curricula. Melbourne Continuation School, founded in 1905, was initially justified for its vocational role in educating future school teachers. In larger Victorian country towns, agricultural high schools were founded—scientific approaches to agriculture were more easily justified. Nevertheless, the new state high schools consolidated around the 'general' course, based on modern and classical subjects—including the languages that were most likely to be found in the private and church corporate/grammar schools. Tate was not overly concerned. He had wanted such curricula in the state high schools from the beginning. Ironically, agricultural courses in rural high schools were not very popular. Parents, it appeared, mainly wanted the new high schools to deliver the same high-status curriculum as the private and corporate schools. In 1912, the continuation school was renamed Melbourne High. The private purposes of families helped subvert official intentions for government secondary schools. Similar stories can be told about Hobart and Launceston high schools.

Not all attempts at agricultural secondary schooling failed. From 1913, South Australia's Murray Bridge continuation class—later a high school under A.R. Hilton—saw students erect brush fences, practise crop rotation, test fertilisers, grow flowers and vegetables, plant an orchard and develop irrigated crops such as lucerne. The school formed an agricultural bureau, sponsoring milk tests and conducting pruning competitions (Thiele, 1975, p. 150).

Reforms such as these occurred in all Australian states. Educators like William McCoy had trans-Australian careers. Beginning in New South Wales, he adapted the Peter Board vision to his posts as Director of Education, first in Tasmania and then in South Australia.

Queensland was the slowest to reform. Early adoption of Board's new primary syllabus was tokenistic, and older inspection and pupil testing regimes persisted. John Anderson, as head of the Department of Public Instruction (1878–1904), regretted the retreat of the 'mental discipline' approach to education; instead, there were children wandering about studying 'grubs and plants and weeds' (Meadmore,

The universities provided syllabuses and public examinations for secondary schools. Merit was proven through examination success. Here girls and boys, having sat a paper for the University of Adelaide's junior public exam, wait to be dismissed. Western Australia, c. 1907. (State Library of Western Australia, 009692PD)

2003, p. 389). So much for nature study, one of the quintessential New Education subjects! With the departure of Anderson, and also Chief Inspector Ewart by 1910, and the accession of J.D. Storey and Reginald Roe, reform proceeded apace. Six state high schools were opened in 1912, all in regional towns. They offered three courses: the general academic, commercial and domestic science. In 1914, a teachers' training college was finally established, but there were continuing restraints. High schools were not opened in towns where the more exclusive state grammar schools had been established. If anything, the scholarship system that supported the state grammar schools and restricted popular access to secondary education was reinforced.

In Alfred Williams, South Australia also had a reforming Director of Education. Backed by both Labor and the Liberals in government, free high schools were established from 1908. Williams argued that:

> The establishment of District High Schools is an attempt to make the opportunities of education accessible to all who are worthy and able to profit by them, however remote their homes may be. In a sparsely settled country . . . it is difficult to give that equality of opportunity which is the democratic ideal; but during the past year we have taken a step towards its realisation. (Director of Education, 1908, *SA Parliamentary Papers [SAPP]*)

Here we see not only the idea that academic 'merit'—proven through worthiness and ability—should be rewarded, but the concept that 'equality of opportunity' should prevail. This latter phrase was destined for a long history in Australian education policy.

New Education ideas in South Australia had been promoted through the annual conferences of the public teachers' union. Williams, as union president then Director of Education in the crucial period, was an effective propagandist for the ideas of Anderson, Knibbs and Turner. He also promoted the ideas of G. Stanley Hall from the United States, especially those relating to child study and the needs of the newly discovered adolescent. Reforms gathered pace. From within the Education Department, Lydia Longmore was entrusted with a new commitment to kindergarten development and Alfred Edquist to nature study. New curricula for primary and secondary schools were produced and teacher training and teacher working conditions were improved. School medical inspections began in 1909. William's successor, McCoy, took on the task of increasing the range of secondary schools. Alongside the high schools dominated by university-controlled public examinations would be a range of super primaries with Education Department curricula. Thebarton Boys Technical High was opened in 1919, and from 1924 there were central ('super-primary') schools that would eventually convert into single-sex junior technical schools.

Although William Neale's career concluded in Tasmania in 1910, under his directorship a school of domestic economy was established, the compulsory education of blind and deaf-mute children initiated,

Nature Study, and regard for nature in general were significant in curriculum reform along New Education lines. Here schoolboys prepare to plant trees on Arbor Day at Montacute, South Australia, c. 1912. (National Library of Australia, vn4983136)

and teachers and schools—public and non-government—registered. A number of 'inefficient' private schools closed as a result. Medical examinations were instituted, supervised from 1908 by a schools medical officer. In secondary education, continuation classes came first, then Hobart and Launceston high schools in 1913. By then, McCoy was in charge. His attempts to promote secondary industrial, commercial, teachers' and domestic courses, as well as the general academic, were not always successful; nevertheless, new intermediate high schools in Burnie and Davenport extended the accessibility of secondary education. As occurred in other states, pressure towards the academic 'general' course undermined wider curriculum diversity.

Technical and domestic education

Each of the Australian states responded to the demand for more effective technical education for boys. Sometimes new directorates were established within Education Departments. In Tasmania, a technical branch was founded in 1917, and junior boys' technical schools in Hobart and Launceston in 1919. In Victoria in 1911, Donald Clark was appointed by Tate as chief inspector of technical schools. His advocacy, planning and supervision in the area involved epic effort over many years. He argued that half of the employable males in Victoria would end up as primary producers and industrial workers. It was foolishness that there was virtually no post-primary education meeting their needs, or national ones. Clark argued in 1915 against the hegemony of the general academic course: 'In a young country such as this, we should be teaching our people to do something . . . the time will come when almost the whole of our secondary schools will become vocational schools . . .' (Turney, 1975, p. 330) Frank Tate was not persuaded. In South Australia, another enthusiast, Charles Fenner, was put in charge of technical education. The independence of the School of Mines and Industries slowed technical school expansion there until the 1940s. The establishment of technical courses and schools was part of Peter Board's reforms in New South Wales.

Technical education was for boys. Variously named domestic science, domestic arts, domestic economy, home economics, home science—and more—over the twentieth century was for girls. It gave rise to subjects not only in new secondary schools, but also the last year or two of the primary curriculum. Domestic science was a curriculum reform that addressed perceived social problems. Through training girls in domestic science, the working-class family could be transformed. In the period of the White Australia policy, the curriculum took a role in encouraging a healthier, more numerous white population, essential for national survival. One of its side-effects was to increase the gendered character of the curriculum. In many post-primary schools, girls had less of mathematics and other academic subjects as a result. In South Australia, Alfred Williams in 1911 was not particularly concerned—after all, 'the great end and aim of a woman's life is to be the honourable mistress of her own home, her healthy vigorous children who are well disposed to all that is right and good' (quoted in Hyams, 1988, p. 150).

Educational reform: Improving children and youth

The eugenics movement in Australia was often more benign than in parts of Europe and the United States, where interventions in the 'breeding' of 'unsatisfactory populations' could take disturbing forms. These populations were marked by their apparent tendencies towards criminality, immorality and mental retardation. It was often argued that the deficiencies coincided with their racial and ethnic origins. Interventions were sometimes justified by the emerging social sciences. Social Darwinism led to the belief that there were fit and less fit populations. The less fit apparently could be a danger to others and themselves.

Aboriginal people—usually argued to constitute a less-fit population—were objects of much eugenic interest. The consequent social administration could be fatalistic. The best that might be done would be to 'smooth the pillow of a dying race'. Other approaches involved reinvigorated regimes of segregation and training, and new efforts to separate children from their parents.

On the frontiers of white settlement, the politics of race could be fierce, and access to a public school was an area of conflict. At Oodnadatta in South Australia, white mothers sought the exclusion of children from Afghan families in the small public school, causing a quandary for the state. Non-attendance of Aboriginal children in the school was ignored by all, but pleas for the exclusion of other children drew mixed reactions from government officials. At Oodnadatta, the Education Department's health officer did not support the case of the white mothers, some of whom falsely argued that Afghan children were riddled with venereal disease, and were less clean than most white families (Theobald, 2001).

New state instrumentalities railed against the apparent incompetence of working-class white, as well as Aboriginal, families—especially those mothers who, it was argued, raised their children with little concern for cleanliness, morality, nutrition and discipline. The new domestic science curriculum for girls was a partial response to this view. In the words of South Australia's Children's Council, in Adelaide early in the century:

> Young girls from 12 to 16 are permitted to parade the streets at late hours, aping the worst manners of their elders, forming very undesirable companionships, hearing conversations anything but edifying, and witnessing and participating in conduct calculated to blunt finer feelings. (Report, 1901, *South Australian Parliamentary Papers*)

> Groups of boys of ages varying from 7 to 15 roam the streets and parks, smoking cigarettes, playing pitch and toss, garden robbing and haunting the back entrances of business establishments. These boys and youth ought either to be at school or in some youthful occupation. Their condition is one of moral peril and graduation from these nurseries of vice too frequently takes place. (Report, 1903, *SAPP*)

In 1903, a New South Wales Royal Commission on the decline of the birth rate argued for a new policy towards working-class families. Working-class larrikinism was a problem for the inner cities generally. Social reformers, whether directly influenced by the eugenics movement or not, proposed solutions that would improve population quality. Environmental solutions included slum clearance, sewerage and clean water provision, more parks and playgrounds, and even new garden suburbs, where stand-alone houses with their own gardens would be surrounded by neighbourhoods remarkable for their trees and grassed parks. Institutional solutions included prolonged schooling—especially for the newly identified 'at-risk' adolescents.

An argument that middle-class children should be schooled away from the inner city became persuasive. Schools without playing fields, surrounded by slums and associated poverty and immorality, were a problem. Some schools remained, like SCEGGS, an Anglican girls' school in seedy Darlinghurst, Sydney, but others went. In Melbourne, when the high school split into boys' and girls' schools in 1927, the boys departed for the suburbs: sports grounds were possible in South Yarra. The girls, though, were left in the cramped, apparently rat-infested, inner city building until it was condemned in 1930. William Adey, the first headmaster of Adelaide High School, was trapped in the difficult west of Adelaide's square mile. He complained of being surrounded by working-class hotels, from which drunkenness and riot all too frequently spilled out. The boys and girls of his school could hardly avoid taking a morally perilous interest (Campbell, 2001a).

More kindergartens for the very young were part of the effort. Advocates such as Lilian de Lissa believed in their capacity to reform working-class life—social reform could proceed from educational reform. The kindergarten might achieve spiritual and cultural transformation not only of the children educated, but also their mothers. Australian Education Departments also established kindergarten classes, with some sending staff, such as Martha Simpson in New South Wales, to learn direct from Maria Montessori in Italy. In every state between 1895 and 1912, Kindergarten Unions were founded. Despite early interest, Education Departments eventually became reluctant to enrol infants. The Kindergarten Unions, attracting philanthropic support, developed as major providers. Establishing kindergartens and training colleges was a fit mission for well-educated middle- and ruling-class women. They were often at the centre of turn-of-the-century child-saving movements. The Lady Mayoress of Melbourne in 1914 was a supporter, proudly announcing that even 'highly strung' infants from Chinese and Assyrian families had been persuaded towards orderliness through the kindergarten (see Spearitt, 1979; Snow, 1989; Weiss, 1993; Gardiner, 1982).

As the compulsory provisions of the *Education Acts* were tightened, primary schooling became more significant in the lives of Australian children. They were expected to attend school every day, and were excused attendance only on the presentation of a note, usually arguing illness. Unlike the older elementary school, the primary school increasingly concentrated on a particular age group—the 5 or 6 to 12-year-olds. The new word 'primary' suggested a next step, towards 'secondary'.

We have already noted the argument that adolescents needed schools dedicated to their age group alone. They were at special risk of being corrupted by too early an entry into the adult workforce. Wise adult supervision in youth clubs, newly age-graded sporting clubs, church fellowships—and secondary schools—provided an answer to the larrikin problem. A more orderly, better educated youth would also be of national benefit. The new schools could be used for mass

The kindergarten signified a new approach to the education of infants. Froebel's approach preceded that of Maria Montessori, but her ideas had a great impact early in the century as this classroom shows. Western Australia, 1920. (State Library of Western Australia, 004538D)

medical examinations—useful in correcting the shocking health of new recruits discovered in the colonial call-ups for the Boer War at the turn of the century. Schools could be used for military training as the Great War came closer. Amendments to the national *Defence Act* of 1910 demanded that schools improve the fitness of boys through parade-ground drill and perhaps training in rifle shooting. Physical training began to be imagined as a compulsory school subject. The domestic science curriculum made its contribution, as we have seen. In the language of eugenics, improvement of the race would occur; national survival and prosperity would be a consequence.

The school leaving age was usually raised a year—to the fourteenth birthday—in this period. Where the developing institutions of adolescence were inadequate, there would be a different approach to the juvenile offender. Older approaches common in the colonies from

The militarisation of schools in the lead up to the Great War. The Commonwealth cadet scheme preceded the introduction of universal military training for boys from 1911. Monkland Primary School unit, Gympie, Queensland, c. 1906. (State Library of Queensland, 77011)

early in the nineteenth century, such as the sending of boys to the training ship *Sobraon*, moored in Sydney Harbour, were modified. There should be new children's courts, and new and sympathetic reformatory institutions and regimes. Children and youth needed to be categorised more scientifically, from the incorrigible to those capable of rescue. The former should not be allowed to corrupt the latter.

Interventions in the lives of children and youth—their rescue from their local circumstances—engaged a range of voluntary organisations as well as the state. Imperial philanthropy saw the Fairbridge organisation collect young people living in various institutions in England. They were sent to Western Australia (and other parts of the Empire), to Fairbridge farms, where their schooling would be sufficient to turn them into useful farmers. The first party arrived in 1913. The legacy of such child migration schemes remains highly controversial (see Sherington and Jeffery, 1998).

The Great War

The 1914–18 war saw the engagement of schools in work supporting the war effort. Empire Day, established after the Earl of Meath's visit to Australia in 1910 and commonly celebrated in schools, helped prepare the way for much of the jingoism that overtook many public schools and most of the Protestant church colleges. There was initial enthusiasm in Catholic schools, but less following the conscription campaigns and the 1916 Easter uprising in Ireland.

In the Protestant colleges, there was an immediate linking of school purposes to the cause of the British Empire. Pride was taken in old scholars and teachers who volunteered for military service. Such schools, as well as the more exclusive of the privates, helped produce the officer class. The outstanding Australian general John Monash was educated at Scotch College. The war legitimised the role that such schools considered they played in nation-building. Many chapels were built as war memorials in the early post-war period.

The cult of British Empire loyalty became part of the official culture of public and Protestant schools in the early twentieth century. Raising the flag on Empire Day, 1913 at Coopers Glen Public School, New South Wales, 1913. (Mitchell Library, State Library of NSW, BCP 02073)

The new Scotch College in South Australia, founded in 1922, was dedicated 'to the sons of Scotland' who had served. The great majority of ordinary soldiers were educated in public schools. Australian war casualties, both in the Ottoman Empire and France, produced grief for school communities, but also a military tradition that might be celebrated judiciously.

Those state high schools founded before the war shared the approach. Unley District High in South Australia, founded in 1910, was impacted in several ways. The recruitment of male teachers caused staff and curriculum difficulties. Students and parents were encouraged to raise money for the relief funds, and war saving was encouraged. Old scholars in uniform were invited to talk to students and staff. The domestic arts staff and students helped cater for grand war-winning fetes. As the war drew on, the cooking curriculum was modified—with more emphasis being placed on invalid cookery. Sometimes the baked results were sent down to the Keswick Military Hospital. Girls knitted socks and made up parcels for troops. Compulsory cadet training for boys took on new urgency. In stories for the school magazine, girls imagined themselves as nurses in France; boys saw themselves as soldiers on the Western Front, part of the heroic effort to defeat the Hun. And in 1919, the school Honour Board was completed. Some 90 old scholars had fought, nine had died—one of illness and another of gas poisoning—while the other seven had been 'killed' (Campbell, 2010).

After accounts of the fighting at Gallipoli by Ellis Ashmead-Bartlett and Charles Bean were published, Anzac commemorations were introduced across most Australian schools. The sacrifices of Australian soldiers, for King, Country, Flag and Empire, and sometimes freedom and democracy, entered school curricula. Education Department children's papers, interested since 1901 in celebrating the new nation, now had the beginnings of a legend that would sustain citizenship education into the indefinite future. The story of Simpson and his donkey, assisting wounded men on the murderous slopes of Gallipoli, was considered suitable for primary school children. Lawrence Binyon's *For the Fallen*, 'They shall not grow old, as we that are left grow old . . . /We will remember them' became a secular liturgy for schools on Anzac Day.

Other war effects were variable. In Queensland, teacher salary increases were deferred, but then a succeeding Labor government provided to children, free of charge, the school newspaper; copy, drawing and exercise books; lead pencils and erasers. In 1917, the experimental rural school at Nambour was founded with its agricultural, practical curriculum, and its sensitivity to the economy of the local community. In Western Australia too there were budget cuts justified by war. Children below the age of 6 were excluded from public schools, and kindergarten classes suffered accordingly. In Victoria, Frank Tate devoted the public school system and the school paper to fundraising and fostering imperial loyalty. In South Australia, despite the war, secondary technical education was finally organised, the school leaving age increased and public high schools consolidated by the 1915 *Education Act*.

Lutheran schools experienced hostility arising from the war fever, even if German as the language of instruction was in sharp decline by the early twentieth century. In South Australia, all of the Lutheran primary schools were forcibly closed. The argument that these were 'Australian schools' failed despite the long-ago, early nineteenth-century Prussian and Brandenburg origins of pupils' grand- and great-grand-parents. Persecution was strong in other states, especially on the ground of 'inefficiency' if English was too little used for instruction, but most Lutheran schools managed to remain open in Victoria and New South Wales (see Hayes, 1978).

Aboriginal schooling and racism

We have already noted the new ideas informed by Social Darwinism and eugenics that impacted negatively on Aboriginal communities. Intelligence testing promoted by the new discipline of psychology also impacted badly. It would take another half-century before educators routinely acknowledged that 'intelligence' was dependent to a great degree on the cultural and language circumstances of children's families. Enlightened criticism of Aboriginal schooling existed, but

Despite the 'Advance Australia' banner, a group portrait on the last day before the Hahndorf Lutheran School was closed on 30 June, 1917. Lutheran schools were too German for the South Australian state government during the Great War. (Butler, 1979, p. 94)

such views had little influence. A Queensland inspector wrote about the Barambah Native School in 1917:

> If the object . . . is to keep the children quiet, and out of mischief during the daytime and train them to be lazy . . . it is a success, but if the aim is to cultivate their intelligence, to give exercise to their self activity, to train them to be industrious and self reliant with a fair knowledge of their class work when leaving, the school is a failure. (quoted in Haebich, 2000, p. 394)

In New South Wales, Peter Board's new curriculum (1916) for Aboriginal children set low standards for achievement. It was unhelpful in terms of recommending teaching methods and suitable resources. Its inspiration was a pre-New Education idea: that Aboriginal boys needed only to be prepared for low-paid farm labour, and girls for domestic service.

The exclusion of Aboriginal children from public schools following the demands of white parents continued, even though the Protection

Board thought lighter coloured children could attend. The white manager of the Walhallow Aboriginal Station had an Aboriginal wife, and was distressed that his children were excluded from the public school. The case went to the Director of Education. Peter Board thought that the children—especially since they were light in colour—might be allowed in if they were 'clean'. By the time this concession was made, however, the children had been accepted into another public school where the teacher was less punctilious. At Wanaaring, a demand for Aboriginal exclusion was withdrawn when the consequence was likely school closure for want of sufficient enrolments. The racism involved in the politics of exclusion varied from community to community. A teacher at Karuah Public School, Annie McLennan, wanted to treat all of her pupils impartially and equally. But that did not suit white parents, who drove her to distraction as they specified the conditions under which their children might associate with Aboriginal children. Eventually full exclusion was implemented at Karuah. Aboriginal children were again dependent for their education on missions, and then a separate native school. The Karuah public school was not desegregated until the 1950s (see Fletcher, 1989a, 1989b).

At Huskisson in New South Wales an Aboriginal man who had attended public school years earlier found his grandchildren excluded. Apparently the problem was caused by the fear of competition between Aboriginal and white fishermen: excluding Aboriginal children from the school might drive Aboriginal fishing families away. In some places, Aboriginal children were not enrolled in school—their parents knew what to expect if they tried.

The Cootamundra Domestic Training Home for Aboriginal Girls (1911–68) combined the effort to segregate and separate girls of mixed parentage from their families with an aim to assimilate them through training as domestic servants for white families. The parallel institution for boys was the Kinchela Boys Home, which experienced a history of brutality and abuse towards its inmates. These separations of children from their families continued to wreak social devastations into the twenty-first century. Such approaches were common across the Australian states. In Western Australia from 1915, A.O. Neville began his career as policy-maker, administrator and Chief 'Protector' of Aborigines. He concentrated his efforts on segregating and training children of mixed descent. Carolup (1915–22) and Moore River (1918–51) settlements were established for this purpose, but Moore River also included unmarried mothers, juvenile and adult offenders, the elderly and the very poor. They contained schools with basic curricula, but the settlement conditions and regulations were no better than those of 'internment camps'.

Private and corporate schools

Private schools continued to decline as church corporate and state schools grew in number. In Melbourne, the poet John Bernard O'Hara's South Melbourne College lasted from 1889 to 1916. O'Hara cultivated wealthier families, taking pride in the academic successes of his students. He escaped from one of the causes of private school failure: the collapse of respectability. Having fallen in love with a pupil, Agnes Law, who was pregnant to him at 19 years of age, O'Hara succeeded in hushing the fact, but the school did not last. In 1915 Frank Tate was able to persuade his Minister of Education that government scholarships should be reserved for the new state high schools, despite the opposition of O'Hara and many of his fellow non-government school heads. By 1916, he was tired and ill. Enrolments were declining and the school's finances were in trouble. The college was taken over by the Methodist school, Wesley College (Pawsey, 1990).

The growing influence of athleticism and games led not only to new sports grounds but also new inter-school sporting associations. Some were exclusive, with one measure of a school's status being its membership of the top athletics associations (Sherington, 1983). School uniforms also became more common. Though many of the church corporate schools had boarding houses, virtually none could survive without day students.

Girls' schools also developed Arnoldian characteristics, such as prefects, houses, school songs and games. Many of them took pride in their public exam results, scholarships and old scholars' university

By the early twentieth century, games, especially rugby, football and cricket were essential features of Protestant boys' church schools. Then Roman Catholic schools also began to play. But could the students devoted to games also pass exams like those of the new state high schools? The rugby team of the Catholic St Stanislaus College, Bathurst, New South Wales, 1904. (State Library of NSW, BCP 05125)

successes. In this period—at least early on—first-wave feminism and advanced schooling for girls were associated. The domestic science curriculum was often resisted, being seen as diverting girls from an academic education equivalent to that of their brothers. Their teachers were almost always single women, well educated and not averse to encouraging clever girls into professional careers—including, but not only, teaching. At the same time, such girls' schools, including the state high schools, hardly resisted the knowledge that most girls would marry.

In this period, as a result not only of the New Education but other enthusiasms, the idea of experimental or alternative education also developed. Peter Board in New South Wales encouraged such an experiment in a public school, Brighton-Le-Sands, on Botany Bay. The curriculum included gardening and manual work. Active, practical learning methods were encouraged as the New Education demanded.

It is to non-government schools that we look for other alternative schools (see Petersen, 1969, 1970). From 1916, the Theosophists decided that the regeneration of humankind and preparation for the coming 'world teacher' might be advanced by schooling. Vegetarianism, eurythmics, coeducation, gymnastics, a literary curriculum based around myths and legends attractive to children, and even some rather vague sex education and the engagement of children in the governance of their schools, were all part of the program. Glen Carron, Morven Garden and the King Arthur schools existed for a time as Theosophist schools. The Turramurra College, also in Sydney, based some of its ideas on the American Homer Lane's teaching that self-government would advance the development of children. In 1922, the school partially implemented the Dalton Plan. Some 50 boys worked in a largish schoolroom on individual and collective project-assignments. Self-expression was encouraged through creative writing, music and craft, and the death of 'class instruction' in favour of 'individual learning' was heralded. Involved in 'trying' their fellow students for misdemeanours, students rejected corporal punishment—caning—as suitable punishment. This school did not survive the 1920s, unlike the girls' school Ascham (1886–), which also worked with the Dalton plan. The opening of the Presbyterian Knox Grammar (1924–), with more traditional pedagogy and curriculum, and lacking the disabilities of most private schools, seduced much of Turramurra College's enrolment.

The church corporate schools continued to send large numbers of matriculants to the early twentieth-century universities, and certainly to the professional faculties such as Medicine and Law. They continued to educate and acculturate elements of the middle class, including the professional and governing elites. Many graduates originating from public high school also found their way into the more prestigious professions, but increasing numbers were Arts and Science graduates, necessary for the production of secondary school teachers. There were substantial increases in the numbers of women enrolled.

In the Catholic primary schools, there was little in the way of reform. If curricula tardily followed the new syllabus statements emerging from the Education Departments, religious instruction remained wedded to performing the catechism. Selleck (1978) argued that there was a defensiveness, a sense of persecution—almost a ghetto mentality—in the Catholic schools. This situation was not improved by the pro-conscription campaigns in World War I that were condemned by Catholic Archbishop Mannix. Resentment over the withdrawal of state funding festered, and the goal of placing all Catholic children in Catholic schools had yet to be achieved. Nevertheless, there was often a strong sense of the Catholic school belonging to its local community. With parishes increasingly responsible for sustaining Catholic schools, the connection between locality, church, priest, sister and brother teachers, family and school contrasted with the centralisation of the state system.

In the secondary area, Catholic high schools and colleges—each run by orders of brothers or nuns—developed differently. They were always single-sex schools. Some were elite in character, such as schools of the male Jesuits and the female Society of the Sacred Heart. After World War I, there were intermediate and technical schools established, often by the Christian and Marist Brothers. There was less done for girls, partly because the expense of establishing girls' domestic science schools was considered prohibitive.

In this period, Catholic girls' schools became more interested in pursuing public examination success along with the cultivation of faithful Catholic wives and mothers. Despite this, diminution of the accomplishments curriculum—usually close to the interests of the more bourgeois of the female orders—was resisted in some schools. One reminiscence of schooling at Kincoppal, a Society of the Sacred Heart school that operated, in Sydney in the 1920s, portrays the school's atmosphere:

> After Mass we had breakfast in the refectory under the chapel . . . Because so many of the nuns spoke French, if we spoke at all we had to speak in French at breakfast. Conversation as such was not allowed at any meal. One girl sat behind a rostrum at the end of the refectory during the evening meal and read aloud. The school had an inexhaustible supply of novels to do with the torturing of English priests at the time of Henry VIII and Elizabeth I, the rack being their favourite torture

instrument. They made grim reading and grim listening. (quoted in Niall and Britain, 1997, p. 155)

Most of the Catholic boys' collegiate schools became devoted to success in public examinations. The making of professionals, the making of a Catholic middle class, achieving uplift from the old Irish working-class origins—these were the goals of many schools. Rigidity and authoritarianism were hardly confined to the culture of Catholic schools in this era, but there were more than the usual problems in the Catholic school sector (O'Donohue, 2001).

Teachers and teaching

The range of work done by teachers and the kinds of institutions within which they were employed varied widely in the period 1901–25. Teaching was hardly a unified profession—and for some, 'profession' was quite the wrong word. Many—especially in the church corporate and private sector—regarded themselves as gentleman and lady teachers, educated rather than trained. Lilian de Lissa in South Australia in 1910 recklessly compared, in her words, the more spiritual and cultivated kindergarten teachers with the 'dumb-driven cattle', the public school teachers. She soon regretted the statement. Nevertheless, as de Lissa argued, kindergarten students 'learned to regard their duties in a true missionary spirit—not as a profession, but as a religion' (quoted in Whitehead, 2010, p. 93).

Early in the century, public school teachers consolidated their unions. Usually they incorporated characteristics of the 'professional association'. Union meetings had been platforms for disseminating the New Education. Future and current directors of education participated in the conferences, but there was also a tendency towards the industrial side. Improved promotion opportunities, salary determinations, teacher transfer rights, superannuation and more were pursued in this period. As public school teaching became a mass occupation, and as the new arbitration courts in the states began to determine salary awards, the unions considered the possibilities. That process might lead to membership of state labour councils. In 1918, the New South

Wales Teachers Federation was founded, combining older teacher associations. Despite Peter Board's disapproval, it showed an early interest in industrial arbitration.

In Western Australia, there was a teacher strike in 1910, and a new militancy arose. For public school teachers, balancing aspirations towards middle-class respectability with working-class approaches to pursuing better wages and conditions became a feature of their union histories. There was another issue of importance. The gap between the salaries of men and women teachers seemed to be strengthened by early determinations of the Commonwealth Conciliation and Arbitration Court. Women and children were to be considered dependants of male-wage earners. Women's wages could be less than men's because men apparently supported them.

In Catholic schools, the proportion of religious to lay teachers rose from 42 per cent in 1900 to 73 in 1925. In 1900 and 1930, the ratio of women religious in relation to teaching brothers and priests was about 9:1. Concern over salary scales was of little concern in the Catholic sector, as vows of poverty, chastity and obedience organised teachers' working lives.

Even though the New Education promised a transformation of teaching, it is best to remain sceptical about how much change occurred in classrooms. Whatever changes were underway were often slowed by the war and its aftermath.

Alexandr Yashchenko was a distinguished Russian zoologist. He made a journey to Australia in 1903, during which he visited schools in Adelaide, Melbourne and Sydney. He witnessed geography and science lessons, and reported that they were about the learning of facts. Teachers were skilled at evoking correct answers from their pupils in rapid-fire questioning. Maps were drawn on blackboards and in student books, with physical features and towns accurately filled in. What impressed him most was the discipline involved—rather more in the public schools than the church corporate schools he visited. Memorisation was at the heart of it all. What the teacher taught, or what the textbook or syllabus stated, would be learned and delivered back on demand. In a couple of cases, he commented on more active and creative methods of teaching, but these were rare.

What Yashchenko did not write about as a spur to such teaching methods was the necessity to prepare young people for frequent, often all-important public and school examinations. (Yashchenko, 2001.)

Primary schools maintained timetabled routines, largely devoted to working through graded readers, the taking of dictation, the learning and chanting of multiplication tables, the doing of sums and rather terrifying performances demanded by 'mental arithmetic'.

Much of the new work in civics, geography and history referred to Britain and Empire, though Catholic schools were more than sensitive to Irish perspectives. Lists of significant dates and monarchs were rote learned. Heroes of Empire, such as Nelson, Wellington, Clive and Wolfe (sometimes with the minor addition of women such as Florence Nightingale or Grace Darling), often occupied pages in children's readers. As national consciousness grew, explorers of Australia—Cook, Flinders, Bass, Hume, Hovell, Blaxland, Wentworth, Lawson and Eyre, and the tragic ones who died in the wilderness,

Arithmetic out of the classroom and into the real world. Children measure the length of a school wall with yard-sticks. The sign held by the older girl announces the total length at 10 yards. A primary school in Victoria, c. 1914. (State Library of Victoria, pc003177)

Leichhardt, Burke and Wills—were added to the curriculum. Learning about these men and women performed excellent service, inculcating Empire loyalty and national pride. The claims of Australian Britons to the lands of Australia at the expense of Aboriginal peoples were legitimated as the sacrifices of pioneers and explorers were noted. After all, had not the admirable Aborigine, Jacky Jacky (1833–54), sensibly assisted the surveyor-explorer Edmund Kennedy in northern Queensland? Had not his heroic contribution to white settlement been officially recognised by the colonial government? The routes that explorers had taken encouraged mapping skills, as dotted lines crossed the continent.

The Great War added a pledge of loyalty to the daily or weekly life of many school children. Dorothea Mackellar's poem 'My Country' (1904) soon entered the curriculum. The second verse, beginning 'I love a sunburnt country . . .', was usually learned by heart.

Most Australian states had developed teachers' colleges by the time of the Great War. In some cases, their principals were also university professors of education. Lecturers in the colleges began to disseminate up-to-date knowledge about teaching methods, curriculum and school organisation. Alexander Mackie, the principal of Sydney Teachers College, edited one collection in 1919. By the time of the third edition (1924), a new 'science of education' was being produced by educational psychologists such as Cyril Burt. Mackie argued that it would assist in the distribution of students to suitable curricula and classes. The production of 'reliable norms' of scholastic performance would be of benefit to teachers. Other chapters made a virtue of the New Education spirit and teaching methods. T.T. Roberts attempted a taxonomy of different kinds of lessons: Information, Drill, Problem, Aesthetic and Exhortation, each demanding different mixes of methods involving the oral, text-study, observation, conversation and so on. He argued for the material assistance that good school architecture, furniture and teaching aids could bring, and the importance of testing—both formal and informal. Yashchenko had noted problems with teaching in his lesson observations. A number of classes had been taught in unsuitable schoolrooms, not classrooms. The relative absence of aids in many classrooms was noted, but not in the demonstration rooms of Melbourne's training college. Frank Tate showed him round, proud of the facility.

•

At the end of this period, the universalisation of schooling had progressed substantially. Compulsory attendance, increased school leaving ages, a range of post-primary or secondary schools for adolescents and kindergartens for the very young were more available. A cost of increased universal schooling was increased differentiation between children, courses of instruction and schools themselves.

There were social as well as educational consequences. New 'rungs' in the 'educational ladder'—so important to policy-makers such as Tate, Board and Williams—had been added, though Chief Inspector M.P. Hansen in Victoria, even in 1923, thought that 'greasy pole' was the more accurate metaphor (quoted in Turney, 1975, p. 337). Opportunity to mount the ladder in the public school system was supposed to be based on proven merit. The ladder could only be climbed if hard work, aptitude and increasingly, intelligence were demonstrated. Some groups—for example, families of the new middle class—did especially well out of the new state high schools. New middle-class fathers were dependent for their employment on the emerging white-collar and semi-professional jobs that were being created in the expanding public service and business. The old middle class, rural and urban business owners—including wealthier farmers—and those based in the older professions tended to stick to the private and corporate schools for the education of their children (Campbell, 1993).

There was little advance for some groups, especially Aboriginal children. In comparison, many middle-class girls found new educational and employment opportunities as higher education, clerical work and professional careers became more readily available. Constance Davey made her career in South Australia. Graduating from the University of Adelaide during the war, she completed a doctorate in psychology at the University of London. In 1925 she was appointed a psychologist within the Education Department of South Australia. She specialised in the testing of 'retarded' children and slow learners, creating that state's first 'opportunity class' for such children. She began a vocational guidance program. Hers was a career that had been unavailable in nineteenth-century Australia. Some working class girls also had new opportunities that were dependent on higher education, especially through the teachers' colleges. But other working-class girls ended up in the new domestic science schools and courses that usually closed off opportunity to them. Working-class boys in the new technical schools were better off. Their courses directed them towards apprenticeships and employment as tradesmen.

If the genuine private schools continued to decline, the new state secondary schools were the outstanding addition to the institutions that schooled young people. The academic high schools were occasionally criticised for imitating the Arnoldian institutions of the church corporate schools—uniforms, prefects, houses, school colours, magazines and songs, games such as cricket, rowing, hockey and more. High school principals such as Alexander Kilgour of Fort Street and William Adey of Adelaide High hoped early on that their schools might develop a certain independence from the education bureaucracies that produced them, but that was not to be. Kilgour finally conceded that the significant corporate entity was the Education Department, not the school. They would be cogs in the machine (Webster, 1981). At the same time, the high schools confirmed the new importance that merit gained through public examination results would have for future job prospects (Proctor, 2002). At Adelaide High, Adey knew that the state high schools would be condemned as exam factories. He regretted that the high school was 'too often looked upon as a place merely for the preparation of a boy in order that he may by and by become the possessor of £1,000 a year and a motor car' (quoted in Campbell, 2001a). Nevertheless the age of patronage in winning desired employment based on membership of some families, ethno-religious groups and social classes retreated a little as new credentials opened careers to talent.

Throughout this process, age and gender relations, and what it meant to be middle or working class, changed. Youth, now described as adolescents by experts, had begun to be separated from both paid employment and serious unpaid domestic labour, though the process took longer for working-class boys, and certainly girls. Very young children—even working-class children, despite the mistrust of many of their mothers that kindergarten teachers were interfering with their families' lives—began to experience childhood differently.

Apparently schools had much to offer in making the nation. According to many, a more orderly, loyal, better trained and educated, and altogether improved population was resulting from reformed schooling. The New Education was significant, but public schools and their teachers remained subject to highly centralised, authoritarian bureaucracies. From World War I, state Directors of Education began to meet regularly. There would be coordinated approaches to educational problems, such as the administration of intelligence testing. Economic benefits as well as the more diffuse national benefits were expected. But then, the Great Depression was not far away, and there were other threats. Too many young people were taking Hollywood films in the new garish picture palaces far too seriously. And then there was the threat of Bolshevism. Such fears required the national anthem ('God Save the King') to be sung more regularly, and in many states there were loyalty pledges—'I honour my God, I serve my King, I salute my flag'—introduced into schools. Some teacher enthusiasts, though, encouraged children to think about the more internationalist League of Nations ideals as well.

Further reading

See McCallum (1990) and Miller (1986) for analyses of new forms of social administration of children. On educational progressivism in the United States, see Tyack (1974), and on its Australian influence, see Dunt (1993). Standard histories cover the arrival of the New Education—for example, Barcan (1980, 1988) and Austin and Selleck (1975). Selleck (1968) remains the authoritative study. For the reforming directors of education and others see Crane and Walker (1957) on Peter Board, and essays in Turney (1983) on Tate, McCoy, Smith, Smyth and Mackie. The best biography is Selleck (1982) on Frank Tate. For adolescence and the rise of the high school, see Campbell (1999a, 1999b). On child-saving, eugenics and other attempts to reform unsatisfactory populations, see Roe (1984) and Rodwell (1992). State high school histories include Campbell (2010), Gregory (2005), Horan (1989), Parker (2006), Proctor (2002) and Rasmussen (2010). Nearly all church corporate schools have at least one published, commissioned history, though critical approaches are rare. There is a dearth of scholarly histories of primary schools, though much can be gleaned from the various centenary compilations (see Burkhardt, 1995). On physical training in schools, see Kirk (1998), and domestic science, Matthews (1983) and Bessant (1976). On nuns teaching in Catholic schools, see O'Brien (2005). A critical view of Catholic education is O'Donohue (2001), as opposed to the standard—though indispensible—history by Fogarty (1959). On Aboriginal schooling, Fletcher (1989a, 1989b) remains essential. On kindergartens and early childhood, see Gardiner (1982), Spearitt (1979), Brennan (1998) and Whitehead (2010).

CHAPTER

5

The socially useful school 1926–1950

By the mid-1920s, seven or eight years of primary education was a conventional part of children's lives, especially in the cities and towns. For many families, the experience was two generations deep, as the first cohort of children to be subject to mass compulsory schooling had children or even grandchildren of their own. Primary schooling was a prolonged commonplace experience that children shared with their parents. Few children, however, remained at school beyond the compulsory years. Full secondary schooling was still the experience of a minority, as was pre-school. Kindergartens were usually the preserve of either the well-to-do or the very poor.

School populations were mostly white and of British and Irish origin. Although Australia remained a nation where more than 90 per cent of the population was of Anglo-Celtic stock, there were areas of the larger cities—Sydney and Melbourne in particular—where other European migrants, including refugees, became increasingly visible. Several thousand Jewish refugees arrived during the 1930s, ahead of a much larger wave of non-British post-war migrants from the late 1940s, but there was no systematic Asian migration as yet because the White Australia policy remained in place. While Indigenous languages and cultures continued to survive against the odds in some parts of the country outside the schooling systems, growing numbers of Aboriginal people were mastering the kinds of curricula taught in Australian schoolrooms. They included members of the growing Aboriginal civil rights groups. Many Indigenous children, however, still had limited access to schooling.

The majority of people lived and worked in the cities, despite the economic importance of the rural sector. By 1928, a third of the population lived in Sydney or Melbourne. The Depression and World War II not only interrupted the plans of the schooling administrators of the 1920s but also had their effects on the families who populated the schools. For example, people moved around during the 1930s and 1940s as Depression and war affected family life. Birth rates fell to record lows.

This was a period in which a new generation of progressive educational ideas and school improvement plans emerged, despite successive waves of nationwide hardship. The exigencies of the Great Depression and World War II relegated spending on public schools

Education for industrial progress—before the Depression. Fort Street schoolboys inspect a lathe at the Australian Manufacturers' Exhibition, Sydney, 1927. (State Library of NSW, Home and Away, 6301)

to a low priority. During the 1910s and early 1920s, the main focus had been on expanding provision, including the establishment of public secondary schools and teachers' colleges in all states. In the mid-1920s, there was optimism that Australia was entering a new phase of economic expansion, which schools would support.

The growth mostly stopped or even reversed during the 1930s and 1940s, but discussions about how to organise and manage children in the schools intensified. Two main ways were proposed by which schools might become more socially useful. One was by sorting and streaming young people according to new international ideas and beliefs about intelligence, ability and aptitude. The second—more homegrown—arose during World War II, and saw schools as a basis for social reconstruction.

Questions for Australian schooling in the late 1920s

Whereas most leaders of the public school systems in the early twentieth century had risen from school teaching through the education bureaucracies, by the late 1920s there was also a growing education intelligentsia based in the new teachers' colleges and universities, many members of which had postgraduate qualifications from the United Kingdom or the United States (see Dunt, 1993).

Australian educationists began to publish substantial accounts and analyses of education in Australia as well as books about education theory and practice. New ideas and theories were spread by such organisations as the Australian Council for Educational Research (ACER), founded in 1930 with a generous grant from the Carnegie Corporation in the United States. The ACER was headed by K.S. Cunningham, who had a doctorate in educational measurement from Teachers College, Columbia. The 1930s and 1940s saw the ACER begin the publication of a series of reviews of education in Australia, which collected and analysed data from every state—as a resource for educationists, administrators and policy-makers. A precursor to these national surveys was G.S. Browne's (1927) widely disseminated *Education in Australia*. The book describes the institutional structures of education during the mid-1920s, and provides an insight into what the senior men of Australian educational administration and research considered to be key achievements, problems and issues of the day (see also Cormack 2012).

Browne was Vice-Principal of the Melbourne Teachers College at the time of the book's publication. He put the book together, he said, to encourage the development of a national approach to education. His introduction listed a number of common characteristics shared by the Australian states. They included youth, Britishness, a sparsely populated interior and new opportunities for meritocratic progression through free public schools. The work of the state Education Departments was clearly the main game, but he also mentioned Catholic schools, 'conducted without one penny of subsidy from the Government', and church and secular corporate schools—comprising a 'valuable part of the educational fabric' but only available to the 'prosperous classes' (1927, p. xxi). The centralised administration of state schooling was one topic canvassed in the book, as something that set Australia apart from other Anglophone nations. Browne argued that tight central control had been historically necessary to secure the equitable spread of schooling across a thinly populated continent: 'The truth is that centralisation . . . ensures that the children of the rural pioneer receive as good an education as the children of the banker or artisan in the city.' (1927, p. xvii).

The early directors of public education, such as Frank Tate, had argued that the problems of centralised uniformity had been solved by their New Education-inspired leaderships, yet Browne's book reported that centralisation was still contested. Educationists in America and Europe tended to view centralised systems as characterised by 'soul-killing uniformity, mechanical teaching, and the ruthless crushing of original ideas amongst the teachers' (1927, p. xvii).

Other preoccupations on display in *Education in Australia* included the provision of post-primary schooling, the training of teachers, schooling of children with disabilities and pedagogical experimentation. Cecil Thompson, Queensland Inspector of Schools, included the following in a list of 'World-wide educational tendencies that would affect Queensland':

> The thought given to the education of the adolescent, and almost general acknowledgement that *all children*, except the unfit, should benefit by secondary education of some type.
>
> The recognition of the needs of country districts and the justification of their claim to equality with the city child as regards educational opportunity.
>
> The advances made in the psychological study of the individual child and the consequent modification of curricula. (quoted in Browne, 1927, p. 307)

The category 'adolescent' was relatively new in educational discourse, and the association of adolescence with schooling would become increasingly strong across the twentieth century. Public high schools had been founded in all states, but there was uncertainty about how to manage the majority of young adolescents who would not be proceeding to an academically focused high school. Chapters in Browne's book were dedicated to this category of student, under the sub-heading 'The twelve to fifteen problem'. The states reported different approaches to the development of junior secondary schooling, including such institutions as central schools, domestic science schools for girls, junior technical schools for boys and rural schools in the country. But development was haphazard. New South Wales, which had begun to establish such schools in the 1910s, was already reorganising them by the mid-1920s. The curriculum of the rural schools, for example, was being revised in response to the demands of their clients to restrict the time spent on agriculture and increase the study of 'town skills' (1927, p. 79).

Nor was the other end of schooling yet settled. Most children remained at home until they started school, with starting ages varying from state to state. Some spent time in nursery schools or kindergartens. The Kindergarten Union in each state ran philanthropic institutions in the crowded inner cities, combining education with social work. There was a clear line of demarcation between the governance of schools and the privately run kindergartens. As Percival Cole of New South Wales put it, 'The Kindergarten Union receives a subsidy from the Department of Education, trains its own

The transformative power of the high school. Little girl into tough flapper, a modern adolescence organised by the curriculum, leadership and social opportunities of the government high school. (Artist: Joshua Hall. *Unley High School Magazine*, 5: 1, 1926, p. 21)

teachers, organises its own schools, and redeems the slums' (quoted in Browne, 1927, p. 32). Each of the states reported the uptake of kindergarten methods in the infants departments of the larger public schools, with Montessorian methods starting to supplement or replace Froebelian organisation. Wallace Chubb, Senior Inspector of the Western Australian Education Department, reported an active debate in his state about the best age to start school. In 1920, the admission age had been raised as a cost-saving measure. Chubb expressed his concern:

> The loss of that initial year may not be serious in the case of children who come from good homes, where their physical, mental and moral development is carefully watched over by parents [but] . . . there are many children of four and five years of age whose home environment, if not bad, is at any rate not as good as the child's welfare requires. Some of these little ones live in poor houses where the mother has to go out working, or where the main playground is the street. (quoted in Browne, 1927, pp. 334–5)

The report of each state included an account of the schooling of the 'abnormal' child, a growing field of interest. There was a lot of variation, not only in the kinds of provision made but also in the terminology—much of which is offensive to modern ears. It was clear that Education Departments increasingly considered that young people with disabilities should attend schools. In Tasmania, classes had recently been established for 'sub-normal' or 'retarded' children, who were selected by a series of tests and examinations overseen by a Supervisor of Special Classes. In Western Australia, on the other hand, few 'feeble-minded' children were receiving schooling.

Each of the states reported on innovation or experimentation. Many described their first steps in the adoption of apparently scientific systems of psychological measurement. As we saw in the previous chapter, the schools were a proving ground for the application of psychology to 'normal' populations (see Wright 2011), and Cole for New South Wales and Browne for Victoria wrote about the development of standardised tests to establish class and age 'norms' on a statewide basis.

There was another side to modernity in the improved operation of the school. Browne was one of a number of his contemporaries seeking to implement Deweyan progressivism by translating it into concrete pedagogical techniques, in order to enlist the child actively in their own learning. Here the United States led the way, with such schemes as the Dalton Plan, Caldwell Cook's 'play-way', the Platoon and Winnetka teaching systems, and the Project Method.

Different states had different requirements and arrangements for the training of teachers. The main institutions were the state teachers' colleges, of which the Sydney Teachers' College was easily the largest, with more than a thousand students in 1926—more than three times the number of the next largest, Melbourne. The other states developed similar institutions, with a widespread consensus that teachers needed more sustained preparation before they entered the nation's classrooms. They likely needed a full high school education followed by two years at teachers' college.

All the states except New South Wales still had some teachers training in versions of the nineteenth-century pupil-teacher system. Kindergarten teacher training was run by the Kindergarten Union in each state. Small teachers' colleges were also funded from time to time by Catholic orders and other religious denominations; however, with no mandated minimum teacher training standards, 'unqualified' or poorly qualified teachers often found themselves in classrooms.

The Great Depression and schools

Australia's economy suffered during the Depression, with higher rates of unemployment than many other developed nations. Unemployment reached a peak of nearly 32 per cent in 1932. Public expenditure was heavily cut, resulting in large-scale reductions to state Education Department budgets. Some students stayed longer at school, as many male youth were unable to find employment. Others left earlier than they might have done, including many young women. It depended on the work that was available locally. Women's employment was not as hard hit as men's, so a wage might be preferable to prolonged schooling, especially if other family members were unemployed.

During the worst of the Great Depression many schools assisted children in poverty. At Belmore North Public School, free soup and bread is distributed. Sydney, 1934. (State Library of NSW, Home and Away, 4367)

Depression hardships added a new inflection to the older discourses about the uses of schooling and employability. Social class, gender and race could all be engaged in revised ways to organise and justify new discriminations in the labour market.

In 1926, the demand for teachers in small rural schools had led the Victorian government to open country teachers' colleges at Ballarat and Bendigo, but these were closed down in 1931. New South Wales planned country colleges too, opening Armidale in 1928. However, the Depression saw plans for others at Wagga Wagga and Bathurst postponed. One motivation behind the Armidale venture was the department's belief that teaching at Sydney Teachers College under Alexander Mackie had become too theoretical (Cleverley, 1972, p. 82). In 1930, the principal of the newly established Armidale Teachers' College, C.B. Newling, asked his first batch of graduates to write to him about their placements, many of them in small rural schools.

Their letters offer a snapshot of the experiences of new teachers—very young women and men—at the beginning of the Depression.

> I like teaching, Mr Newling. Of course at times I get angry and annoyed but I am trying to develop a sympathetic outlook towards the children.
>
> •
>
> In my first class I have nine children, the ages ranging from five to ten. Two of them, one nine and one ten, began school for the first time only a couple of months ago. They come four and a half miles on horseback.
>
> •
>
> For the first five months I taught in a corridor. Since June I teach part time in a room. At present I have 72 on roll and when in the corridor the children sit 3 in each desk while 12 children have no desks at all. It is while in the corridor that I have most difficulty in teaching . . . However I find that some of the difficulty is overcome by using teaching aids such as reading and number cards.
>
> •
>
> Music has a wonderful power breaking down the wild habits of some of the urchins who have come off the street . . . Nature Study topics will lead the most self-conscious child to talk and forget himself. (quoted in Reid and Martin, 2003, pp. 54–60)

The detail and severity of Depression measures varied from state to state, but the same kinds of economies were considered across the country. The largest savings came from reducing public school teachers' salaries and increasing class sizes. Other kinds of budget cuts were less effective fiscally, but nevertheless served as a declaration by governments of their economic prudence. Early on, teachers and their unions tended not to resist wage cuts too strongly in order to protect jobs.

The Depression exposed those areas of public education such as teachers' colleges and high schools that were considered by some policy-makers to be extraneous to the government's core education business: the public primary schools. Western Australia accepted no new students into its teachers' college after September 1930, and the college was closed in late 1931. By 1933, teachers were in such short supply that it became necessary to employ untrained monitors. The college was reopened in mid-1934 in a by now almost derelict building. In South Australia, fees were reintroduced into public high schools in 1934 at the urging of conservative groups such as the Taxpayers' Association and the Chamber of Commerce. They remained in place until 1943. The Vice President of the South Australian Chamber of Commerce was reported as saying, 'Boys, who are going to be labourers, as it does not make them better labourers, do not need higher education' (quoted in Miller, 1986, p. 189). The savings achieved by the government, however, were less than they might have been as a result of the strategies of the Director of Education, W.J. Adey, who carefully exploited the exemption provisions. His department granted almost everyone who applied for it exemption from high school tuition fees, obeying the letter but not the spirit of the new regulations. Despite this, and in contrast to New South Wales where fees were not reintroduced, high school enrolments declined. In New South Wales, enrolments increased dramatically—especially among boys.

One response to the Depression in New South Wales was the passing of the *Married Women (Lecturers and Teachers) Act* in 1932. In good economic times, it had been a convention that women resign on marriage. During the Depression, however, a small but increasing number of women stayed on, causing consternation in the Education Department—and elsewhere. Women were paid less than men of the same level and were therefore less expensive to employ, but conventional wisdom held that it was wrong for a married woman to take a job that could be given either to a man with a dependant family, or a new teachers' college graduate. The Act removed all married women from the permanent teaching service, allowing for them to apply to be reappointed as temporary teachers if they could demonstrate financial hardship or if it was 'in the public interest'. As temporary teachers, they could only work on short-term contracts.

Surprising many officials in the Education Department, most of the 800 or so married women in employment were actually found to be in need. By the time the Act was repealed in 1947, there was a teacher shortage so the labour of married women was in demand. By that time, 10 per cent of the New South Wales Department of Education workforce was made up of married women teachers in temporary employment (Theobald and Dwyer, 1999).

The response of the public schools to the Depression is easier to observe than that of Catholic, private and corporate schools because of the lack of public information, including reliable statistics of any kind. Certainly the Depression did nothing to diminish the commitment of the Catholic bishops to their primary school systems. The nuns who comprised the majority of teachers in Catholic schools must have found it difficult, however. By the mid-1920s, it was already difficult to recruit enough young postulants and the existing nuns were usually overworked. Within many schools in poorer districts, unpaid tuition fees required increased levels of forgiveness by communities of sisters. The associated deprivations were assumed by them (O'Brien, 2005, p. 206).

Most of the last of the private-venture schools closed during the Depression. They were unable to compete as schooling grew more complex and more highly regulated, and as fees became more difficult to collect. Surviving sole proprietor-principals found it all too hard. This period had its challenges for the church corporate schools, too. The experience of Abbotsleigh, an upper middle-class boarding and day school for girls in Sydney's then semi-rural north, offers an insight into how a school's fortunes were shaped in part by the Depression.

Sold to the Church of England by a charismatic and well-connected lady principal in 1924, the school struggled for the next six years as a new, quieter employee-principal struggled both to live up to the reputation of her beloved predecessor and to manage the demands of an interventionist board of governors. In 1930, a building program was put on hold, tuition fees were reduced, a boarding house was closed and there were successive reductions in staff salaries. The headmistress left by mutual agreement, complaining privately to a friend that 'I am coming to the conclusion that half the world are megalomaniacs'. By 1935, however, salaries had been restored, enrolments were rising and the replacement headmistress would remain at her post for the next 23 years (Emilsen, 2000, p. 98).

Public schooling: The right child in the right school

In the late 1920s, at about the age of 13, June Wallis (pseudonym) found herself educationally adrift after a series of family crises. June's family had fallen on hard times and her parents were too depressed or distracted to enrol her in a secondary school. A serendipitous encounter with a local teacher eventually led to her selection for the public high school in Parramatta, but once she left school she did not know what to do with her life. After the loss of her husband in World War II, an unplanned life as an independent woman meant she had to attend seriously to the business of paid employment. She felt herself to be totally unprepared (Proctor, 2004).

The educational and vocational path of George Walters (pseudonym) was bumpy too. George found himself unable to gain entry to an academic high school in the mid-1930s, despite the urging of his mother, who had travelled with him to Sydney for the purpose from a tiny settlement in the Snowy Mountains. In common with many parents of the time, George's mother had dreamed of a prestigious high school education for her son. Eventually he was enrolled at Parramatta High, but regretted that his mother had not advised him to go to a technical school instead. He did not 'shine' at the academic high school. He thought he might have done better at a technical school because he 'had a flair' for that kind of learning. He was a practical man who was 'good with his hands'. He believed that certification from a technical school would have made his career path a lot smoother (Proctor, 2004).

Both of these stories speak to an idea that became increasingly popular during the 1930s and 1940s. It was crucial to find the right educational 'fit' for children and adolescents. In fact, June eventually made a career in the nascent field of vocational guidance. She became convinced by the possible good consequences of psychological testing and measurement—systematically regulated and administered by the state—being able to avert, for people like herself and her parents, the sorts of setbacks and wrong turnings they had experienced in their lives.

Public education administrators, policy-makers and others spent much of the first half of the twentieth century talking and writing about, and trying to design, schools and school systems that would ease children into the right school setting and then into the waged or unwaged employment that best suited them and the nation. They had two main methods at their disposal. One was the assessment of the interests, abilities and needs of either individual children or categories of children. The other was related: the arrangement of different kinds of post-primary schools and post-primary curricula. During the 1930s and 1940s, there were a number of experiments and developments in curriculum reform, psychological testing and measurement, and vocational and therapeutic 'guidance'. While the hypothetical student in the debates and discussions was conventionally male, girls too were caught up in the educational movements of the times. Often this meant that reformed technical—mainly manual arts—curricula for boys were paired with domestic science for girls.

'Ability' became an important guiding concept, coming from new educational research and theorisation in the United States, Britain and Europe. Australia's educational intelligentsia became absorbed into this movement through study and travel. The continued rise of intelligence testing during the 1930s and 1940s distinguished ability from achievement. Achievement and effort might be obvious to any classroom teacher, but the identification of potential required specialised knowledge and training. Highly intelligent children could sometimes be lost. At the same time, age and school grade became more closely matched during this period, with social promotion in a cohort making inroads into the older demand that children master an assessment standard prior to grade promotion (Trethewey, 1994). 'Backward' and 'advanced' children, it was argued, should where possible remain with their own age group—but, if possible, in classes with a separate curriculum planned specifically for them. Schools were increasingly organised into infants, primary and secondary classes. Boundaries between these were becoming sharper and more clearly defined.

In Australia, the potential of psychology as a new social science had been associated with schooling from early in the century. During the 1920s and 1930s, school psychology services for testing and measurement were consolidated. Two key moments in the life of a school student were identified in particular. Aptitude testing might help teachers direct children more efficiently into the appropriate course of study at the end of primary school. And vocational guidance and testing would help send the students in the right direction for their future occupation.

Although this kind of testing did not become universal until the 1950s and 1960s, its continuing development played an important role in the way schools were conceptualised during this period, especially in discussion and planning for the future expansion of secondary schooling. The institutional base and legitimacy given to educational psychology by its uptake in schools was important in the foundation of psychology as a profession (Wright, 2011, pp. 87–125). Not everyone was impressed, however. In 1937, one New South Wales school principal declared that 'intelligence tests at school are of little value [and vocational guidance is] an anaesthetic to lull the people into thinking that something is being done for the unemployed youth' (quoted in Hughes, 2002, p. 40).

The category of students most in need of schooling reform, it was widely agreed, were the 12–15-year-old girls and boys who were not best suited to enrolment at an academic high school. The late primary and early post-primary years—the years towards the end of compulsory schooling—were the focus of attention from educationalists, administrators and psychologists. David Tyack's analysis of a bifurcated progressivism fits this period. School administrators and others built on the achievements of the 1910s and 1920s in the style of the 'administrative progressives' of the United States (Tyack, 1974). That is, they placed their faith in social efficiency measures in schools achieved by bureaucratic organisation and by the use of social sciences like psychology for the standardised testing and measurement of young people, then the streaming and placement of them into different schools and pathways. Belief in the power of schooling to offer the appropriate education for groups of children headed in different adult directions was given further impetus by the Depression. It fuelled anxieties about the futures of children, including the place of schools in educating citizens and workers of the future.

The public examination-passing elite from Canterbury Boys High. But did Australia in the Depression need boys like this? Many conservative supporters of the church corporate schools worried that high school boys competed too well with the 'private' school boys for the limited number of remaining pleasant and well-paid jobs. Sydney, 1935. (State Library of NSW, Home and Away, 12185)

While all schools grappled with issues of how best to align curriculum and culture with clientele, the public school systems had by far the most difficult task. They were charged with managing the talent and development of whole state populations. Primary school courses of instruction, common to all children, were to disaggregate into differentiated post-primary schools, streams and courses. Creating the right mix of streams and other ability or vocational groupings, and institutions and courses within schools or across systems, was a matter of intense deliberation. Channelling children into the right places was a challenge. All of this was underpinned by questions and discussions about the relationship between schooling and future employment. How close was this alignment to be, and what was its nature? What should be the role of public schools in providing technical or vocational education?

Gender-specific vocational training. St Mary's Commercial College (Catholic). Thousands of girls aspired to the new workplace, the office, that followed the invention of modern business and bureaucratic practices from the late nineteenth century. New South Wales, 1937. (State Library of NSW, Home and Away, 8161)

Provision for super-primary schooling other than the high school varied from state to state. While the institutional forms of 'primary' and 'high school' remained relatively stable, there was considerable variety and movement in the 'twelve to fifteen' sector. In the Sydney suburb of Parramatta during the 1930s and 1940s, for example, post-primary students were catered for by a full high school as well as a boys' intermediate high school which became a central school in 1944; a boys' junior high established in 1944 and a Home Science school that was renamed a Domestic Science school in 1942. More efficient interventions in children's futures were encouraged by the raising of the leaving age from 14 to 15 in the early 1940s.

Several states experimented with technical schooling for boys. For example, in the 1920s New South Wales had established a post-primary school called a junior technical school where boys would study for two years before attempting a specialist 'Junior Technical Certificate'. But in the 1930s, junior technical schools in New South Wales effectively became junior high schools, offering more or less the same three-year course that was offered by high schools and culminating in the all-purpose Intermediate Certificate. In Victoria, the articulation between the junior and senior technical schools, technical colleges and industry was stronger, making them arguably more successful than the New South Wales schools (Hyams and Bessant, 1972, pp. 142–54).

In the mid-1920s, William McCoy—brought to South Australia from Tasmania in order to reorganise public education—established a system of vocationally oriented central, then technical schools. Administratively, the schools were first annexed to primary schools. Success in a course with a commercial, technical or domestic arts focus might lead to the new secondary school for boys, Thebarton Technical High School. A vocational guidance scheme was inaugurated in South Australia in 1929 in order to guide students into the right kind of course, although substantial implementation was held back by the Depression.

One group of students, or potential students, who had been the subject of discussion and some anxiety comprised children and adolescents in rural areas. There were several reasons for concern. One was that country children who travelled to the towns or cities for higher schooling might be lost permanently to their rural communities:

> Every new step in the provision of educational facilities in the town meets the same objections—that it is attracting the youth away from rural pursuits; that it is draining the country of its strength. (quoted in Phillips, 1985, p. 215)

Another was the apparent rejection by school clients of government school attempts to provide practical curricula suited to country children. Designers of post-primary curricula were often frustrated by families' apparent preference for traditional pen and paper subjects.

Solutions to the problem of providing schooling to the rural population included practical measures such as the funding of school buses. In the late 1930s, Tasmania had some success with post-primary

The tedium of the ordinary classroom. Students in a rural high school, Deniliquin Intermediate High, New South Wales, c. 1935. (State Library of NSW, At Work and Play, 06192)

'area schools', which enrolled all children between the ages of 12 and 15 in a given district. The Hagley Area School outside Launceston entertained 'hundreds' of visitors, and was celebrated in a newsreel film (Browne, in Maslin, 1948, p. xiii). Its emphasis on cooperation and citizenship included such features as a school parliament:

> Our main objective has been to convert a School into a Juvenile Community . . . a microcosm of society, where the virtues and standards we ultimately desire in our citizens may be practised by them in their youth. (Maslin, 1948, p. 3)

Its focus on the needs and interests of the school's local community included the running of a 'full-sized farm', partly funded by a donation from the Broken Hill Company (Maslin 1948, p. 29). In addition to the common junior curriculum of reading, spelling, arithmetic, history and so on, the school's timetable included subjects like needlework, laundry and horticulture for girls, while the boys studied saddlery, blacksmithing and agriculture.

The New Education Fellowship

Australian educators had always looked overseas—especially to Britain—for educational ideas and models. However, the influence of American theory and practices was making inroads. The 1920s and 1930s were a time of fervid internationalism in the Anglophone world. In 1937, the New Education Fellowship (NEF), an association of progressive educationists based in Western Europe, toured a popular and influential conference through Brisbane, Sydney, Canberra, Melbourne, Hobart, Adelaide and Perth, sponsored by the Australian Council for Educational Research (ACER).

The NEF had been founded in the 1920s by a group led by the Englishwoman Beatrice Ensor, a Theosophist who combined this progressively oriented semi-religion with her years of experience as a school teacher, principal and county schools inspector. In the 1920s, the NEF had been influenced by spiritualism and early psychoanalysis, but by the 1930s the focus was more practical—perhaps system oriented—with its membership increasingly characterised by people who were employed as senior educational administrators and academics in universities and teachers' colleges. By the time its conference arrived in Australia, the NEF was an influential mainstream organisation.

The conference's follow-up publication, edited by ACER director Kenneth Cunningham, *Education for Complete Living* (1938), became a manual for reform well into the post-World War II era. The kinds of ideas championed by the speakers included the following: schools should provide practical training in democracy and good citizenship; schools should nurture everyone, no one's 'talent' should be 'wasted'; schools ought to be closely connected to their local communities; public examinations are constraining and unproductive, especially when tied to over-prescriptive syllabuses; schools should not be narrowly academic; they should include the arts and practical subjects, catering to the 'whole' child; schools should support psychological and physical health and development; provision of pre-schooling should be expanded and developed; and among many other prescriptions, the pre-schooling enterprise should include education in good mothering (list adapted from Campbell & Sherington, 2013, pp. 34–5; Cunningham, 1938).

The NEF conference was a major event. Government and non-government schools in all states gave teachers time off to attend lectures, many of which were broadcast over the radio. There was also daily coverage in the newspapers, constituting unprecedented public interest in education. Cunningham, the ACER's director, wrote:

> For the first time in Australia all sections of the education world pulled together in a common effort. University professors sat on committees with people in charge of kindergartens; private school teachers rubbed shoulders with those in the public school system in a way that has never happened before. (quoted in Hyams and Bessant, 1972, p. 163)

There is no doubt that many teachers were inspired by New Education movements in their various forms from the late nineteenth century.

Others were sceptical, resistant or immune. At Unley High School in Adelaide, several teachers declined to take a day off to attend the NEF lectures, choosing instead to stay at school marking tests and preparing lessons (Campbell, 2010, p. 102). It is likely that the daily lives of most children, teachers and schools were barely touched. Christina Stead (1990), a former teacher, included the following school staffroom vignette in her novel *For Love Alone*, set in the 1930s:

> 'I hate it, I hate it,' said the fair woman, rocking herself. 'If I can only keep the kids down, I don't care if they never learn a line. That Milly Brown came in with a note from her mother again this morning about ink on her dress. I wish some of the mothers had to take care of my class for a whole day.'
>
> 'I wish that too,' said Mrs Keeling. 'They'd wake up.'
>
> Teresa burst out with: 'Why do you stay in it if you hate it so much?' (1945, p. 113)

It was not New Education-style progressivism.

The NEF conference sponsors, including state Education Departments, sought advice about the future organisation of Australian education. Isaac Kandel, a professor at Teachers College Columbia, stayed on in Australia. He was thoroughly critical of a number of features of Australian education, including its centralised bureaucratic management and the reliance on public examinations. One of the dangers of centralisation that he identified was a lack of engagement with school parents and communities. The cultivation of public support, he argued, was essential in creating a constituency both for innovation and for adequate levels of financial support for schools. Good education and efficient schooling had become separated.

Schooling Aboriginal children

In the same year as the New Education Conference—1937—the first national conference of (all non-Aboriginal) representatives of Aboriginal Protection Boards (or equivalents) from each state and territory was held. The conference was significant for its endorsement of 'assimilation', including the principle that Aboriginal children should be educated to the 'white standard', which meant basic literacy and numeracy. The delegates agreed that Aboriginal children could only keep up with white children to Grades 3 or 4.

For many Aboriginal children, it would still be decades before schooling became a routine part of life, although the conference was most concerned with those who were living in or near the towns and cities. The Western Australian Chief Protector of Aborigines, A.O. Neville, a leading advocate of forced child removal, was a strong presence, expressing an unwavering mistrust in the capacity of Aboriginal families to manage their own lives. Meanwhile, large numbers of Aboriginal children continued to be excluded from government schools. In New South Wales, they could be either denied entry or forced to leave at the request of any white parent. There are many letters in the Education Department's correspondence archives from Aboriginal communities objecting to this treatment. The following comes from a letter written to the King of England by a Batemans Bay woman in the mid-1920s:

> I beg to state that it is months and months since those children were at school and it is a shame to see them going about without education.

> At Batemans Bay there is a Public School, and why are those children not allowed to attend, when the School is Public? Another thing, Your Majesty, we have compulsory education, why are they not compelled to attend school?

In the case of Batemans Bay, the Aboriginal community prevailed, with the support of the school principal and the local inspector of schools, and the children were readmitted (Fletcher 1989b, pp. 125–7). Aboriginal children in many areas continued to be denied adequate schooling, and if they were able to attend school, it often came at the price of tensions within their own communities and with local white families.

In the late 1940s, A.O. Neville guessed that across Australia three-quarters of Aboriginal children were receiving no schooling at all (Beresford and Partington, 2003, pp. 46–7). In making sense of such a statistic, it is important to keep in mind first the great diversity of Aboriginal experience and second the distinction we maintain in this book between schooling and education. Nganyintja Ilyatjari, a Pitjantjatjara woman born in the late 1920s, was one of the first children to attend the Ernabella Mission school in the Anangu Pitjantjatjara Yankunytjatjara Lands in Central Australia in the early 1940s, later becoming an assistant teacher there. Her account of the education she received outside the classroom from kin and community was originally recorded in the Pitjantjatjara language. By observing and listening to her elders, she explained, she learned to find and prepare food, to build shelters and about her culture:

> I lived as a child at a place called Angatja. My father, mother, grandmother, older brothers, aunties and uncles taught me there and I learned from them . . . It was like school and we became very knowledgeable and we did all our own work. (quoted in Hyams, 1988, pp. 5–6).

Catholic schools

Most Catholic families who wished to do so were now able to find a place in a parochial school. It is not known exactly what proportion of Catholic school children were enrolled in Catholic rather than public schools, but it was likely around 80 per cent by 1945 (Selleck, 1978, p. 89). The percentage had risen since the late nineteenth century and was to decline again over the next 20 or 30 years. The schools remained staffed mostly by nuns, brothers and priests, and the catechism remained the basic teaching tool in daily religious instruction: 'The Catholic . . . requires that his child will soundly learn and firmly keep the Faith of his Fathers' (1978, p. 91).

Those who enrolled children in state schools did so in defiance of their bishops and priests. Control of primary schools remained local, organised around the administrative unit of the parish. Parish priests played an important role in their management and operation. This gave them remarkable administrative autonomy compared with state schools, but there is little indication that their curriculum or pedagogy varied very much. They followed the government schools closely—except for religious instruction. Where state registration was required, the schools were regularly inspected by inspectors from Departments of Education. It was important for the schools to be able to demonstrate their parity with the public schools.

Secondary schools were operated by the various religious orders. Catholic schools would never become as centralised as state schools, but the establishment of the first state Catholic Education Office in Victoria by Archbishop Mannix in 1932 was an indication that substantial local autonomy was unlikely to last much longer.

Corporate schools for girls and boys

Small but significant numbers of mainly middle- and upper-class children were enrolled in church and secular corporate schools, even if only for a year or two to gain some polish (McCalman, 1993, pp. 113–34). Retention rates were higher on average than in the public schools, and the schools' graduates were disproportionately represented amongst university students. In a period before university entrance was very accessible, however, outstanding examination results were not always the main focus—especially for boys. Team sports and extra-curricular activities were important, as were charitable works. Most of these schools were denominational.

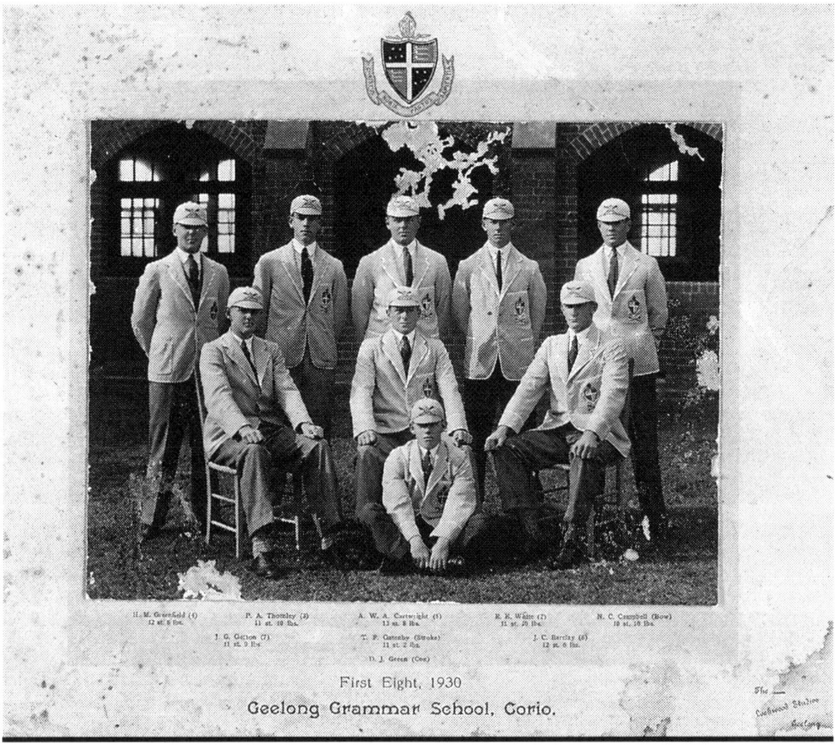

Schooling for ruling. Geelong Grammar School's first rowing eight, including John Gorton, seated on the left, a future prime minister of Australia. Victoria, 1930. (National Library of Australia, vn4632475)

Students learned respectability, manners and leadership, in their gendered forms, and made lifelong personal connections. The schools continued to model themselves mainly on the British greater public schools, with their Arnoldian practices. They played a substantial role in the making of a distinctive Australian middle and ruling class.

It remained common for staff and principals to be recruited from Britain. Their headmasters and headmistresses sometimes became public figures, such as James Darling of Geelong Grammar in Victoria, or Winifred West of Frensham in New South Wales. Both—perhaps unusually in comparison with most of their peers—were leaders in implementing progressive educational initiatives. Heads of the corporate schools were typically answerable to, and sometimes in conflict with, boards of governors comprising churchmen, local businessmen or professional people. During the 1930s and 1940s, many joined either the Headmasters Conference (1931) or Headmistresses Association of Australia (1947), both organisations modelled on British equivalents.

Schooling during and after World War II

At the beginning of World War II, Australian schooling comprised a mix of public, Catholic and other non-government provision, with government schools enrolling just over three-quarters of Australia's school students. Most children left school soon after their fourteenth birthday, and the main business of the state Departments of Education was in running the huge and widely dispersed primary school systems. Up to 30 per cent of school children in New South Wales were enrolled in rural schools, and up to three-quarters were enrolled

Despite the war, grade two with teacher at Drouin State School, east of Melbourne, Victoria, 1944. (National Library of Australia, an24229822)

in these schools in other states. Having scarcely recovered from the effects of the Depression, the public schools were often run down, and a number of the improvements planned by the state Education Departments had not eventuated.

Teachers' colleges in most states had barely been restored, let alone developed. Their enrolments would soon be threatened again by military enlistment and the opening up of paid work for women during the emergency. The low birth rate of the depression years would continue, affecting school enrolments.

Voluntary enlistment in the armed forces was high. More than half a million people—mostly men—served overseas. Unlike in Europe or East Asia, the war and home fronts were mostly separate for Australians. Nevertheless, there was a well-founded fear of invasion from late 1941, with 1942–43 the years of highest disruption to civilian life.

During the war, there were shortages of school supplies and equipment. In 1942, a number of schools were evacuated in Western Australia and Queensland. Darwin was evacuated ahead of the Japanese bombing and there were voluntary evacuations elsewhere. Students and their teachers participated in Air Raid Precautions, including the digging of trenches in their schoolyards. Many fathers were absent and in danger. As during the Depression—though for different reasons—many families were on the move.

By 1945, there were plenty of children who could not remember the country in a time of peace. Queensland's Director of Education called for sensitivity in the schools:

> The material effects of wartime conditions will in time be overcome; the mental and moral effects on the child's life of certain war-time conditions will not be easily countered, and will require sympathy, tolerance and a well planned education. (quoted in Spaull, 1982, p. 272)

Small numbers of young people in schools from the 1930s were refugees or, after the war, children of 'displaced persons' from the Central and Eastern European theatres of war. In 1950, the annual magazine of Parramatta High School, in Sydney's west, carried some articles by Latvian students, alongside the usual prize lists, English

Air raid drill for war in the Pacific. Training children in the event that Japanese bombs might fall on the Flinders Street Primary School, Adelaide, 1942. (State Library of South Australia, B 21652)

compositions and sports results. The following extract is from an account of an apparent reprisal killing:

> It was a sunny autumn morning during the Second World War, at the end of September, 1944 when the Russian troops came suddenly into Tuckum (a town in Latvia) where I used to live . . . Five years have gone by but I can't forget . . . and I will never forget. (*The Phoenix*, 1950, pp. 57–8)

There were serious teacher shortages during and after the war. Many married women who had resigned either by convention or legislation were invited back into the service, albeit on lower rates of pay and usually in temporary positions without career paths or salary increments. Retired teachers were re-employed, and many rural schools were closed for lack of staff. Class sizes were increased and there was emergency recruitment. Short training periods in teachers' colleges became shorter. In 1942 the Queensland and Victorian Education Departments temporarily raised the starting age of children from four or five to six years, despite the protests of parents. In the secondary schools, there was an acute shortage of mathematics and science teachers. The teacher shortages delayed the moves in several states to dismantle their pupil-teacher systems. Teachers won some concessions under these circumstances, including salary increases—often the first since the 1920s—under new awards in all states from 1945 to 1946. Women, comprising the majority of the teachers, were paid 75–80 per cent of male salaries for the same work.

The war not only extended the shortages of the Depression but also intensified the calls for reform that had arisen in its wake. By the 1940s, there was considerable public interest in education. In 1945, the *Sydney Morning Herald* identified a community mood that was, 'never so great or widespread . . . Never before have there been so many committees concerned with education reconstruction and never before has there been such a spate of talking about teachers and their work' (quoted in Spaull, 1982, p. 170). Idealistic declarations such as that made by the secretary of the Victorian Teachers Union in 1944 became common:

> The war has roused us from our complacency . . . we need a tolerant and better-informed people . . . Are we to put our trust in the competition among nations to devise means of destruction, or, through a right system of education, to foster co-operation and goodwill? (quoted in Hyams and Bessant, 1972, p. 167)

In the post-war nation, better schooling would build a better, fairer country, a stronger community and a more peaceful world. The educational reform agenda usually emphasised the social and citizenship purposes of schooling. That often included the demand for equality of educational opportunity, raising the school leaving age, broadening the secondary school curriculum to cater for all students, better vocational guidance, decentralisation of administration, the improvement of teacher status and even the abolition of external examinations.

The role of public school parents' groups during this period was also important, and marked a change in the politics of schooling from earlier periods. The 1940s marked the approximate beginning of the activism of parent organisations in Australia. In South Australia, Parents and Citizens (P&C) Associations were founded across the state high schools (Campbell, 2010, p. 109).

A lasting contribution of the 1940s reform movement was the introduction of 'political arithmetic' to the study of Australian schooling. While the growing field of educational psychology demonstrated a scientific basis for individual differences in academic attainment, the even newer field of educational sociology looked to social, structural explanations for educational inequality. During this period, a loose coalition of academics and others pioneered the kinds of class-based analysis that would, over the next 70 years, demonstrate robust correlations between parental wealth, social class, and schooling achievement.

Influential and widely cited pamphlets and essays by writers such as John La Nauze (1940) and Norman Henderson (1942) used statistical data such as school leaving age and university entrance figures and household income figures from the national census to demonstrate the inequalities experienced by public and non-government school students in particular.

The great educational ladder of opportunity, ran the argument, was not working for all students. This was not only a social injustice but represented a waste of talent. Henderson's analysis of the 1933 census demonstrated that more than half of Australian household heads

> had to keep a home going for a year on what it costs to fully provide for one boy at a certain Melbourne private school for the same period! . . . And this in what we call a democracy whose catch-cry is 'Equality!' (quoted in McCallum, 1990, p. 112)

Discussion of curriculum reform also continued during the war and into the post-war period. The main achievements during the 1940s were probably developments in the new social studies and in physical education, which finally replaced drill-based physical training.

Curriculum and teaching

During the 1930s, progressive educators in Australia had advocated the repackaging of the traditional courses in history and geography into interdisciplinary, civically focused 'social studies' courses. Concern to educate children about the broader context of the war provided an impetus. Social studies courses became part of the core study of primary schools in the post-war period, while separate studies of history and geography tended to persist in secondary schools—especially at the more senior levels. However, social studies was often regarded with suspicion by conservative groups such as the hierarchies of the Catholic Church and conservative politicians. In 1944, the content of a proposed social studies course in New South Wales so alarmed a number of church and parent groups with its treatment of such topics as the history of the labour movement that they lobbied successfully for its amendment (Bessant and Spaull, 1976, pp. 28–9).

The way for the new social studies subjects had been paved by the earlier incorporation of war news into the curriculum for older children. All state Departments of Education had continued to produce their children's magazines for schools. These were important sources of fresh teaching content during the war, when other publications were in short supply. Many included information about the war—such as public service explanations of austerity measures and articles about weapons and aircraft. In South Australia, the educationist Adelaide Miethke, in her capacity as director of the state's Schools Patriotic Fund, oversaw a two- or three-page supplement in each edition of *The Children's Hour*, which was designed to foster patriotism and support morale. During 1944, the Victorian equivalent included a series of articles about Poland, Norway, Holland and China by G.S. Browne titled 'They fight for freedom'.

The use of radio programs in schools had begun before the war, broadcast through the still young Australian Broadcasting Commission (ABC). Educational broadcasting incorporated war-related information into programming.

Concern for the fitness of the youth of the nation, partly in response to the threat from fascism in general, and Japan in particular, saw a series of national and state meetings in the late 1930s advocating new approaches to physical education. A Council for National Fitness was established by the Menzies government in 1939 and a federal *National Fitness Act* passed in 1941. The Act provided small grants to the states for the promotion of physical fitness through schools and teacher training colleges as well as through youth clubs and municipal centres. Each of the six universities was given initial funding to establish lectureships in physical education. The Act was a significant intervention by the Commonwealth government into school education (Irving, Maunders and Sherington, 1995).

In New South Wales, the impressive Education Minister, David Drummond, was instrumental in the 1938 appointment by the state government of a Canadian teacher, Gordon Young, as Director of Physical Education. He and his group rapidly began the process of transforming the physical education curriculum in New South Wales, supporting the training of the first specialist physical education teachers and spreading the message of physical and mental fitness through the developing National Fitness Association.

In Victoria in 1937, a medical doctor and sports scientist, Fritz Duras, who had been expelled from his university in Germany for his Jewish ancestry, was offered a position at Melbourne University to set up Australia's first university course in physical education, with a grant from the Carnegie Corporation. Young, Duras and others like them were dismissive of the older forms of training. They had been based on mass, repetitive drill with nineteenth-century military origins.

The threat of an imminent war and the international rise of fascism and militarism provide one context for understanding physical education, especially as it concerned boys, but there was an expression of longer term concerns about girls too. The care of girls' growing bodies and their future children had been a preoccupation since the late nineteenth century.

This was a strong field for women reformers, such as the kindergartener and parent educator Zoe Benjamin, whose publications included *The Schoolchild and His Parents* (1950). The eugenicist Marion Piddington, whose husband had been chair of the 1903

Physical fitness for the struggle between democracy and fascism, between white and emerging 'coloured' peoples. Later physical education would move away from the mass drill approach represented here. Drummoyne Primary School, Sydney, 1934. (State Library of NSW, Home and Away, 1229)

Royal Commission into the decline of the birth rate in New South Wales, was one of a number of people to advocate more explicit sex education in public schools—a matter which she argued was too important and too technical to leave to the haphazardness of the family (Bongiorno, 2012, p. 166). These ideas can be connected with other progressive movements, such as the promotion of the idea that schools (and residential areas) needed adequate playground space.

Commonwealth government and education

The war was an important moment for state–federal relations. The Uniform Tax Agreement of 1942, which effectively transferred most company and personal income tax powers to the Commonwealth government, would transform education funding later in the century.

It was predictable that when the war was over and the men came home—if there was not a new depression, as many feared—there would be a surge in the youthful population, and only one government—as opposed to the six state governments—would have the tax revenue to respond satisfactorily.

There was some direct Commonwealth intervention in preschooling, an area that hitherto had been almost wholly in the private and voluntary sectors. In 1939–40, the Lady Gowrie Child Centres were established, named for the Governor-General's wife who had been active in their foundation. The centres were a response to widespread concerns in the 1920s and 1930s about the morbidity and mortality rates of mothers and children, especially those living in poverty. Founded in inner city slum areas, the Gowrie centres were model pre-schools and research centres. They were generously funded—initially at least—with £100 000 from the federal public health budget, and included an intensive program of medical, health and psychological evaluations of the children in their care. Parent education was considered crucial, and parents had to guarantee their children's regular attendance and provide information about diet, routine and behaviour at home. They accepted only 'normal' children—those without diagnostic classification—and those who had Australian-born parents (Brennan, 1998, p. 41).

During the war, there was some provision made for the care of children of women working in essential industries, but there was continuing significant opposition to the idea of mothers' employment outside the home. Such assistance was quickly abandoned at the end of the war.

Commonwealth investment in post-school education included the Commonwealth Reconstruction Training Scheme, established in 1944 to provide scholarship and stipendiary support to returning servicemen and women for education and training, including teacher training. Some senior secondary schooling was also supported. More than 300,000 people took advantage of the scheme. A Commonwealth Office of Education was established in 1946.

•

In 1948, the ACER identified a number of 'signs of a new vigour and vitality' in Australian education:

> Everywhere there is a flood of ideas pressing hard through existing channels, dammed back in places by the slowly yielding barriers of traditional practice, in others by unyielding barriers of insufficient supply, both human and material. (Waddington, Radford and Keats, 1950, p. xiii)

This was written before the 1949 election that consigned Labor to 23 years of opposition. The new Robert Menzies-led Coalition government of Liberal and Country Parties was not as anxious as the Curtin, and then Chifley, Labor governments to reconstruct post-war Australia in quite the same planned way. Possible federal interventions in public schooling were put aside as the 'forgotten' Australians, the middle class to whom Menzies had appealed in 1949, were to be given room to fulfil their aspirations, uncluttered by intrusive government interventions—or, as the conservatives liked to put it, 'the dead hand of socialism' (see Brett, 1992).

State governments retained almost total power over public schools, and where non-government school registration legislation was in place, had influence over private and corporate schools for the whole of the period of this chapter. Schools and school systems varied in their capacity to imagine and implement school reform. As many responses to the Depression showed, even the universalisation of secondary schooling was not quite accepted as orthodoxy in the period. It was not universally believed, for example, that most of a young person's adolescence should be spent in a school.

As we have seen, educators of this period were not short of innovative ideas in terms of new kinds of schools, teacher training and curriculum reform, but the Depression and then the new war were obstacles around which it was difficult to negotiate. One of the most significant legacies of this period for the near future of schools and schooling would be the teacher shortage. It had been too easy to close and restrict entry to teachers' colleges. There would be another schools emergency, despite the want of a new depression or a significant outbreak of 'hot' as opposed to 'cold' world war.

Further reading

On the education intelligentsia, see Dunt (1993), and on psychology and psychological testing, see Wright (2011) and McCallum (1990), with Holbrook (1987) useful for vocational guidance. On the ACER, see Connell (1980) and on Carnegie Corporation philanthropy in Australia, see White (1997). On teachers and teacher training, see Hyams (1979). On married women teachers, see Theobald and Dwyer (1999). On Australia during World War II, see Spaull (1982). For Catholic schooling, see Selleck (1978), O'Brien (2005), O'Donoghue (2001) and Fogarty (1959). On the NEF and educational reform, Cunningham (1938) is essential reading. Godfrey (2004) and Campbell and Sherington (2013) write on its impact respectively for public examination reform and secondary schooling. On Indigenous schooling, see Fletcher (1989a, 1989b), Haebich (2000) and Beresford and Partington (2003). David Kirk's (1998) argument about schooling the bodies of school children through new approaches to physical training is essential reading. On reorganising the primary school, see Trethewey (1995). On corporate schools, see McCalman (1993) and Sherington, Petersen and Brice (1987). Gronn's (1992) work on the headmaster of Geelong Grammar, James Darling, is important. For early childhood, see Brennan (1998). Browne (1927) remains a great contemporary start to understanding the period.

CHAPTER

6

Equality of opportunity 1951–1975

At the beginning of 1951, the Melbourne broadsheet the *Age* carried the claim: 'For Australia, this next half century is one of unlimited promise—promise of development, of growth into economic adulthood.' (1 January, 1951) This kind of optimism is not unusual in texts from the 1950s, including texts about schooling. Nor was it unusual to imagine Australia as a teenager, just as the nation had been imagined as an infant at the turn of the twentieth century. The quarter-century between 1951 and 1975 was, in retrospect, a period that was perhaps more confident and less troubled than others in the twentieth century, notwithstanding the baby boom emergency for schools, the crises of the Cold War and the youth rebellions of the late 1960s.

There was considerable growth and development in Australian schooling, during which teachers, students, administrators and policy-makers were finally at liberty to consider their schools without the constraints of depression and war. There had been nearly two decades of austerity. Now there was a long boom and relative peace despite military commitments in Asia. Moreover, school education seemed more important than ever before. Schooling was a topic of public interest—and even national importance. This was the period during which the national government finally interested itself in schooling.

Socially, there was a 'revolution in rising expectations'. This was a phrase used by contemporary commentators to describe the increasing educational aspirations of families for their children. As in other Western and Anglophone nations, there was more demand for secondary schooling. Whereas, a few decades earlier, the classroom had been peripheral to 'real life' for many or most, by 1951 primary schooling was embedded in the lives of children, families and communities. Between 1951 and 1975, secondary schooling would become similarly universal and conventional—at least to the age of 15 or 16. It was still only a minority who completed the final years of high school and fewer still who continued to tertiary study. Nevertheless, by 1975 these senior secondary school and university students were sizeable and growing minorities. Early childhood education grew too, as did some of the debates over its purpose and direction. By the 1970s, there were new contests for legitimacy and government funding between the advocates of the traditional kindergartens, who saw themselves as safeguarding the interests of the child, and feminist groups such as the Women's Electoral Lobby (WEL, founded in 1972), which advocated expanding child care to facilitate the economic independence of women (Brennan, 1998).

The public schools were still managed and run by very large state Education Departments, but there were some small shifts in power away from the head offices. For Catholic schools, there was a power shift in the opposite direction: away from the parishes towards central Catholic Education Offices. With the largest increases in child populations since the nineteenth century, school systems were under strain. The baby boom and massive post-war immigration meant that schools were filled to bursting point during the 1950s and 1960s. The number of students enrolled in the primary and secondary schools rose from 975 000 in 1945 to 2 839 000 in 1972 (Karmel, 1973, p. 139). As a social studies school textbook expressed it in the mid-1960s:

> If you have been attending school in the 1950s and 1960s the whole of your school life has been spent in an atmosphere of turmoil and uncertainty . . . You may not have been aware of all the problems that

> have been worrying your teachers and parents, but you must have been aware of the crowded conditions in which you were probably taught at primary school and secondary school . . . You were born in a high birth-rate period. But the teachers you needed were born, or should have been born, during the depression of the 1930s or the war years of the 1940s—a low birth-rate period. (Austin, 1966, p. 55)

There were shortages of teachers, of buildings, of school materials. The Catholic schools came close to collapse.

In the 1960s and 1970s, the federal government moved decisively into the field of school education. This was the era of the re-establishment and entrenchment by both conservative and Labor governments of what in the history of Australian schooling is known as 'state aid'—that is, the direct funding of non-government schools by the state. Many of the other developments outlined in this chapter have close parallels in other nations, but state aid is a peculiarly Australian issue, shaped by the specificities of Australia's federal system of government and its history of religious sectarianism.

In the 1960s and early 1970s, 'community' was a term increasingly used to suggest ways in which individual schools should be more directly responsive to their students and their families. But public interest could also be political. The 1960s and early 1970s saw rising activity from what political scientists of the period called 'pressure groups'—notably over state aid. There was increased public action by school teachers, too. The 1960s and early 1970s saw increased militancy from the public school teacher unions, including strike action. In the early 1970s, there were even brief signs of activist school student organisations, such as the Victorian Secondary Students' Union, originating in the anti-Vietnam war movement.

Changes in school populations presented challenges or added richness and excitement, depending on one's perspective. There were increasingly large student numbers in classrooms. From the 1960s, the secondary schools were required to manage not only the larger numbers, but more academically diverse cohorts of students. From the late 1940s, Australia had begun to encourage migration from non-English speaking countries (as well as the United Kingdom), including the resettlement of Central and Eastern European refugees, and then Southern European immigration including large numbers of Italian and Greek immigrants. Most migrant children found themselves in public schools, but Catholic schools were attractive to migrants from Catholic countries such as Italy and Poland. In the late 1960s, many of the baby boomers themselves began to enter teaching, having been supported through their training by government-funded teachers' college bonded allowances.

The 1950s, 1960s and early 1970s were a time in which the category 'teenager' truly embedded itself in popular discourse. Teenagers were objects of concern and anxiety, even alarm. In the 1950s, there were moral panics about 'the generation gap', about American comic books, about sexual precocity, about hair and fashion, and about suspect peer groups. The Hollywood movie, *Rebel Without a Cause* (1955) showed an angry James Dean dicing with death after falling in with the cool crowd at school. In 1972, the Australian government held heated discussions about whether to ban *The Little Red Schoolbook* (Hanson and Jenson, 1969; also T. Stephens in *Sydney Morning Herald*, 1 January 2003). This was an internationally controversial publication that originally had been written for Danish school students. It was frank about drugs and sex, and encouraged school students to think critically about school structures and discipline. The use of leisure drugs other than alcohol and tobacco typified much youth culture around this time, even though many young people were then—as now—cautious, abstemious and conservative. New sociological and psychological studies of youth were published. Disturbed children increasingly were referred to child psychologists.

Inside the classrooms—especially in the primary schools—by the end of the 1960s, there was some take-up of progressive curricular and pedagogical ideas such as inquiry methods of learning, 'projects', creative arts and music, and group work. These were encouraged by the expanding teachers' colleges, which were disaggregated from the state Education Departments and reorganised as Colleges of Advanced Education in 1973. (The CAEs also incorporated the Kindergarten Teaching Colleges.) At the same time, the old approaches to student categorisation—'the dull, the normal and the brilliant', as Freeman

Gendered rituals for modern teenagers in the modern high school. Boy asks girl to dance at the Telopea Park High School social, Canberra, 1964. (National Library of Australia, vn4590171)

Butts (1957, p. 4) put it, persisted. But there were some signs of a rebellion against the types of educational psychology that supported the intelligence-test foundations of school and student administration.

At the end of this 1951–75 period, there was fresh recognition of the relationships between social class and inequality. They informed the landmark report, *Schools in Australia* (Karmel, 1973), commissioned by the first federal Labor government since 1949. A Commonwealth Schools Commission was created in the same year to provide policy advice, carry out research and allocate federal funding to schools. The Commission introduced programs to address the disadvantages associated with poverty and a range of other causes. Aboriginal and Torres Strait Islander schooling, the schooling of people from non-English speaking backgrounds and gender inequality were the targets of some of its programs. Its report, *Girls, School and Society*

(Committee on Social Change and the Education of Women, 1975) was highly influential. The Whitlam-led federal Labor government is sometimes held responsible for a brief but glorious age in Australian education. Although critical of a number of aspects of that government's educational policies, writing only three years later Bessant and Spaull (1976, p. 138) concluded: 'One thing appears certain: the heady, champagne days of 1973 for Australian schools have passed from the scene. They are quickly being replaced by old suspicions and new doubts . . .'

Pressures for the expansion and reform of schools

W.F. Connell (1993) characterised the 1950s as something of a dead period in between the energy and ambition of post-war reconstruction and the new dawn of the 1960s. The schools, of course, were busier than ever, but the argument is that they were growing and expanding haphazardly, without vision or coherent planning. During this period, the Australian Council for Educational Research (ACER) was an organisation that saw itself as a modernising force in Australian schooling. In 1957, it published an influential monograph by Freeman Butts. Like Isaac Kandel, who had visited in the late 1930s, Butts was a Professor of Education at Teachers College, Columbia, in New York. His survey of Australian schooling is worth summarising here because the issues he raised continued to be important or contentious.

Butts (1957) was highly critical of Australian schooling, concluding his monograph by calling for a 'great educational revival'. 'Somehow,' he argued, 'the fires of educational enthusiasm and aspiration for a better education must be kindled' (1957, p. 79). Like Kandel before him, Butts was critical of the centralisation of educational administration in the state Departments of Education, which led, he argued, to rigidity and lack of innovation. He also expressed concern over Australia's 'dual system' of education, divided into public and (mainly) Christian denominational schools, especially Catholic schools. He saw the dual system as potentially dangerous to Australian egalitarianism and religious tolerance, arguing in no uncertain terms against any introduction of direct state financial support to the non-government sector of schools.

Butts saw hierarchies everywhere he looked: between primary and secondary schools; hierarchies of class and gender in the organisation of schools; and artificial hierarchies of value in the organisation of the curriculum—especially at the secondary level. He described an oppressive reliance on external examinations in secondary schooling and found Australian curricula to be unimaginative and narrow. High-status subjects, including mathematics and languages, lacked excitement. Technical subjects and schooling laboured under the opprobrium of being low in status. Teaching tended to be old style, with limited student participation or engagement. Regular examination of schools and teachers by the state Education Department inspectors, he argued, was a disincentive to trying new things. Moreover, teachers were inadequately trained. What needed to be done, according to Butts, was to energise and reinvigorate the public schools through decentralisation, local community engagement and parent participation, and the reform of curriculum, pedagogy and teacher training.

These sorts of critiques—which came both from insiders and outsiders—had sporadic influence, but in the face of post-war population growth, Australian schools had no choice but to change in some way. Table 6.1 shows the expansion of the different school sectors in the period. The most immediate pressure was from the increase in the child and youth population. At the same time, the retention of young people in school for longer periods was actively encouraged by government policy and by developments in the labour market. In South Australia, for example, the decision taken in 1946 to increase the school leaving age to 15 was implemented in 1963.

In an economy marked by expanding industry as well as increasing numbers of white-collar and professional jobs, including school teaching, better and more educational credentials were required. Moreover, there was a growing *belief* in education: 'The extension of education became more than the spread of skills and knowledge, or the widening of citizenship. It was the universal expectation of personal advance and a better life via learning' (Marginson,

TABLE 6.1

Enrolment growth in each education sector in comparison with population and labour force, Australia, 1955, 1965, 1975 (indexed as percentage increase)

Year	Primary schools	Secondary schools	Higher education	Technical education	All education	Population (all ages)	Labour force
1955	100.0	100.0	100.0	100.0	100.0	100.0	100.0
1965	130.8	220.2	270.6	203.7	157.3	123.3	123.7
1975	142.8	314.2	887.0	294.4	202.7	151.0	161.6

Source: Marginson, (1997, p. 21).

1997a, p. 34). And it would be governments that would provide such opportunities. There was a commitment to government-sponsored educational growth that reached well beyond Australia. In both Britain and the United States in the 1960s, public investment in schooling was aimed at economic growth *and* at '[eliminating] poverty' (1997a, pp. 11–14). Following Keynesian economic ideas, there was a great confidence from much of the population, as well as governments themselves, in the capacity of governments to build, regulate and manage the necessary infrastructure required to support social and economic reform and growth. An abiding commitment to public sector leadership lasted in Australia—as in most capitalist nations—from the 1940s to the 1970s. A consequence for the education sector was that public, government schooling expanded while the non-government schools tended to do little more than hold on.

The transformation of secondary schooling

The population surge moved through the primary schools into the secondary schools. From the late 1950s, secondary schooling started to become a mass experience in Australia in the way that primary schooling had done towards the end of the nineteenth century. In 1947, just over one in ten teenagers aged between 15 and 19 had been enrolled full-time in a school or higher education institution. In 1961, the proportion was around one in four; in 1975, it was more than four in ten. Proportions were slightly higher for boys than for girls throughout the period (Marginson, 1997a, p. 23). This placed great pressure on the public and Catholic secondary schools that enrolled the bulk of young people.

The question was how to provide schooling for all these new students. As was common in Australian education, overseas inspiration was sought. One possible approach was provided, by successor policy, from the 1918 statement 'The cardinal principles of secondary education' from the United States. The other was the line of policy arising from the 1926 Hadow Report in England. (On the significance of these reports, see Krug, 1969 for the United States and McCulloch 2002 for England.) The US model suggested collecting all young people of a certain age into one school; the English model suggested arranging them in different kinds of schools according to aptitude, ambition and gender. The US report argued for the organisation of secondary schools around 'principles' or educational objectives, rather than sets of subjects or bodies of knowledge. The principles included such things as health, 'worthy home membership' and civic education.

The United States was a pioneer of comprehensive secondary schools, though the students within them were likely divided into 'tracks'. Intelligence testing and its ally, vocational guidance, produced the knowledge leading to tracking and 'streaming'. There were considerable social effects arising from these technologies of student management, not the least the concentration of poorer and African-American children in those parts of the curriculum not preparing young people for college and university entrance.

In England, the Hadow report of 1926 effectively suggested leaving the existing academically focused secondary schools as they were, but supplementing these by developing more practical, vocationally oriented post-primary alternatives for other adolescents. By the late 1960s, England too was moving towards comprehensive schooling, but it was the United States more than England that was seen as a potential model for the future of secondary schooling in Australia. England was too compromised by its recent history of tripartism (separate grammar, technical and 'secondary modern schools'). Some Australian school leaders continued to look to England, however. They included the supporters of academically selective high schools, who were attracted by the tradition of the English 'grammar schools', and the older corporate, independent schools that sought to be Great Public Schools along the lines of Eton, Rugby and so on. On the whole, English secondary schooling appeared to consolidate social class tensions and divisions; the United States was less inclined to do so—though a common criticism in Australia of American education was that academic quality had been sacrificed for democracy.

Comprehensive government secondary schools were developed throughout Australia as the older differentiated post-elementary, or super-primary, systems began to be dismantled. There is no single definition of a comprehensive high school, but in its simplest form it can be thought of as a neighbourhood school that enrols everyone, regardless of academic merit or aptitude. A stronger definition includes specific attention to the absence of selection on the basis of 'ability to pay fees, religious attachment, ethnic or racial origins, or indeed any previous academic attainment or "ability" or "intelligence"' (Campbell and Sherington, 2013, p. 6). If everyone was welcome in this new school, arguments nevertheless remained about its internal organisation. Crucial questions included: How rigidly and to what extent were students to be sorted, tracked and streamed once enrolled? Which subjects would be studied in common and which apart? To what extent were students' courses to be shaped by their own interests and to what extent mandated by the schools' assessment of their 'ability'? Could there possibly be parity of esteem across the curriculum, or would some tracks and subjects (and their students) be considered better than others?

Coeducational, comprehensive government secondary schools for youth of the baby boom. Kurri Kurri High School in the Hunter Valley, New South Wales, 1956. (State Library of NSW, Home and Away, 28922)

Tasmania, Western Australia and New South Wales moved more quickly to comprehensive systems of secondary education than did Queensland, Victoria or South Australia. Very slow at providing universal access to any kind of secondary schooling, Queensland introduced automatic progression to a secondary school in 1963. The leaving age was 14, which was about the same age at which its pupils had finished primary school, so until the mid-1960s when the leaving age was raised to 15 and the transfer age to secondary school lowered to 13, there was a substantial cohort of school students who had never entered a secondary school. Nevertheless, by the end of the 1960s a comprehensive secondary school system was in place. Victoria and South Australia, however, retained their separate technical high schools into the 1970s.

Tasmania and Western Australia were the first states to 'go comprehensive', with Hobart and Launceston secondary schools comprehensive by the early 1960s. The Western Australian Department of Education shifted to comprehensive secondary schooling by the mid-1950s, inspired by an activist Director of Education, Thomas Robertson. In 1958, the Education Minister announced that all public secondary schools would henceforth be comprehensive and coeducational. Despite protests by an alumni group, the 'Old Modernians'—old scholars of the prestigious Perth Modern School—even it went comprehensive in the 1960s (Tully, 2002, pp. 95–6). The junior technical high schools were swiftly phased out in Western Australia.

New South Wales officially adopted comprehensive schooling in its public secondary schools with the *Education Act* of 1961, though the distinctions between the different kinds of post-primaries—technical, domestic science and academic—had been lessening through the 1950s. The new secondary schooling arrangement, which also added another year to the junior part of the secondary school, was called the 'Wyndham Scheme' after the director of the Education Department, Harold Wyndham. It had taken a long time to negotiate, partly because Catholic school leaders had been concerned about the expense of staffing and housing an additional year for all students at school (Hughes, 2008, pp. 55–76).

The Wyndham Scheme was the outcome of a long consultation process. A committee to inquire into secondary education in the state had been set up in 1954 and reported in 1957. The deliberation period had been accompanied by extensive public meetings and consultations, which demonstrated not only that there was considerable public interest in school reform, but also that the idea of automatic progression to high school was popular. Under the Wyndham Scheme, it was envisaged that all students would attend secondary school until the end of the fourth year at about the age of 16, with a much smaller number persisting to the Higher School Certificate at the end of the final two years. A curriculum of core subjects plus options in the first four years would cater to a range of interests and aptitudes. In contrast with Western Australia, however, New South Wales retained a handful of academically selective and single-sex schools. In the future, the former would provide an institutional base and a set of arguments against the comprehensive schools as market-based economics made their comeback, along with a critique of assimilation as the best kind of migrant policy (Campbell and Sherington, 2013).

There were many reasons for the move to comprehensive high schools, and they enjoyed widespread popular support at least until the end of the 1970s. There were democratic arguments about ease of access and equality of opportunity. Comprehensive schools extended educational opportunity and solved the problem of children's scholastic pathways being determined by a set of tests taken at age 11 or 12. They made economic sense because it was less expensive to run one large general school in a district than a number of smaller specialised ones. Going to a local secondary placed less stress on transport infrastructure, and all children in a family could attend the same school if it were coeducational. Finally, in a nation with an increasingly diverse immigrant population, the schools would be good for assimilation.

In New South Wales, it was the supporters of the academically selective high schools who were most opposed to the new arrangements—sometimes bitterly so. The historian of the prestigious Newcastle High School painted a picture of a city divided by either opposition or allegiance to the well-known Newcastle Boys and Girls

High Schools, when each year some children were chosen for entry and others rejected (Armitage, 1983). There was a sustained campaign from the schools' supporters to maintain academic selectivity. As had occurred in Perth, on the other side of the country, the campaign failed. The campaigns defending of some of Sydney's selective high schools, including Fort Street, Sydney and North Sydney Boys and Girls High Schools were more successful (on Fort Street High, see Horan, 1989).

The non-Catholic, non-government secondary schools were less affected by the changes of the period than were the government and Catholic schools, given their narrower enrolment bases and limited education responsibilities across the social classes. Where the populations of the government secondary schools changed, the elite non-government schools continued to cater for much the same traditional secondary school clientele. Part of the difference can be seen in such schools through their superior retention rates. Stronger rates were associated with the wealthier social classes, even within government schools. A study of government high school students in the 1960s found that more than three-quarters of 'high' socio-economic status teenagers remained at school until the final year, compared with fewer than 15 per cent of those from a 'low' socio-economic backgrounds (Karmel, 1973, p. 18).

The non-Catholic, non-government schools (together with the elite Catholic schools, independent of the Catholic education offices) had long catered for a middle-class or upper middle-class clientele. In 1972, the retention rates from the first to the final year of high school were 87 per cent in the non-Catholic, corporate schools, 35 per cent in the Catholic systemic schools and 28 per cent in government schools (Karmel, 1973, p. 19). The public secondary schools managed a small increase in their share of enrolments in the decade to 1975.

Teachers and teaching

The teaching force grew even faster than the student population as class sizes were reduced in the 1970s. In the early 1950s, teachers comprised 9 per cent of state government employees. By the mid-1970s, the figure was 17 per cent. Between 1960 and 1975, school enrolments increased by 44 per cent, but teacher numbers grew by 105 per cent, from 74 289 to 152 431 (Marginson, 1997a, p. 27). From the 1950s to the early 1970s, the average age of teachers dropped, and the rapid expansion of secondary schooling challenged the previous dominance of primary school teachers in the profession.

By the 1950s, there was near-universal support among administrators and policy-makers for extending the periods of pre-service teacher training—or teacher 'education', as contemporary reformers insisted it must now be called—but many teachers were rushed through their training during the 1950s because of the pressure of the baby boom. In South Australia, there was the infamous 'pressure cooker course'. Other teachers were called back from retirement. Discrimination against married women necessarily faltered. Nevertheless, pre-service teacher education eventually expanded and courses grew longer.

Three baby-boom teachers for the last of the baby-boom teenagers. In the staffroom at Rosebud High School, discussing the teacher union newspaper. Victoria, 1971. (National Library of Australia, vn4589240)

New South Wales was the first state to offer equal pay for equal work for women teachers, mainly due to a well-organised campaign by the New South Wales Teachers' Federation (Spaull, 1977). The decision was taken in 1958, although it was not until 1963 that all women teachers received equal pay. Despite the support of key men (and women) in the union, not all male teachers were impressed:

> I was Deputy Infants Mistress at [a school in Broken Hill in western New South Wales] and it was my job to see that the garbage bins were emptied. And the deputy principal used to do all the emptying of garbage bins with the big boys. But on the day that we got equal pay they weren't emptied. So I went over and asked him what was the matter with my garbage tins. 'Why weren't they emptied?' And he said, 'Today you got equal pay. You can empty your own garbage tins.' (Interview by H. Proctor, 12 March 2000)

By the early 1970s, public school teachers in all states had been granted equal pay for equal work, marriage bars had been removed and it had become possible for women to be principals of co-educational primary schools or heads of subject departments in co-educational high schools. In the mid-1970s, however, women remained well under-represented in senior positions, despite comprising more than 50 per cent of all teachers. For example, in South Australia in 1973, only two of 92 headships of the largest ('Class 1') primary schools were occupied by women (Committee on Social Change, 1975).

Since the nineteenth century, the positions of school inspector and superintendent had been prestigious in the state Departments of Education. They were the conduits of policy between head office and the schools. In the 1950s and 1960s, with some variation from state to state, the inspectors' responsibilities included the assessment and grading of individual teachers. Inspectors would regularly visit each school in their jurisdiction, observe lessons and evaluate the proficiency of each classroom teacher. The system declined from the early 1970s, partly because of its expense, partly because of the transfer of authority to school principals and partly because of hostility from classroom teachers and their unions over the assessment role.

The national teacher union body, the Australian Teachers' Federation, became a more important force after 1950 when it absorbed the former Federated State School Teachers' Association of Australia. There were large differences in culture amongst the state teacher unions, but overall teachers became more militant during the 1960s and their relationships with the state Education Departments grew more confrontational than they had been in the past. From the mid-1960s, there were occasional strikes. This caused some conflict within the profession, as some teachers urged a closer identification with other workers in trade unions, while others—more conservative—were horrified by such an association. In Victoria, there was a series of splits on these and other grounds. Primary, high school and technical teachers each had separate unions. Elsewhere, single unions of government teachers were just able to manage the centrifugal interests of different teacher groups. Non-government school teachers began to found and consolidate unions too, especially in the Catholic sector, as the proportion of lay teachers rose.

In 2010, Robyn Lee Long remembered her primary schooling in suburban Sydney in the 1950s:

> I graduated to 'ink monitor'. I had to empty all the inkwells . . . every morning and fill them up with fresh ink that the teacher had mixed up from a powder dissolved in water. We wrote copperplate letters . . . with a 'Slope Card' underneath, so that all of our loops and letters were slanting in the same direction . . . Pupils like me, who started off left-handed, were smacked on the knuckles with a ruler . . . so that we would learn to write with our right hand (which wouldn't smudge the ink so much). (Artarmon Public School, 2010, p. 36)

This vignette could have been written at almost any time in the previous half-century, and perhaps further back, but 'ink monitors' and compulsory right-handedness faded out in the 1960s with the spread of ballpoint pens and more sympathetic approaches to individuality.

Primary classrooms in particular began to become less authoritarian and more creative, especially from the mid-1960s. Teachers' colleges and school authorities alike encouraged teachers in the delivery of 'child-centred' lessons that might include experimental music, improvisational drama, discussions and hands-on activities. New curriculum aids such as Cuisenaire rods—little coloured blocks to help with mathematical understanding—were imported from overseas. Syllabuses and textbooks were rewritten to build reasoning, understanding and explanation around the content matter of both new and traditional subjects. The 'New Maths' was introduced amidst controversy. Enjoyment and meaningfulness became important criteria for a successful lesson. 'Schooling is a significant segment of life which for all children ought to be enjoyable and fruitful in itself, not merely a preparation for later life.' (Karmel, 1973, p. 94) Many educational reformers pinned their hopes on the democratic possibilities of social studies in the classroom, a subject that expanded into the high schools (see Campbell, 2010, pp. 160–1). Nevertheless, the Karmel Committee still found, when its members undertook a series of school visits in the early 1970s, that many Australian classrooms remained over-controlled and unimaginative. Some teachers—and parents too—actively resisted the new methods and topics, finding them insufficiently structured.

The progressive pedagogical and curricular expressions of this period were part of an international movement. Also influential was a separate set of ideas from the United States that prioritised the organisational logic of the curriculum. Ralph W. Tyler's *Basic Principles of Curriculum and Instruction* (1949) was widely read in Australia, and his model for rational, outcome-based curriculum development was eventually to be more influential than the work of many others that were more in the Deweyan mould.

Catholic schools: Vatican II and reform

O'Donoghue (2001) describes mid-century and early 1960s Australian Catholic schools as authoritarian, dominated by a dogmatic Irish brand of Catholicism and promoting rigidly conventional gender roles. The Second Vatican Council, 1962–65, initiated by the reformist Pope John XXIII, prompted some changes. Some of these changes to school practices are depicted in the ABC television mini-series

Brides of Christ (1991). The teachers—mostly nuns—and students of a girls' school work to determine what it means to be Catholic women in the changing world of the 1960s. Such reforms as the liberalisation of dress for nuns might not seem like much now, but they were experienced as a marked alteration in the daily lives of the nuns and their students.

At the same time as being unable to cope with the post-war increase in school enrolments, Catholic schools were losing the labour of religious (nuns, brothers and priests), as fewer young people took up vocations. In 1950, in the archdiocese of Melbourne, 80 per cent of teachers in Catholic primary schools were religious. By 1971, the figure was 32 per cent and falling (Selleck, 1978, p. 95). Moreover, the religious were ageing while the rest of the teaching population was getting younger. Catholic schools had depended since the late nineteenth century largely on the labour of nuns. This not only imbued schools with a certain character, but also made them relatively cheap to run. Lay teachers were not only arguably less wholeheartedly committed to the faith, but also had to be paid near-market wages. There were even some arguments coming from within the Catholic system, under great stress in the 1960s, that its schools ought to close down.

As we have seen, pedagogical and curricular changes were afoot in all schools during this period; the climate and spirit of Vatican II allowed and even encouraged Catholic schools to engage in more progressive pedagogies and more socially relevant curricula—and, crucially, to change the way in which religion was taught: it became less the rote repetition of the catechism and more about meaning. These kinds of change did not go uncontested. In Victoria, the lay activist B.A. Santamaria fought against many of the reforms ushered in by Vatican II until his death in 1998.

State aid and the federal government interventions in the nation's schools

The Goulburn (New South Wales) Catholic school strike of 1962 is generally regarded as an important event in the history of the Catholic

A new spirit in the schooling of Catholic children following the Vatican II Council. Guitar-playing teaching sister and students, St Peter's School, Surry Hills, Sydney, 1971. (National Library of Australia, vn3084811)

struggle for state aid. It was precipitated by a New South Wales government determination that improvements needed to be made to the toilets at a Catholic primary school in Goulburn in order for the school to remain open. The auxiliary bishop of Canberra-Goulburn argued that if government regulations required better toilets, then the government should pay for them. After a long-running dispute (1957–62), a public meeting of churchmen and parents suddenly voted to call a shutdown of all Goulburn's Catholic primary schools in 1962:

> This meeting of the Catholic community of Goulburn expresses its bitter disappointment at the failure of the State Governments—present and past—to recognise the justice of the claims of Catholics to a fair share of the public purse for its education system and wishes to draw public attention to the almost insurmountable plight in which Catholics find themselves. (quoted in Hogan, 1978, pp. 68–9)

On Monday, 16 July 1962, nearly 2000 Catholic students arrived at their local public schools seeking enrolment. At such short notice, only about a third of the children could be found a place. The strike lasted a week. Had it gone on longer, the Education Department might have had time to make room, but the image persisted of hundreds of children being turned away from public schools. The protest was followed in the press throughout Australia, with editorial comment mainly hostile to the Catholic cause, but in the longer term the action became an important symbol in the overturning of the century-old colonial state aid settlements. In the end, however, it was federal rather than state money that would eventually rescue the Catholic schools.

Before the 1950s, there was a view among state and federal politicians that the introduction of direct government financial assistance to non-government, especially Catholic, schools would be 'political suicide' (Wilkinson et al., 2007, p. 20). This changed tentatively in the 1960s and dramatically in the 1970s. School funding first became a federal election issue in 1963 when Prime Minster Robert Menzies used a policy speech to promise direct grants for the development of science teaching in secondary schools. It was a reversal of a previously long-held position, and Menzies took even some of his own colleagues by surprise with the announcement. The States Grants (Science Laboratories and Technical Training) Bill of 1964 included provision for direct federal grants to both government and non-government secondary schools for the building of dedicated science classrooms. Not much money was involved compared with what was to come, but this bill was often regarded as 'the thin end of the wedge' for direct federal aid to schools—especially to Catholic and other non-government schools. School library funding on the same non-system discriminatory basis followed later, in 1968. While schooling had remained as a 'residual power' of the states at Federation in 1901, Section 96 of the Australian Constitution allowed for grants for special purposes. This is the section under which successive Federal governments have provided funding to both government and non-government schools.

In the chemistry laboratory of Marcellin College (Catholic), Randwick, New South Wales, 1963. A year later the Menzies federal government provided grants for science laboratories in government and non-government schools alike. (National Library of Australia, an24474454)

There were several reasons for the introduction of federal funding to schools in the 1960s and early 1970s. Public school parent and teacher bodies had been lobbying for federal government assistance for decades, as state governments were hard put to provide enough schools and teachers for the post-war baby boom. Then there was the disastrous Labor Party split in 1957, with the possibility that the 'Catholic vote' might be attracted away from Labor—or back again—by government generosity towards Catholic schools (Bessant and Spaull, 1976, pp. 97–141). Both public and Catholic schools were criticised during the most difficult days of the Cold War. The communist Soviet Union's successful launching of Sputnik in 1957 terrified Western governments. In the post-Hiroshima, post-Sputnik world, science education was of national importance, and the schools—regardless of their public or private status—were ill-equipped. It made sense that the first major foray into direct funding of schools was through support of school science laboratories—and the anti-communist 'Catholic vote' was available for possible seduction by doing so.

By the early 1970s, all the main political parties supported state aid, and in 1972 the then leader of the opposition, Gough Whitlam, campaigned hard on the issue of education funding. In a famous election speech at Bankstown in Sydney before the 1972 election, he promised that spending on schools and teacher training would be the fastest growing item in the federal budget: 'Sure—we can have education on the cheap . . . but our children will be paying for it for the rest of their lives' (Australian Labor Party, 1972). Whitlam's championing of education was part of a new vision for the role of national government in the support and improvement of social infrastructure:

> If Australia is ever to have decent schools and equal opportunities . . . the national government must be directly involved . . . My basic proposition is this: that any basic service or function of our community which can be hitched to the star of the Commonwealth grows in quality and affluence. Any function or activity which is financially limited to the States will grow slowly or even decline. Further, a function will be fairly financed to the extent that the Commonwealth finds the money for it. A function will be unfairly and inadequately financed if the whole burden falls upon the States.

The problem of inequality was front and centre. Education, argued Whitlam, was 'the key to equality of opportunity'. Whitlam also promised a pre-school place for every child, 'because pre-school education is the most important single weapon in promoting equality and in overcoming social, economic and language inequalities'. In the late 1960s, the Liberal-Country Party Coalition governments under Menzies' successors had started to allocate grants to pre-schools. Labor's program was more ambitious, although by the time it was implemented it fell well short of a place for every child.

One of the first actions of the new Labor government in December 1972 was to set the terms of reference and appoint the members of the Interim Committee for the Australian Schools Commission. It would be chaired by Peter Karmel, with Jean Blackburn as deputy. Its task was to assess the state of all Australian schools, and recommend priorities and processes for the delivery of needs-based grants to eligible government and non-government schools. The committee was directly appointed by the government, but its membership included people who could be seen to be representative of the main institutions concerned with schooling: universities, technical education, Catholic, public and other non-government schools. Its members were professional educators or education bureaucrats. The report was published on schedule in May 1973, in time for almost immediate implementation through federal budget allocations.

In the abundant economic climate of the time, Karmel (1973) recommended a huge increase in the funding of Australian schools, with a particular emphasis on the most needy. Of its proposed funding for 1974 and 1975, nearly 70 per cent was earmarked for government schools and just over a quarter for non-government schools, with the remainder in joint system programs (Marginson, 1997a, p. 47). He also recommended a program of additional targeted funding for 'disadvantaged schools'. The reasons for this were clear: '[T]he poor,' argued the report, 'are disadvantaged in their relative lack of power in society, in the absence of any cushioning against adversity, and in the paucity of the kind of experience which is helpful to success in school and society.' (Karmel, 1973, p. 93) There was an emphasis on local community engagement consistent with broader Whitlam government principles of devolution and community-building:

> The Committee is neither able nor willing to be prescriptive about the forms which school–community relations should take, but values experimentation. Educationally, and from the point of view of efficient use of resources, it would make good sense to have the school as the nucleus of a community centre. Joint planning, and even conduct, of schools by educational, health, welfare, cultural and sporting agencies could provide additional facilities for the school, allow the community access to its resources, and thus generally increase its fruitfulness. In

> this way a link could be forged between school, family, peer group, and the society at large. (1973, p. 14).

The report also advocated the development of more productive working partnerships between teachers and parents (1973, pp. 13–14).

Other Karmel recommendations targeted the development of school libraries, special education for 'handicapped' children and the fostering of school innovation more broadly.

The report attracted considerable public support and the consequent Bills—the Schools Commission Bill and the States Grants (Schools) Bill—passed through the hostile Senate with the support of Country Party senators, after the government agreed to an amendment affirming government funding for the wealthiest non-government schools. The most dedicated resistance came from an organisation of parents, teachers and other public school supporters, the Council for the Defence of Government Schools (DOGS), who took its opposition to the funding of non-government schools to the High Court of Australia in 1973.

The increase in federal funding to schools, and the interventions associated with the funding, affected schooling at the grassroots level almost immediately. In fact, the impact was often spectacular. Within two years of the publication of the Karmel Report, funding had increased from $364 to $1091 million (Marginson, 1997a, p. 46). By 1975, however, the Whitlam government's programs were under threat, following the international economic crisis of 1974. The 1975 Labor budget included cuts to Schools Commission programs that were supposed to be temporary, but Labor lost government at the end of 1975 and the direction of the Schools Commission would change under the succeeding Liberal-National Party coalition government of Malcolm Fraser.

The 'disadvantaged' and the fight for equal opportunity

It is difficult to avoid a narrative for this quarter-century of progress from the staid and unenlightened 1950s to a heady post-1968 progressivism. Such an approach would be a considerable over-simplification, but there is some truth to it. There were two broad strands of reform. The first was about what went on inside schools as progressivism made an impact not seen since before World War I. The second addressed social and economic inequality. Four groups in particular were the targets of attention: Indigenous children, non-English background migrant children, girls; and working-class children.

Indigenous children

In the 1950s, Aboriginal people faced new complications as well as new promises. The practices and regulations enforcing separate schooling slowly began to be dismantled across the nation, and more serious attempts were made to provide access to schooling for Indigenous children living in remote areas. During the 1960s, most explicitly discriminatory legislation was repealed or dismantled amid successful civil rights campaigns. But there were competing visions for change. Aboriginal rights activists worked to raise public consciousness from the perspective of human citizenship rights and (gross) economic inequality. Others remained within an assimilationist or even paternalistic paradigm. Aboriginal people were conventionally framed in colonial terms as objects of policy rather than participants in policy-making—or indeed as citizens. For example, a contributor to an ACER review of Australian education reported that it was quite possible to educate 'a primitive people to that stage where they can take their place in the Australian economy' (ACER, 1956, p. 48). The forced removal of children from their parents and communities continued—though increasingly controversially—despite the spread of new psychological theories about the significance of the mother–child bond.

There was a wide variation in the schooling experience of Indigenous children. Some families had been attending school for generations. Others, including many children living in remote areas across the north of Australia, first encountered schools and classrooms in the 1950s and 1960s. In the 1950s, on a remote cattle station in the Northern Territory, the children of the Rembarrnga people were apparently very keen to learn to read and write. Their teacher was just as keen to encourage Western conventions of dress when she reported in 1957: 'A nice bunch of intelligent youngsters . . . Chalk, pencils, readers etc. would be appreciated but clothes are an absolute necessity' (quoted in Collishaw, 1999, p. 127). A former pupil of the school later recalled a combination of school and work on the cattle station:

> 1958, I start school. I went to school for three years. Then after that I went mustering . . . Every year during the school break we used to go out to the stock camp [to work] for a couple of months . . . We used to write with ashes [charcoal] first and writing on tea chest. No paper or pencil. For one year anyway. Then we got all our gear. Then after, we got uniform. (quoted in Collishaw, 1999, p. 127)

Part of the platform of the Whitlam Labor government was 'to restore to the Aboriginal people of Australia their lost power of self-determination' (in Broome, 2010, p. 230). In 1975, the

Aboriginal communities remained subject to ongoing efforts to 'protect' and Christianise them. A Sunday school for children at Cundalee, Western Australia, 1956. Change was coming. (State Library of Western Australia, 130463PD)

Schools Commission established a committee that would become the Aboriginal Consultative Group, drawing its membership from Indigenous people across Australia. Nevertheless, the obstacles facing most Aboriginal children remained considerable, even by the mid-1970s. The removal of formal enrolment bars did not necessarily make the schools welcoming places. Further, schools often exerted the same old pressures on Aboriginal families: the attainment of 'European' education was likely at the expense of Aboriginal culture. Australian history textbooks and other school literature continued to routinely denigrate, patronise, marginalise or simply ignore Indigenous people, their lives and contemporary culture. Stories of forced dispossession and frontier violence were not yet part of the school curriculum. Despite the difficulties, and the lack of schooling of parents and extended family, the period from 1950 to 1975 saw huge increases in the numbers of Aboriginal children completing primary school and proceeding to high school. Even so, the numbers remained well below comparable figures for other groups.

Migrant, non-English speaking children

The teaching of non-English speaking children was new territory for most schools and teachers. Stella Ferrari (pseudonym) started high school in Adelaide in 1961. Along with the other first-year students, she had to complete the by now conventional set of tests to determine her attainment so far and her potential. As a result, she was streamed towards the bottom end of her cohort in class 1D. Stella was from an Italian family and had previously attended school in Italy and Egypt. Her confidential school record card included the comment that on arrival she 'only' spoke Italian and French. Not only did her schooling precede the introduction of English support classes, but her fluency in two languages was considered a handicap rather than an advantage (Campbell, 2010, pp. 118–21). Her fate was similar to that of most students placed in low streams. She left school early without much success in the assessments that counted: the public exams.

There are many similar stories for this period. Andrew Reimer's wry memoir describes an almost surreal experience of being placed in a class for slow learners on his arrival as a Jewish refugee from Hungary, unable to understand a word anyone said:

> I was surrounded by a world where things happened, where things were done, where certain actions had consequences, without possessing any ability to discover what was expected of me. What was the strange chant that the class took up at one point? Why did one of the boys get called out to the front to receive a couple of whacks with a stick? What was the point of the teacher's joke that sent the whole class into gales of laughter? (quoted in Niall and Britain, 1997, p. 250)

This sink-or-swim approach was replaced by a remedial strategy, with the patchy introduction of special English support in the 1960s. By the early 1970s, there were increasing attempts to go beyond mere assimilation and to celebrate diversity and 'multiculturalism'—another project of the Whitlam Labor government.

Girls

In 1974, the Commonwealth Schools Commission established an inquiry into girls' education. Its terms of reference included an examination of the extent, causes and broader social ramifications of girls' under-achievement at school and the recommendation of programs 'to assist girls so that they have as many careers and life choices open to them as boys' (Committee on Social Change, 1975, pp. 1–2). *Girls, School and Society* was the first major report by an Australian government on sex inequality (the term 'gender' was not yet in currency). The people who contributed to it, either as committee members or consultants, included such leading feminists as Elizabeth Reid, Eva Cox, Clare Burton and Anne Summers. Jean Blackburn edited the final report. It was explicitly grounded in the 'the new feminism', which had 'opened up new ways of looking at education as part of the process through which differing expectations are passed to boys and girls growing up' (1975, p. 1). It was trailblazing in the way that it not only measured the material details of girls' under-achievement—which were considerable in Australian schools in the early 1970s—but also, by using the then new explanatory concept of the 'hidden curriculum', identifying the power of the culture,

Girls are lined up for a vaccination campaign in the 1950s. Schools were useful for mass medical examinations and treatments. Randwick Junior Girls High School, New South Wales, 1956. (State Library of NSW, Government Printing Office 2, 07718)

curriculum and organisation of schools to produce inequality. *Girls, School and Society* was among the most successful of a new wave of liberal-progressive reports spawning policies that worked their way through the schools, contributing to broad social change. It was realistic in its approach:

> The Committee is well aware that action in schools and education systems will not alone achieve the changes in Australian society necessary to ensure sex equality and to open up wider options in it for both sexes. It will, however, assist in the development of social changes and it is a necessary part of more widespread action (1975, p. 168)

Working-class children

Much of the preceding discussion of disadvantage and inequality is also about social class. This includes Aboriginal children from rural working-class families, girls from families where fathers were unskilled workers, migrant children whose fathers were usually in working-class jobs, and pre-school children from the working class, whose lives were much less likely to be touched by the kindergarten than those of middle-class children. These were the children most likely to be placed in the 'disadvantaged' category. The least well-resourced school system was the Catholic, with a great number of working-class children educated within it.

Even though the language of social class and class inequality would be subsumed by terms such as 'low socio-economic status', 'disadvantage' and 'poverty' towards the end of the 1951–75 period, it retained sufficient power to galvanise the labour movement at least to seek fundamental shifts in government social policies, including those about education. Late in the period, the Karmel Report (1973), which led to the establishment of the Schools Commission, was highly responsive to this approach. The Disadvantaged Schools Program, and similar programs, targeted the problems associated with working-class schooling. In the process, the Schools Commission put aside as irrelevant the old religious divisions. Catholic schools would be targeted to the same degree as public schools; the primary test of new funding under such schemes would be the disadvantages associated with social class, not who owned or controlled the school.

•

This period of school history began with the intention of the newly elected (1949) government of Robert Menzies to sustain an interpretation of the Australian Constitution that would allow no federal engagement with schools. Education was the business of the states. It is fair to say that, at this point, the ruling Liberal Party was overwhelmingly a party of Protestants and the middle class, with little sympathy for a Catholic, mainly working-class set of schools. In the 1960s, this approach had been destabilised, and by the mid-1970s it was completely overturned. This is the last chapter in which the issue of religious sectarianism plays a large part in the narrative.

Children of the baby boom often survived the overcrowded schools, the often poorly trained teachers and an instrumental curriculum. It certainly helped that post-school employment opportunities continued in abundance. This was also the last era in which post-school employment was not overly dependent on an individual's success at school.

Nevertheless, the seeds planted in progressive educational reform ideas—especially from the 1930s and 1940s—came to germination in this era—once the emergency of the baby boom had been dealt with. The curriculum underwent a process of reform that would allow an escape from the rigidities of centrally prescribed textbooks. As inspectors and controls of the old type retreated, many public schools and their teachers experimented with new forms of instruction. Public examinations were reduced in number, and in Queensland in the early 1970s they were abolished altogether.

This era also marks an apotheosis—the high point for government schools in Australia—despite a challenge from a small group of alternative schools, and even the popularity of a de-schooling movement. New approaches to secondary schooling through the establishment of the comprehensive high schools, which involved improved retention and a growing share of enrolments, saw advantage gained against the non-government sectors. The older non-government schools were beginning to look a little moribund. The comprehensive high schools were *the* schools of the new outer suburbs, of the rapidly expanding populations in Australian cities. Reforms to the universities and institutions of further education, and new—mainly federal—government scholarships saw genuinely accessible pathways established from schools into higher education. Such ladders of opportunity had been imagined at the beginning of the twentieth century, but the 1960s and 1970s saw new opportunities for working-class and lower middle-class children to stay at school, and go on to further education.

This is not to shift attention from the arguments that increasingly defined the era in relation to inequality and disadvantage. They were real enough, but change appeared possible, and by the 1970s was material for many. It appeared that a new age for youthful opportunity had begun, even if some—including many middle-class children—appeared ungrateful, given the new youth cultures and even student rebellions that gathered despite the disapprobation of older Australians.

Further reading

Bessant and Spaull (1976) provide a critical history of education policy, and Marginson (1997a) does the same for the post-1960 period. The final two 'round-ups' of Australian education published by the Australian Council of Education Research (ACER, 1956, 1964) cover a wide range of topics. W.F. Connell's (1993) history from 1960 remains an essential compendium. See Kociumbas (1997) for childhood. On secondary schooling, see Campbell and Sherington (2013) for New South Wales, Tully (2002) for Western Australia and Goodman (1968) for Queensland. Primary schooling lacks an authoritative monograph. See Brennan (1998) for the pre-schools. On Harold Wyndham, see Hughes (2002). On the restoration of state aid to non-government schools, see Wilkinson et al. (2006). On Aboriginal schooling, see Haebich (2000). On Catholic schooling, see O'Donoghue (2001) and Selleck (1978), and on the campaign for school funding, see Hogan (1978). For an insider's view of Catholic education politics in Victoria, see O'Brien (1999). On teachers, see Spaull (1977). For school woes in the 1960s, see McLaren (1968) and McLean (1969). On gender politics in schools in the 1970s and 1980s, see Yates (1993). For the Karmel Report and federal education policy, see Dudley and Vidovich (1995), and on the lead-up to the constitutional issues around education, see Spaull (2001). See Sherington, Petersen and Brice (1987) for the corporate, independent school sector. For the Disadvantaged Schools Program, see Connell, White and Johnston (1991). The Karmel Report (1973) is essential reading. The educational arrangements of Australia's non-mainland trusts and territories have their own histories that are not discussed in this book. For a good account of Papua New Guinea's educational history, see Cleverley (2007).

CHAPTER

7

Towards a market of schools 1976–2000

In this last quarter of the twentieth century, there was unprecedented change in Australian education. The shifts in policy—some of which accompanied economic restructure—had a profound effect on schools, and on the lives of teachers and students. Schooling became more important than ever in the lives of young people and their families. By the end of the century, most Australian students—male and female—stayed on at school until the end of Year 12. The children of the 1980s and 1990s were more likely to have had parents who had prolonged experience of secondary school, whether in Australia or overseas. It was these better educated parents who became active 'stakeholders' in education—for example, as potentially expert choosers of different kinds of schools for their children. School education continued to be an important issue in elections through the 1970s to the 1990s, and federal government education policies increased their significance in comparison with those of the Australian states.

A new orientation of the nation towards global economic competitiveness occurred. Different approaches to training the workforce coincided with the collapse of full-time youth employment from the late 1970s. Demands were made of the senior secondary curriculum—which, until the early 1970s, was not normally expected to engage youth universally. The senior secondary school developed a custodial character, as older youth—especially working-class youth—found themselves in schools for longer than they wished. Schools, state

Education Departments and national agencies undertook curriculum reform in response, but there was a catch-up character to it. State governments increased the school leaving age beyond 15 years. From 1976 to 2000, Year 10 to 12 retention rose from 42.6 to 74.4 per cent, yet policy-makers argued that it was not enough.

This era is marked by the rise of neoliberalism in economic and social policy. The effects in Australia included the privatisation of government instrumentalities. Public–private partnerships in infrastructure development became common. The argument usually went that public ownership of services was expensive and inefficient; reform was more likely to occur if enterprises competed for customers in markets.

Though contested, there was an inexorable reorientation of schools and systems to the new policy agendas. The history of the Australian Schools Commission from the mid-1970s through the 1980s exemplified the process. An early emphasis on the funding and encouragement of diversity *and* equality in schooling was constrained. Though the Schools Commission had never been funded well enough to make a transformative impact on 'disadvantaged' students, the commitment to 'equality' dropped away. By the early 1980s, the Innovations Program and the Education Research and Development Committee that directly addressed disadvantage had gone and the flagship Disadvantaged Schools Program did what it could with no new funding. The Commission was in the process of being transformed from an agency giving major support to public education and its improvement, to an agency underwriting the costs of non-government schools: 'driving deeper the wedge between public and private schooling' (Connell et al., 1982).

Table 7.1 shows the decline of the public school systems in this period, as neoliberal ideas colonised the policies of both Coalition and Labor governments. Table 7.1 is not simply about the decline of government schools, but the effects of school consolidation as all schools managed the after-effects of the 1945–65 baby boom.

More important than the number of schools was the change in the proportions of young people in the different school sectors. Completing secondary school grew in importance over the twentieth

TABLE 7.1
Number of schools in Australia by sector, 1976–2001

	1976	1981	1986	1991	1996	2001
Government	7 306	7 531	7 589	7 470	7 088	6 942
Non-government	2 138	2 261	2 496	2 510	2 542	2 654
Totals	9 444	9 792	10 085	9 980	9 630	9 596
Government % increase		*+3.1*	*+0.8*	*−1.6*	*−5.1*	*−2.1*
Non-government % increase		*+5.8*	*+10.4*	*+0.6*	*+1.3*	*+4.4*

Source: Australian Bureau of Statistics (2001).

century as the labour market demanded higher educational credentials. Late in the century, anxieties in this area acted to the detriment of government high schools. From 1976 to 2000, their share of secondary enrolments was substantially reduced as Table 7.2 shows, though the contraction was less in the smaller states and territories.

By 2000, there had been a market of schools established, though rural and remote areas saw less of it than larger urban areas. The school market was enabled by federal government schools funding. Competition within public systems occurred along with the fight with non-government schools for enrolments. In the public sector, restrictions on who could go to which schools diminished. The end of neighbourhood public school zoning was not only brought on by

TABLE 7.2
Changes in the numbers of full-time Australian secondary students enrolled in government and non-government schools, 1976 and 2000

Year	1976		2000		1976–2000
School sector	N	%	N	%	% change
Government	850 626	75.9	862 214	64.2	−11.7
Catholic	186 794	16.7	283 094	21.1	+4.4
Anglican	35 748	3.2	66 262	4.9	+1.7
Other non-government	47 465	4.2	131 974	9.8	+5.6
Totals	1 120 633	100.0	1 343 544	100.0	

Source: ABS (2001).

competition policy, but the decline in school-going populations. In competing for enrolments, government and non-government schools sought to differentiate themselves, usually by promoting curriculum specialisations or various social exclusivities.

If a new settlement was emerging in the schools sector, confusion continued in the 'pre-school' area. Attempts to produce workable policy were piecemeal. Older models of kindergarten enrolment became incompatible with new employment patterns for mothers. Educational research insisted on the importance of the early years of childhood in later school success. As federal governments attempted to unify the sector and incorporate it into broader schools policy, public funding grew—but its cost to families also expanded, and access remained patchy. Providers included communities, churches, profit-oriented businesses, school systems and more. The pre-school sector was the most privatised—even market-driven–sector of all. It was riven by controversies over the desirability of long day-care in comparison with stay-at-home mother care. Indeed, there was a problem about 'care' as opposed to 'pre-school education'. Was vocational college training satisfactory for carers, but university education necessary for pre-school teachers? What did 'care' mean without educational stimulus, or the education of infants without 'care'? Parents often found the sector too complicated and expensive to access easily (Elliott, 2006). Histories of institutions such as the Lady Gowrie Child Centre in Melbourne provide insights into the challenges. Established in response to English ideas about child training, by the end of the twentieth century the Lady Gowrie Centre was dealing with the new Italian influence from Reggio Emilia. Negotiating the need to charge fees, but providing for families who could not afford them, and responding effectively to changing public funding regimes, demanded ever more skilled management (Waters, 2000).

As Australian schools became more diverse and competition-focused, new and old hierarchies of schools were consolidated and established. Multicultural policy, emerging in the post-White Australia era, was responsible for some of the changes. Many new non-government schools were founded for groups defined by their peculiar ethno-cultural, religious and national characteristics and

The modern preschool. Computer keyboard and telephone, as well as coloured pencils, paper, glue and cut-outs. Bonython Preschool, Canberra, 1996. (National Library of Australia, an13225911)

histories. Other schools remained exclusive in terms of social class, as discriminations were practised on the basis of the ability to pay fees, probable learning and behaviour problems, and entrance tests favouring academic potential. Issues around gender also affected schools. There was a remarkable turn-about in the popular debate concerning educational disadvantage and gender. In the 1970s, the issue was the problems that girls might have in classrooms and in gaining credentials that might lead to higher education and employment. During the 1990s the 'boy problem', extant from the late nineteenth century, was rediscovered. New programs were framed to support boys as the new disadvantaged sex.

Social change and schooling

In 2000, the principals of public primary schools in Australia were surveyed about their schools, the adequacy of government resourcing and the future of public schooling. Their replies said much about the relationship between schools and a changing society. Many pointed to the problems arising from the 'breakdown of traditional family structures'; others focused on the depredations wreaked by new levels of drug and alcohol abuse. Many children apparently had 'poor social skills', producing increased levels of disruptive behaviour. There was a need for new cooperation with welfare agencies to manage the difficulties. Most principals expected that public primary schools would be required to increase their share of children from families in poverty and breakdown (Angus, 2001).

Such issues had been identified 25 years earlier by a Royal Commission on Poverty (Fitzgerald, 1976). What was new was the despondence of the principals who believed that governments were unwilling to assist. They believed that government schools were being socially and educationally residualised.

The 'breakdown of traditional family structures' had long been an issue for the creators of public school systems in Australia, where 'traditional' families barely existed for substantial segments of the population in the convict and then gold-rush eras. The reform and discipline of 'unsatisfactory' families had been an early mission of public schools. Later, their operators developed a history of blaming 'broken homes' for students who 'failed' or were unhappy at school.

The period of this chapter coincides with the rapid expansion of the social sciences in universities. New research addressed the relationships between schools, students, families and society more generally. One study discussed new feminist and sociological critiques of the traditional family: demographic structures, family law reform, changing sex roles within families, the decline of marriage, new kinds of fatherhood, non-Anglo-Australian families, mother-headed households, and lesbian mothers and their children (Burns, Bottomley & Jools, 1983). The most influential study of teachers, students, families and schools was *Making the Difference* (Connell et al., 1982). It examined the relationships of schooling, including the ways in which the ordinary practices of the secondary school likely contributed to social inequality.

During this period, youth culture continued to differentiate itself from official school cultures. Schools were forced to adapt—for instance, school drug policies had to be written. Students required more than formal instruction from their schools—this was the period in which student counsellors were appointed to larger schools across the country. New sexual freedoms and identities became more obvious in school settings. Victoria provides a small example. *Young, Gay and Proud* was published by the Gay Teachers' and Students' Group in 1978. It advised gay and lesbian school students on negotiating their lives.

From the late 1970s, after the recession induced by the oil-price shock and the removal of high protectionist tariffs, the manufacturing industry went into decline, and took Australia's working class with it. Consequent youth unemployment was associated with new panics about youth 'at risk'. There were demands for a coordinated national youth policy, and the further prolongation of schooling was one of the more obvious solutions. Along with contributing to a fall in rates of unemployment, youth retention to Year 12 and beyond could lead more positively to the development of new 'skills' and 'competencies'. These would result in improved access to the labour market. They

Schools adapt for diverse populations. Refugee children from Kosovar at school in the army base at Singleton in New South Wales, 1999. (National Library of Australia, vn3092540)

might also produce a more globally clever, competitive Australia. Improved school retention became one of the 'good' educational stories of the era, as opposed to the other story: of young people no longer able to earn a living wage.

Changing patterns of migration also affected schooling. There were fewer families from Central and Southern Europe, with many more from East Asia, and then the Middle East. Some were middle class—sometimes 'business' migrants. Others came with little in the way of possessions. Many Vietnamese were refugees. East and south-east Asian migrants in particular sought out high-quality traditional academic schooling.

The following brief school histories demonstrate some of the changes occurring in this period.

Six schools and the challenges

Mitcham Primary School

Mitcham Primary School sits in one of Adelaide's more middle-class suburbs. In 1976, the curriculum was enhanced by government funding for a new library, and music and activity rooms. As the 'resource centre', rather than 'library', was fitted out, the teacher-librarians became significant promoters of non-teacher-centred learning.

Following its role in introducing the New Maths, with Schools Commission funding, the school also introduced Italian, a language other than English (LOTE), recognising the presence of many Italian-Australian families in its district. The Commission funded a consortium of schools for the teaching of Italian, including a Catholic primary and a nearby government high school. This was the kind of program the Schools Commission favoured—a sensible curriculum initiative certainly, but one that also encouraged collaboration between public and non-government schools. This made a 'significant contribution in terms of multi-cultural appreciation and tolerance' at Mitcham Primary (Cornwall, 1997).

In the 1980s and 1990s, the school introduced programs for children with 'special needs', funded by state and federal governments. The first of these was the More Able gifted and talented program.

A selection procedure identified students who were then regularly withdrawn from classes for an enhanced curriculum. Their teachers received in-service training. The second was the Learning Assistance Program, concentrating on students with poor literacy and numeracy. The third program was about students with physical disabilities. Children in wheelchairs were withdrawn from their former special school and were 'mainstreamed' into standard Mitcham Primary classrooms.

The first computers arrived free of charge as a promotion exercise by their manufacturer, an example of newly encouraged 'industry–school links'. In 1991, the South Australian Education Department abolished corporal punishment. A major means of running orderly Australian schools from 1788—especially where boys were present—was gone. The 'management of student behaviour' became the subject of staff professional development and departmental guidelines. In 1981 a school council, composed of men and women, took over as the formal means by which parents contributed to the governance of the school. It replaced a committee composed of fathers, and the mothers' club. Most mothers, it appeared, were no longer full-time housewives with time to attend club meetings during the day. These events are specific to this school, but they are also typical of the kinds of changes occurring elsewhere (Logan and Sachs, 1997).

Mainstreaming promised large numbers of children with disabilities access to a broader curriculum and various school and post-school opportunities. It was embraced by many parents and students for reasons of equity. On the other hand, there was resistance from some teachers and schools where there was little additional resourcing for the new students and programs. Government schools enrolled disproportionate numbers of young people with special needs. Late in the century, anti-discrimination laws improved the right of families to access a range of schools, including non-government, for their children.

Unley High School

Across the road from Mitcham Primary was Unley High. By 1983, the enrolments were down, and the school's reputation for magnificent public examination results was tarnished. It had been a decade since streaming was supposed to have ended. The school was expected to become comprehensive, providing for students other than those bound for university. Reforming the school timetable opened a discussion about how the curriculum could be improved. In the process, the school's governance and culture came into question. The participation of teaching staff in curriculum and school decision-making rubbed against the responsibilities of senior staff. Parents and students had an uncertain role in the discussion. New timetabling structures led to competition between subject faculties jostling to exploit new opportunities, or defend existing privileges. For example, the idea that all subjects should have equal time in the curriculum appalled teachers of languages, mathematics and physics, as physical education and home economics expanded their time. Newly conceived school-assessed subjects jostled for students and esteem against the publicly assessed, high-prestige subjects. There were new subjects—health, legal, business, 'modern', technology and computing studies—that reflected new efforts towards vocational relevance. There was a new pastoral care program as well.

Transition education became an important issue in this school, and in others around Australia. Work experience programs for young people would assist their understanding of the labour market. There was a new drive towards increasing the number of significant age groupings within the school. An old American idea—that of the middle school, giving young adolescents their own programs, institutions and leadership opportunities—enjoyed a resurgence in popularity. New teacher training programs supported the movement. At Unley High, a new set of buildings separated 'middle' from senior high school students. Transitions between school and work, school and higher education, primary and secondary education, childhood and early adolescence, early adolescence and middle and late adolescence, would all be supported by new curriculum and new managerial and organisational arrangements within schools.

Unley High eventually became more comprehensive. In the 1990s, it became a 'discovery school' for the use of new information technologies in teaching and learning. The conflicts associated with reformed curriculum, improved student access, equity *and* excellence, new student groupings and assessment, as well as school-based decision-making, were redolent of the era (see Campbell, 2010).

The Parks Community Education Centre and Golden Grove

On the other side of Adelaide were two new schools. Their differences reflected the changing priorities of the Schools Commission and governments. The Parks Community Education Centre was built in the working-class suburbs of the city's west in the 1970s. It attempted to integrate social, welfare and educational services on the one site for a community that was one of Adelaide's poorest. The state Labor government took pride in providing superb community facilities for those who had least. The school was clearly about social justice. Many families in the area were transient, in public housing, sometimes recovering from the imprisonment of a parent, homelessness or other problems.

The Parks school benefited from the Disadvantaged Schools Program. Its teachers largely chose to be there and were collegially prepared for their work. Teaching was innovative. There was an emphasis on educating the whole community as 'home group' teachers visited their students' families. The drama program involved community as well as students. Students improvised plays about their own experiences, touring the productions across the state. Such activity at The Parks helped many young people. Unusually for children from this area, some even went to university. It was a school of national significance, but the government funding required to maintain its activity declined—as, in the end, did its enrolments. It closed in 1996.

The Golden Grove schools complex was part of a new suburban estate developed by the Delfin company. Three schools opened in the complex in the late 1980s: a government high school, a Catholic school and a 'Christian' college. The three schools shared a library, a disabilities program, computing and science laboratories, and technical education, home economics and music facilities. It was a project that suited the times. A choice between schools—public and private—would attract middle-class families. In an era when federal government funding was crucial for new school foundations, there would be savings through shared facilities. This model was a real possibility for future suburban developments.

Our Lady of Lebanon College

In New South Wales, near Parramatta, there was another school—primary at first, then with a secondary annexe—founded in the early 1970s. Its history was closely tied to developing multicultural policy. Maronite Catholics from Lebanon had a presence in Australia from the nineteenth century, but with the civil war of the 1970s there was new migration. The Maronites had their own Catholic rite, so absorption of their children into existing Catholic, let alone public, schools was resisted. Federal funding was crucial to the foundation of Our Lady of Lebanon College. Maronite Sisters of the Holy Family established the school. With the church on the same block, it formed a tight community. Arabic and French were the languages taught, but with a mainly working-class parent body with high unemployment rates, school fees were difficult to collect and good academic results were scarce. It was a school that could barely have existed without Schools Commission and then succeeding federal funding. The funding paid for new buildings, and assistance for its students—especially in the areas of literacy, numeracy, and special education. The Lebanese villages from which its families came remained significant in the life of school, church and community, but integration also occurred as the Lebanon-originated teaching nuns retired and lay teachers and administrators, not always attached to the Maronite tradition, were hired. The demand for Arabic declined. School registration meant satisfying the curriculum demands of state authorities. As a school representing a specific 'ethnic' community, it received many visits from leaders of political parties, as the 'ethnic vote' was courted. Schools such as this had barely existed before the 1970s (see Stephens, 2012).

Mount Druitt High

While Our Lady of Lebanon College eventually prospered, there was a different fate in store for Mount Druitt High School in Sydney's outer west. Founded in 1969, it was one of dozens of public comprehensive high schools established in the 1960s and 1970s in the new outer suburbs. Cheap housing, poor public transport and limited employment opportunities soon led to high rates of unemployment and social welfare interventions. In 1997, there was dramatic publicity for the school. Sydney's tabloid, the *Daily Telegraph*, published a story about the class that 'failed'. Of the school's Year 12 students, not one had received (or applied for) a tertiary entrance score. A comprehensive school in name, it could not provide comprehensive curriculum opportunities (Laughlin, 1997). It was the kind of school that collected unrepresentative shares of children from poor families, a school likely to consolidate social disadvantage. Such schools allowed wealthier non-government schools to concentrate the 'cultural and economic resources' of non-disadvantaged families on their sites. They could specialise in the most prestigious parts of the curriculum: those that maximised the probability of university entrance (Teese, 2000). Mount Druitt High was closed, re-emerging as a junior campus of a larger school—with its enrolment still coming from families with household incomes close to the lowest in Sydney. Public schools in similar situations existed in most Australian cities.

Como High

Como High School in Western Australia represents a different response to the pressures of the period. It was led in the 1990s by a principal who decided to exploit the new neoliberal and devolutionary spirit in public schools policy. She decided to reposition her school in the emerging market of all schools, public and non-government. She would corporatise the school. Its name was changed to the more prestigious 'College'. She recruited overseas fee-paying students. She sought corporate sponsors for programs unusual for public schools. She tried to increase middle-class enrolments by, for example, advertising a golfing program and, where she could, she turned away enrolments from a nearby 'rough' neighbourhood. Eventually the principal came to grief through the misuse of funds, but other public and non-government schools, where the circumstances were amenable, did similar things more astutely (Forsey, 2007).

In these brief school histories, the role of the word 'public' in schooling was being redefined. In the case of Mount Druitt, public schooling became associated with inferior schooling. At Como High, it meant the turning of public responsibilities into meeting the private wishes of more middle-class parents seeking more prestigious schooling. The Parks' story is about a public school actively seeking opportunities for its disadvantaged students. At Golden Grove, the public high school was conceived as just one alternative in a market of diverse schools.

New policy from federal and state governments

The Liberal-National Coalition government led by Malcolm Fraser won a decisive election victory at the end of 1975. It inherited the previous Labor government's Schools Commission, and would develop new priorities as a result.

The 'needs' basis of schools funding was forced to coexist with the idea of per capita entitlement—that is, all families—rich or poor—should receive some support for their children's education. Non-government schools received more federal funding. As early as 1977, the Schools Commission's budget available for equity programs began to be marginalised. Much of what remained assisted Catholic schools as their teacher wage bills soared in the face of declining numbers of religious working as teachers.

Though a new report by the commission, *Schooling for 15 and 16 Year Olds* (1980), was influential, a slightly earlier report from outside the commission emphasised vocational training in the senior high school. There should be a focus on 'school-to-work transition' (Williams, 1979).

The election of the Labor governments led by Bob Hawke and Paul Keating (1983–96) brought a return of the social justice orientation—but not much new funding for public schools. There was some success in slowing the rate of new non-government school establishments, especially where viable existing public schools served an area. The political influence of the non-government schools sector was soon demonstrated, however, as it fought mild attempts to change funding priorities. The 1983–84 campaign to maintain previous levels of non-government schools funding saw the government accused of denying a newly invented fundamental right of citizens to choose a school that suited their children. Labor was bruised by the uproar—a discourse shift in the state aid debate had occurred. The whole non-government sector—Catholic, Protestant, secular, wealthy and poor, Anglo-Australian and non-Anglo—had 'united behind its most privileged members and waged a major campaign of protest meetings, lobbying and media exposure' (Dudley and Vidovich, 1995, p. 91).

New advice to government, sourced from outside the Schools Commission, argued for a 'back-to-basics' curriculum approach. Acceptable standards of literacy and numeracy were to be achieved by schools whose programs should be rigorously evaluated (Karmel, 1985). The sympathy of the federal government for this argument was embodied by a new Minister of Employment, Education and Training. In 1987, John Dawkins replaced Susan Ryan, who had been associated with the equity projects of the Schools Commission. The Commission was finally abolished in 1988. By then, 'economic rationalism'—or neoliberalism—had won the debate over the direction of economic and other government policy (Pusey, 1991). Pressures for school reform around equity issues did not go away, but the Schools Commission was missed as an advocate. From 1987, educational and school reform became part of various industry restructure initiatives. Improved productivity might result from improved workforce education and training. The Organisation for Economic Cooperation and Development (OECD) assumed significance as Australia was judged by the successes of its international competitors. The OECD would be a collector and publisher of comparative statistics relating to literacy, numeracy and measures of more advanced educational performance. What constituted educational success in schools was being radically redefined.

The 'new vocationalism' dominated federal government policy through the 1990s. Ambitious plans by the federal government for nationally coordinated curriculum and training occasionally came to grief as a result of state differences, but the taxing and funding power of the federal government often persuaded recalcitrant state governments. A Curriculum Corporation had been established in the 1980s, jointly funded by the Commonwealth and the states. It assisted an ambition of federal governments to produce nationally consistent curriculum frameworks. The Hobart Declaration, a statement by state and federal Ministers of Education included the Common and Agreed National Goals for Schooling in Australia (Australian Education Council, 1989). The development of student talents, high educational standards and equality of opportunity were among the goals, but another goal required schools:

> To respond to the current and emerging economic and social needs of the nation, and to provide those skills which will allow students maximum flexibility and adaptability in their future employment and other aspects of life.

Other goals concentrated on literacy, numeracy, problem-solving, civics, health and physical fitness. Respect for the Australian cultural heritage included that of 'Aboriginal and ethnic groups'. Improved career education and knowledge of the world of work were required.

This kind of approach was not overturned by the incoming John Howard-led Coalition government from 1996, even though it had a different agenda on some elements of the curriculum. The bias of federal funding towards non-government schools was consolidated.

State governments rethought their approach to schooling. In New South Wales, there was a Liberal-National Coalition in 1988, led by Nick Greiner. It rapidly departed from the Wyndham reorganisation of secondary schooling that had occurred 25 years earlier. New academically selective and specialist high schools were to provide, according to the Education Minister, 'a level playing field between government and nongovernment schools' (quoted in Sherington, 1995, p. 174). Class sizes increased; principals were to have more control over school budgets; the Education Department relinquished its powers over school curricula to a board including representatives of non-government schools and business, as well as teacher unions and professional associations. These and other policies led to mass rallies against the government; as a result the approach was modified. New

South Wales did not go as far in the neoliberal direction as Victoria was about to.

In Victoria, the Liberal-National Coalition government of Jeffrey Kennett (1992–99) sought to diminish public teacher union influence with devolutions of power over teacher staffing and finances to school principals and school councils. *Schools of the Future*, the government's reform manifesto published in 1994, set out the changes. Central and regional support services would be reduced. There would be new performance requirements for teachers and schools, and the introduction of school charters. Competition between state schools for resources and students would be fostered. Initial support for the program—some within the public sector—was wasted as drastic reductions to resourcing followed. A total of 351 schools were closed and 8000 teachers were either retrenched or encouraged to resign (Spaull, 1999). Many of the schools that closed were involved in programs of support for disadvantaged students. The inner city Richmond Secondary College was one such school. For almost a year, activists, students and teachers ran a rebel school, frustrating the government that planned to demolish its buildings and sell the land to developers. After months of occupation, police armed with batons 'cleared' the site (Jolly, 1996).

Expanding the non-government school sector

In 1981, the High Court of Australia ruled on federal government funding of church-owned schools. The case was prosecuted by an alliance of public school supporters, the Defence of Government Schools (DOGS) organisation. DOGS lost the case despite the Australian Constitution's clause 116 disallowing federal governments from establishing religion. The decision signalled the final collapse of the century-old, post-1870s, state aid settlement. New government funding for non-government schools was legitimated. A golden age for non-government schools had begun.

The Catholic systemic and religious order-governed schools were among the beneficiaries. For a school such as St Patrick's Marist College in western Sydney, founded in 1872, the 1970s and 1980s brought both cultural change and financial security. The reforms of Vatican II helped liberalise the curriculum and allowed improved relationships between students, religious and lay teachers. Federal funding allowed the teacher establishment to rise from 22 (1973) to 38 in 1982. The number of Marist brother teachers—seven—remained stable; all the expansion was on the lay side. By the end of the 1980s, the school was almost totally in the hands of lay teachers. The failure of the DOGS case encouraged more confident planning for the future. Unlike the Christian Brothers schools, the Marists were more open to co-education, and St Patrick's took the step in 1985. However, as with many schools in the Catholic sector, there was a problem to be solved. How would schools remain true to the educational visions of their founders if the religious teachers were disappearing? The Marists worked hard to articulate the 'charism' of the order, but it was all a little vague (Braniff, 2001).

Many Catholic schools were sought out by non-Catholic families eager to access non-government school education. Why church schools are supported by non-religious families is not easily explained, although perceptions that church-run schools could be more orderly than public schools—especially in areas with high levels of poverty and perhaps recent immigration—must be part of an explanation.

There was another legacy for Catholic schools that was more of a problem. Widespread sexual abuse of boys by members of male teaching orders was exposed towards the end of the century and into the next (O'Donohue, 2003). St Stanislaus' College, a foundation of Vincentian fathers and brothers in Bathurst, had a particularly unpleasant history in this regard.

The Catholic Education Offices (CEOs) developed the second largest national system of schools. They managed their right to 'block grants' from federal governments, disbursing funds according to their own priorities. This gave the system considerable power over the consolidation and expansion of their school system. Exemptions from anti-discrimination laws were won. They enabled not only the Catholic schools, but other religious schools, to discriminate in favour of teachers and children of their own faith, and exclude teachers

An increasingly rare scene as the proportion of teachers from Catholic religious orders declined. A Marist brother working with boys of St Patrick's School, Dundas, New South Wales, c. 1975. (National Library of Australia, vn3084871)

from employment who were not heterosexual, or respectably single or married.

Older, mainly Protestant, elite schools in the non-government sphere, despite their increased shares of government funding, described themselves as *independent*. If not completely independent of government funding, the word correctly described their independence from systems of schools. Student fees continued to rise despite increases in government funding. Such schools usually became larger and wealthier. New buildings and facilities, not only funded by government but by wealthier old scholars, and new tax-deductible 'building funds' to which parents were required to contribute, made for complex corporate organisations. Business people were recruited to schools' governing councils and school principals became more remote figures. They looked and behaved more like chief executive officers of corporations rather than school heads from the English and Australian past (Sherington, Petersen and Brice, 1987).

At Melbourne Girls Grammar School, an Anglican school dating from 1893, the changes included the establishment of the Merton Hall Foundation, 'with the dual aims of providing capital to maintain the building program and establish an endowment fund sufficient to secure the independent future of the school'. It required a $500 registration fee from the family of each girl enrolled. In 1991, the theme of the annual School Council Seminar was 'School Development—Marketing' (McCarthy and Theobald, 1993, pp. 171–5).

Older Arnoldian conceptions of the 'greater public school' were displaced as neoliberal times saw parents transformed into customers for a service. While games, houses, prefects and chapel remained significant, increasingly important was public examination success as the tertiary entrance scores for the high-status courses such as medicine and law rose. This was a problem for several elite boys' schools at the end of the twentieth century. While elite girls' schools had long celebrated examination success, some boys' schools had continued to treat the overly studious boy with suspicion. A number of elite boys' schools made concerted efforts to modernise during the 1990s and 2000s, modifying the old Rugby and football masculinities with a more 'all round' emphasis, and in some cases a more determined religiosity (Proctor, 2011; Marr, 1999). At the Knox Grammar School in Sydney, slippage in examination performance led to extreme pressure on the school head and staff. Some new non-government foundations such as the Malek Fahd Islamic School followed the secular Sydney Grammar School in enrolling selectively, on the basis of academic merit—other schools could be left to enrol the less able children.

The success story of the post-1970s period (depending on the perspective of the observer) was the rise of smaller low- and moderate-fee non-government schools outside the Catholic system. During the periods of Liberal-National Coalition governments in particular, there were large numbers of such foundations. Many used the word 'Christian' to signify their orientation. Bible-based, and often doctrinally fundamentalist, they offered alternatives to public schools that some parents perceived as wanting in terms of 'discipline' and 'values'. With federal aid, lower middle-class and better-off working-class families could just afford the school fees. The entry of married women into the workforce in large numbers often enabled the devotion of a second family income to school fees. It was a strange phenomenon that, as census after census revealed the growing departure of Australians from church affiliation and religious belief, the number of faith-based schools expanded.

A less successful story was that of the 'alternative' schools that were founded earlier, from the late 1960s into the 1970s. Many of them—those with an emphasis on individual and creative self-expression and close relationships with community—were always going to have a hard time as neoliberalism transformed the purposes of schooling. Concepts such as skills, competencies, training, school-to-work transition, productivity, accountability, measurable outcomes and the like were difficult to accommodate. Some alternative schools, like the Burra Community School in South Australia, existed within public education systems. Others were non-government. Some, like Preshil in Victoria and Marbury in South Australia, found themselves with too many children with behavioural problems; they resisted this kind of enrolment. Others, such as the Collingwood Community School in Melbourne, were well meaning and no doubt provided an education for young people alienated by conventional schools, yet the school's historian has argued that the university academics who conceived it and the teachers who ran it failed to develop a coherent rationale for the school (Kennedy, 2002).

There was a School Without Walls in Canberra from 1974. It had its successes with a minimum of formal classes and the use of broader community resources. There were no uniforms, no bells, no corporal punishment. There were informal relations between children and teachers and a close engagement of parents and community in the work of the school. It responded to educational theorists advocating community integration and de-schooling, who were at their most influential in the late 1960s and 1970s. There was a similar spirit at the Nimbin Community School in New South Wales. Parents, teachers and students had

> such close daily ties that the conventional roles of the teacher and the usual functions of the school have little relevance. Of the fifty or so adults on the school roster, thirty or more are parents of enrolled children and seventeen are involved simply because of their interest in the education of the community's children. (Maslen, 1982)

Most alternative schools in this tradition failed to survive the 1980s.

There was an illiberal group of alternative schools as well. Many small Christian schools adopted American Accelerated Christian Education (ACE) approaches to education. Young people and their teachers did not interact much with the wider community, typified by too much 'liberalism, modernism and secular humanism' (Connell, 1993, p. 224). Children worked on pre-packaged curriculum materials in their study carrels. There were over 50 such schools at one point. State curriculum and registration requirements provided some correctives against their excesses.

Curriculum wars

The period from 1975 to 2000 was an extraordinary one for both curriculum development and changes to pedagogy. There was also a new politicisation of the curriculum. Sometimes Ministers of Education intervened where previously they had left curriculum management to their Education Departments.

In Queensland, a public school parent, Rona Joyner—sometime president of the Festival of Light—objected to commonly used social studies curricula. Under criticism was *Man: A Course of Study* (MACOS) and the *Social Education Materials Project* (SEMP). They were developed respectively in the United States and Australia in the 1970s. Both encouraged an examination of broad social and cultural questions by junior secondary students. An often criticised module from MACOS concerned an Inuit group from the cold north of America. Life was hard. The group could not indefinitely support aged members who were neither mobile nor capable of contributing to finding food, so they eventually were left to die in the cold, as they knew they would. Presumably the social studies classroom would discuss approaches to the aged and ageing in their own societies.

Joyner considered MACOS to be antagonistic to Christianity, an instrument of secular humanism, undermining the values of children's families. She and her allies made little progress with P&C associations within individual schools, but there was something to be said for centralised public Education Departments after all. Joyner persuaded Queensland Premier Joh Bjelke-Petersen. Both MACOS and SEMP were banned in Queensland public schools from 1978 (Smith and Knight, 1978). Although no other state did likewise, a crucial lesson had been learnt by populist neoconservative politicians. There was capital to be gained from attacking curricula that appeared to undermine traditional values. By the 1990s, such politics were common—especially as various members of the Howard government interested themselves in the 'history wars'. In 1993, the historian Geoffrey Blainey had condemned the 'black armband' history that had influenced school curricula. He considered that the Australian history taught in schools had become too negative and pessimistic, with too much attention paid to national crimes and not enough to national achievements.

The rethinking of Aboriginal history since 1788 was at the heart of the history wars. They coincided with renewed Aboriginal activism, and the winning of land rights in cases such as *Mabo*, settled in the High Court in 1992. There were other issues, however. Historiographical shifts appeared to favour relativist, post-modernist influenced narratives, in which many competing truths undermined the firm Truth of the successful nation, guided towards democracy and economic wealth by entrepreneurial pioneers and wise statesmen (Macintyre & Clark, 2003). Fears in this direction led to new centrally produced citizenship curriculum packages, and to the reintroduction of flag-raising ceremonies that had apparently fallen by the wayside following the now vilified libertarian and socialist intellectual and cultural disruptions of the 1960s and early 1970s. The actual impact of these controversies on what occurred in classrooms was probably low.

A third intervention into school curricula came from an alliance of old left and new right intellectuals. Apparently, under the influence of progressive curriculum experts, not only were subjects such as history and English being denuded of grand narratives, canonical literature and the teaching of formal grammar, but so were educational 'standards' falling. It was more than literacy and numeracy; standards in mathematics, science and the other discipline-based subjects that had arisen in the nineteenth century were threatened. According to *The Bulletin* magazine, 'Mickey Mouse subjects' had invaded schools (24 January, 1976). The Australian Council for Educational Standards (ACES) was formed to promote this argument in 1973. These curriculum interventions were not necessarily distinct—personnel and ideas could overlap. Sometimes different elements of the arguments prepared the way for the new vocational training agendas.

At the same time, at least early on, there was a powerful progressive curriculum movement. For some within it, there was no doubt that schools—especially alternative and reformed public schools—might help lead to a more socially just, inclusive society. Victoria and South Australia were centres for these movements. The national teachers' union magazine published a manifesto for a democratic curriculum in 1984 (*The Australian Teacher*, February). Its authors included Jean Blackburn (a stalwart of the early Schools Commission), Dean Ashenden, Doug White and Bill Hannan—all well-known curriculum activists of the left. Parts of the manifesto argued that schools too often reflected and consolidated social divisions. Too often, assessment practices—school-based and public—were more about social administration, the sorting and selecting of young people, rather than education for true democracy.

Garth Boomer in South Australia published his *Negotiating the Curriculum* in 1982. Also in 1982, Gay Hawkins reported on community curriculum and school reform in inner Sydney. Stephen Kemmis published his *Socially Critical School* in 1983, while Malcolm Skilbeck summarised a decade's thinking about the devolution of curriculum control in his *School-Based Curriculum Development* in 1984. The survival of technical high schools in Victoria for longer than in other states allowed unusually high levels of curriculum innovation. Sensible and accessible approaches to sex education, and eventually HIV-AIDS health education, were possible in Victorian schools, whereas in Queensland they stood little chance (see Preston, 2007). By the end of the century, such approaches were less in evidence. A movement to define desired curriculum outcomes and develop standards-based assessment became general.

In this quarter-century, curriculum studies achieved entry into the teacher preparation courses of colleges of advanced education and universities. Curricula in each state were rewritten as power shifted from the older groups deriving from teacher subject associations and discipline-based university academics to the new curriculum experts. Transformations occurred in modern languages, English, biology, technical studies, mathematics and other school subjects. We look briefly at the reform of one subject, home science/economics.

Post-war expansion of secondary schooling had included the entrenchment in the junior high school syllabus of 'domestic science' or 'home economics'. Nearly all girls in government high schools were compelled to study this subject while their brothers were corralled into woodwork or some other boys-only subject. The Willcox family in South Australia was among many who challenged this arrangement in the 1970s and 1980s. The subject was a minor issue for the Willcox Royal Commission in South Australia in the early 1970s. The 13-year-old student Jacquelynne Willcox had resisted compulsory home economics. Jacquelynne told her headmaster that she felt she was being prepared for domestic servitude as a housewife responsible for cooking for and cleaning up after men (Campbell, 2002).

Over the next several years, home economics was transformed, and boys were no longer excluded. The new vocationalism reorganised food preparation—there was considerable advantage to be had in the 'hospitality industry' for girls and boys who knew their way around commercial kitchens. Equal opportunity (EO) policies and EO committees in schools intervened in old and incipient discriminations. In the commercial subjects, a similar process occurred. Boys as well as girls needed 'keyboard skills' as new technology drove typewriting and shorthand out of the school curriculum and

Second-wave feminism and disrupting the gendered curriculum. Boys in the kitchen doing home economics and girls doing metal-work as part of Technical Studies, Unley High, South Australia, 1983. (Campbell, 2010, p. 215)

workforce. Girls would enrol in the business studies subjects, but boys were there as well. The new vocational and education training (VET) subjects, and links with the technical and further education (TAFE) colleges reorganised vocational education in schools. National and state gender policies and projects were often successful in reorienting girls towards parts of the school curriculum, higher education and careers previously considered unfeminine. Despite these successes in removing formal barriers, however, at the end of the century strongly gendered patterns of participation remained in many elective subjects.

Drama across the curriculum. A lesson at Gulargambone Primary School, New South Wales, 1978. (NAA: A6180, 9/10/78/45)

Reforming teaching and teachers

Teaching practices diversified. The Disadvantaged Schools Program and similar projects were responsible for many changes. They often sought to engage students beyond what was possible in teacher-centred, didactic classrooms. Time allocated for teacher professional development became common, assisting in the dissemination of a wider range of teaching methods. Small as well as large groups of students were experimented with, together with the use of resource centres for individual and group projects, team-teaching, extended community interactions, student peer group teaching, abandonment of textbooks in favour of teacher-generated and teacher–student-negotiated curricula, more laboratory work, hands-on practical work, the use of drama across the curriculum. All of these and many more initiatives challenged older conceptions of teaching. New schools architecture responded to the changes. The removal of walls between classrooms occurred in some schools, as did the creation of spaces that could host drama activities, or small-group work, or 'withdrawal' for overwrought students.

Towards the end of the century, some of this diversity was constrained as onerous student testing and reporting regimes developed in response to anxieties about literacy and numeracy teaching, and the accountability of schools and teachers in general.

Changing technology also helped to transform teaching. Overhead projectors became more common. The accessibility of spirit duplicators and then photocopiers made school-based and teacher-generated curriculum materials easier to produce. Ephemeral worksheets, study guides and quick tests ('quizzes') were produced in bulk. Towards the end of the century, computer-generated material assisted teachers. A dream of many educators through the twentieth century, the invention of a 'teaching machine', finally occurred. The use of computers in schools was initially monopolised by male teachers and boys interested in programming, and then girls working on their 'word processing'. But in the 1990s, the computers-across-the-curriculum movement took off, and no curriculum area would be left untouched. In some—usually non-government—schools that charged high fees,

A new domain for teaching and learning. A happy principal surveys teacher and students at work in one of the school's computer rooms. Unley High, Adelaide, 1996. (Photographer: Russell Millard. © NewsPix, DU3312)

students were expected to own and routinely use laptop computers for their school work.

Nevertheless, the standard, teacher-centred classroom was remarkably durable, with its century-old patterns of question and response, and time marked out by bells—no matter that the chalkboards at the front of the room began to be replaced by whiteboards.

The work of teachers came to be better understood in this period. Its complexity was explored as teacher unions made their cases for salary rises. It was also explored by researchers such as R.W. Connell, who produced another significant book, *Teachers' Work*, in 1985. The character of teaching remained responsive to the ages and developmental stages of children and youth, and the kind of school that was its context. Non-government school teachers could be loaded up with extracurricular activities. The work of pre-school or kindergarten teachers remained remarkably different from that of most secondary school teachers. Working in the disadvantaged schools such as Mount Druitt or The Parks was different from working in elite non-government colleges and academically selective high schools.

Under the influence of second-wave feminism, the last of the formal barriers to wage equality, superannuation entitlement and promotion opportunity for women teachers disappeared, but disparities in the representation of men and women teachers across sectors and promotion positions remained. Table 7.3 indicates a little of this, showing the percentages of women teachers in the different sectors.

TABLE 7.3

Female teachers as a proportion of all teachers in Australia, 1976 and 1999 by school sector (%)

Sector and level	1976	1999	Change
Government primary	68	78	+10
Government secondary	45	54	+9
Non-government primary	86	79	–7
Non-government secondary	51	54	+3

Source: ABS (1976, 1999).

Towards the end of the period, believers in the boy crisis in education argued that there were too many female teachers, depriving boys of fit role models. The term 'feminisation' was not only used to indicate the large numbers of women teachers, but to describe an apparent threat to the masculinity of boys and gender-inappropriate teaching methods. This argument was countered, but the idea of a 'boy crisis' entered the popular discourse of education (Kenway and Willis, 1998). In the same period, the moral panic concerning paedophilia possibly affected the recruitment of males into primary teaching.

Some argued that during this period, with all the competing pressures to meet the demands for social inclusion, higher retention and accountability, there was an 'intensification of the teaching labour process . . . [resulting] from increased community demands and from the requirements of a more diverse student body' (Seddon, in Maclean and McKenzie, 1991, p. 62). Where the labour unions of the working class began to decline in this period, white-collar unions such as those of teachers retained their memberships. The state public teacher unions developed their national organisation. A former teacher and president of the New South Wales Teachers Federation, Jennie George, became the first woman elected as president of Australia's national union organisation, the ACTU, in 1996.

Self-determination and Indigenous schooling

For the schooling of Aboriginal children, there were new policies and programs that moved away from the old paternalism. In New South Wales, the last of the mission schools was closed in the 1970s. Many of the problems linked with poverty, racism, and remote and rural locations remained. Nevertheless, the principles of 'self-determination'—or at least partnership and consultation—were increasingly accepted across most jurisdictions. Research into the schooling of Aboriginal children—especially as it engaged the researched as participants with some control over projects—began to deliver new insights. Meridy Malin's studies of Aboriginal children in mainly non-Aboriginal classrooms demonstrated that cultural disjunctions in classrooms were real. Learning was affected by differing approaches to child-raising, child–adult relationships, language usage and expectations such as teacher–child 'eye contact'. From such analysis, Malin (1990) found explanations for many non-Indigenous teachers withdrawing effort and affection from Aboriginal children. Better teacher training and cultural awareness would help; treating Aboriginal and non-Aboriginal children the same (assimilation) would not solve continuing difficulties.

Having fought so long against segregated schooling, some Aboriginal communities decided that their own separate schools were required—but under their control. In towns like Alice Springs, the tension between communities was intense. Separate schooling became a possible way forward. However, the Northern Territory government had only been running its school system independently of South Australia for a short while. Separate Indigenous schooling would be difficult to negotiate.

The Yipirinya School was founded on the initiative of Aboriginal elders in the town camps of Alice Springs. They felt that government schools only paid lip-service to Aboriginal languages and cultural traditions. Their children felt like outsiders. In 1978, a school council was formed and in 1979 classes were started. School registration was only won after a court order four years later. Buildings were constructed with the assistance of federal funding. The school worked on a two-way bilingual and bicultural approach, teaching four Indigenous languages including Arrernte, Luritja and Warlpiri. Each language group had cultural excursions where the students travelled to their country and learnt from elders. The school also followed the curriculum frameworks produced by the Northern Territory government (see <www.yipirinya.com.au>, accessed 26 June 2012).

Less happy was the experience of a government school in Alice Springs, Traeger Park. It was closed by the Territory government in 1991 amid bitter debate over segregated schooling and affirmative action through an Aborigines-only enrolment policy, and what 'equality' in schooling actually meant. The Chief Minister of the Northern Territory argued against separate schooling, claiming it was not 'in the long term interests of Aboriginal children, who have to learn to take their place in the wider community—they have to learn to compete . . . with white children and with white adults' (quoted in Walton, 1997, p. 40). The school was transferred to the Catholic Church, effectively a privatisation—but the affair did not end there. The national Human Rights Commissioner determined that the school had been closed on racial discriminatory grounds. The Commissioner insisted that equitable education did not mean that all students should get the same education.

The reach of schooling remained patchy in the Northern Territory. On outstations, for example, there were 935 enrolments of children in 1989. Aboriginal teaching assistants, but not teachers, worked with the children. Nationally, retention rates as well as average attendances remained significantly lower than for the rest of the population, as Table 7.4 indicates.

Governments began producing Aboriginal education policies and curriculum materials to address long-standing misapprehensions

TABLE 7.4

Comparative retention rates of Indigenous and non-Indigenous students in Australian schools to Year 12, 1994 and 2000 (%)

	1994	2000	Change
Indigenous	32.5	36.4	+3.9
Non-Indigenous	75.6	73.3	−2.3
Difference	−43.1	−36.9	

Source: ABS (2001).

and injustices, although these varied in their effects. It was a period of policy overload. In government schools, it seemed like a new policy was arriving every fortnight. The first of the Aboriginal education policies in New South Wales was published in 1982. Its 1996 revision asserted that Aboriginal students were entitled 'to resources, recognising effects of past inequities, in pursuit of educational outcomes comparable with the rest of the community'. Aboriginal communities had the right to negotiate their children's schooling. Again, Aboriginal children were 'entitled to learn about Aboriginal Australia', including an understanding of Aboriginal communities as custodians of knowledge about their own cultures and history. They were to be free to learn without racism and prejudice. Aboriginal communities and Education Departments were to work as partners in the educational process. Part of the policy was that all children—Indigenous or otherwise—must learn about Aboriginal culture and history (New South Wales Department of School Education, 1996).

By the end of the 1970s, special teacher education courses, Aboriginal school assistant employment and training, special units in Education Departments and professional development programs were all underway. If schooling for Aboriginal children appeared to be better understood and supported, there was also a better understanding of the relationships between school success and the poor health, employment and housing conditions of many Aboriginal people. The *Bringing Them Home* report (National Inquiry into the Separation of Aboriginal and Torres Strait Islander Children, 1997) also pointed to the long-term consequences for children of families devastated by the century's child-removal policies.

•

In conclusion, the period 1976–2000 saw remarkable changes in schools. The social circumstances of schooling led to new ways of dealing with old and new categories of children. The disadvantaged, the gifted and talented, the non-English speaker (NESB), Indigenous students, girls and then boys all were the subjects of new programs. Curriculum could be transformed. In languages, an early emphasis on making 'community languages' available to children from Italian, Greek, Vietnamese and other groups of substantial post-war migration shifted, as 'economic languages'—those of important trading partners, such as Mandarin and Japanese—assumed importance.

Another long-lasting group of schools began to disappear. Older, community-supported, ethnic 'Saturday' schools were wound up as federal governments first supported community languages in schools, and then funded full-time non-government schools for non-Anglo minorities. The Greek-speaking community had supported numerous Saturday schools, though school texts produced in Greece during the dictatorship of the Colonels had been a problem. St John's College in Melbourne grew from its origins as an afternoon school attached to Carlton's Greek Orthodox church. By 1979, it was a day school, and in 1996 it was placed under the jurisdiction of the Greek Orthodox Archdiocese of Australia, continuing 'the work undertaken by the early pioneers who had a dream of establishing the first independent school by Greeks, outside of Greece', as its website proclaimed.

In 2000 the national Human Rights and Equal Opportunity Commission (HREOC) published a report into rural and remote education. It found a great range of reasons why young people—including Aborigines and Torres Strait Islanders—in sparsely settled districts were failing to get an education allowing similar opportunities available to city children. Retention rates had been poor for a long time. In Tasmania in 1977, Year 7 to 11 retention had been 34 per cent in the Eastern Shore district (Hobart), while in the rural Huon Valley it was 14 per cent. The HREOC report exposed the restricted curriculum and teaching circumstances of small rural schools, the lack of access to technical and further education, the expense for families of shifting children to the large towns and cities where more opportunity existed, and the lack of health and welfare services for young people. Programs assisting young people existed from well before the Schools Commission, but the problems remained. Hopes that new information technologies could support the delivery of school curriculum were often disappointed, not the least reason being the inadequacy of telephone lines charged with their delivery. Distance education had changed dramatically over the century, from correspondence lessons, wireless-based schools of the air and now the beginnings of internet-based communication, but each of these modes continued to deliver less of an education than what urban children and youth had come to expect.

By the end of the century, a variety of studies insisted that there had been an over-commitment to correcting the disadvantages experienced by girls in schools. By the 1990s, published 'league tables' of school and student examination results appeared to confirm the discoveries. Girls appeared to be winning the highest marks in most school subjects. Sex discrimination policies were rewritten to include boys, including the new Gender Equity Strategy in New South Wales. Some argued that girls were more competent users of language than boys of the same age, and because boys learned more by doing than talking, curricula and pedagogy required urgent reform. It was a strange turn from Dale Spender's argument (Spender and Sarah, 1980) that girls were disadvantaged because they were silenced in co-educational classrooms as boys demanded too much teacher attention. In response, separate classes had sometimes been established for girls; in the 1990s, it appeared that boys required separate classes. The issues were complex, and some of the debate was caught up in wider gender conflict as some men ruminated on the presence of better educated and more powerful women in their homes and places of work (Gilbert and Gilbert, 1998). Some of it was also about the loss of working-class jobs for young people. It stood to reason that the boys who had previously entered the labour market at the age of 15 or 16, now finding themselves stuck in schools, would not respond well.

Relationships between schooling and the social class origins of children remained strong. The social characteristics of enrolments in government schools—primary and comprehensive secondary—were most likely closest to those of the general population, but much depended on the districts within which schools were located. With the end of strict school zoning and the rise of school markets, some schools rapidly residualised—like Broadmeadows in Melbourne, Elizabeth West in Adelaide and Mount Druitt in Sydney. Other public schools, if situated in more middle-class areas, did better. Many of the most socially exclusive schools were the public and non-government schools that selected their enrolments on academic potential. Highly educated, professionally employed parents were often successful at getting their children into such schools. Some of the most successful selective government schools were populated on a related ethnic basis as well. Many Chinese immigrant families, for example, pushed their children hard in a new kind of Saturday school, the coaching college, to achieve enrolments in selective schools (Campbell, Proctor and Sherington 2009).

If the period began with a new emphasis on correcting inequities in schooling, it ended with a much more diverse range of schools, in which long-standing hierarchies had been consolidated and new ones created. Neoliberal influences placed great emphasis on individual families acting entrepreneurially, exploiting the schooling opportunities available. Federal and state policies and funding supported the reorientation. There was less concern for those who could, or would, not manipulate the emerging school market for their private benefit.

Further reading

W.F. Connell's *Reshaping Australian Education* (1993) takes us to 1985. For the period, there is a rich literature in policy, curriculum, sociology and economics. Studies include Marginson (1993, 1997a, 1997b) and Welch (1996). Government reports, including those of the Schools Commission, are essential reading. On the commission and federal policy, see Dudley and Vidovich (1995). On alternative schools, see Pettit (1980) and Maslen (1982). On curriculum, see Yates, Collins and O'Connor (2011). R.W. Connell and collaborators are responsible for key works. *Making the Difference* (1982) examined the consequences of differentiated schooling, the Disadvantaged Schools Program (1991) and teachers' work (1985). Laughlin (1997), Teese (2000; Teese et al., 1995) and Thomson (2002) write with insight on the difficulties faced by schooling in areas marked by high unemployment and poverty. See reports of the Schools Council (1990) and a Senate committee (1998) on teachers and teaching. On gender and schooling, see Walker (1988), Kenway and Willis (1998), Gilbert and Gilbert (1998) and Connell (2000). On schooling for ethno-cultural difference, see Ozolins (1993), Bullivant (1987) and Kalantzis et al. (1990). Beresford and Partington (2003) is useful on Aboriginal education. On rural and remote schooling, see Human Rights and Equal Opportunity Commission (2000).

CHAPTER

8

The present and future school

In the course of writing this book, we have read the record of Australian schooling from the late eighteenth to the early twenty-first centuries. Some of these accounts find Australian schooling rather satisfactory and look to a future of continuing progress. Others are more critical—either of the schools and systems or of the children and families who populated them. The earliest accounts of schooling in Australia were characterised by anxiety for the moral future of a 'rising generation' in a colony founded in part as a prison. From the late nineteenth century, a common preoccupation was system-building; in the early 1940s, it was post-war reconstruction. Some accounts of schooling written in the effervescent and progressive early 1970s seem more dated from the perspective of a twenty-first century reader than many written in earlier periods. The re-evaluation of Australian education by historians began in earnest in the 1970s, although there are several useful publications that predate this. The purpose of this chapter is to bring the story of Australian schooling into the present, and to speculatively look into the future.

We do not subscribe to the view that the story of Australian schooling is one of perpetual progress, nor that it is one of descent from a golden age (whenever that might have been). The educational past was neither an entirely dark place from which we have now emerged, nor a better place in which every child was well-behaved and knew their spelling and grammar (for example). It is undeniable, however, that the story of Australian schooling is one of extraordinary growth. Schools have sometimes been overlooked in broader histories of Australia, yet they have played an important part in the national story—culturally, socially, economically and even politically. There is no civic institution that has had a greater impact on social and family life.

During the course of the nineteenth and early twentieth centuries, the experience of childhood became almost unimaginable without the school. In the twentieth century, the school captured more and more of adolescence as well as childhood. The school curriculum played a crucial part in the ordering and evaluation of knowledge, and new patterns of labour and employment have determined and been determined by school credentials. The school was a key site for nineteenth-century struggles between church and state and for the sectarian divide between Catholics and Protestants, that lasted well into the twentieth century. First in colonial and then state governments, and much later in federal governments, the size and importance of the education, schools and training ministries only grew.

In the early nineteenth century, schooling as we understand it today scarcely touched the lives of most of the children living in Australia. By the turn of the twentieth century, schools had declared a near-monopoly on basic instruction in reading, writing and arithmetic, and it had been accepted by the government of every colony that the state should provide elementary or primary schooling for all (non-Indigenous) children. Children under the age of about 14 increasingly were discouraged or excluded from participation in paid or productive labour. Although the public schools were run by highly centralised bureaucracies, they nevertheless spawned communities, as did the non-government schools. People made friends at school, formed opinions or prejudices and were sometimes told whether or not they would ever amount to anything. They read the same books, learned the same history and science and played the same playground games. The fact that certain categories of children—notably Indigenous children and many children with disabilities—were either excluded from schools or frequently marginalised within them arguably only increased their power. The historical growth of the school has meant that children have commonly had more schooling than their parents did. This was especially so in the second half of the twentieth century.

In immigrant families from language backgrounds other than English, this generation gap has sometimes been considerable as schools have helped assimilate children into the dominant culture more rapidly and thoroughly than their parents.

In the twenty-first century, prolonged attendance at both primary and high school is near-universal for children and youth. The experience of secondary schooling became both commonplace and compulsory from the 1950s and 1960s, and persistence through to the final year of high school became a majority experience from the 1980s. In 2012, around 80 per cent of students who began high school persisted to the final year (Australian Bureau of Statistics, 2012). The patterns of persistence were uneven, however. They varied with gender and class (middle-class girls were more likely to persist than boys in general) and school sector (with government schools accommodating more of the students who left prior to their final year than either Catholic or independent schools). Indigenous students were still much less likely to remain at school, with 2012 the first year in which a majority did so.

Indigenous schooling is an area of current policy priority, and a significant issue for Aboriginal and Torres Strait Islander leaders and communities (Pearson, 2009). By many measures, Indigenous students experience worse outcomes than non-Indigenous students. In 2008, for example, just over 63 per cent of Indigenous school children met what is considered to be a 'minimum' reading standard, compared with over 90 per cent of non-Indigenous children (Rigney, 2011, p. 40). Significant numbers of Indigenous students—especially teenage boys—continue to be the least academically successful of Australian students. The field is characterised by some of the most innovative and creative practice in Australia, and also some of the most complex disadvantage—sometimes with the two coexisting on the same site. There is considerable diversity from region to region. Schools enrolling large numbers of Indigenous young people are situated in the most urban to the most remote districts. Many schools in middle-class suburbs in Australia's cities have few students who identify as Indigenous. In the Northern Territory, half of primary and two-fifths of secondary students are Indigenous. Where communities experience high degrees of unemployment and poverty, school attendance and school effectiveness are profoundly affected. Then there are the tiny remote government primary schools with few services and amenities, yet strong community ties. For significant numbers in remote areas, English is a second, or even third or fourth language. One of the curriculum development areas in Indigenous education is the encouragement of Indigenous languages where they are still commonly used, and their reinvigoration where they are not.

The most dynamic population growth in Australian education is in the institutions at either end of schooling. In 2008, an Australian government review of higher education recommended that 40 per cent of 25- to 34-year-olds should have a degree-level qualification by 2020 (Bradley, 2008, p. xiv). Increasingly, the final high school credential is used as a qualification for further study rather than direct entry into the labour market. This is having an impact on both schools and higher education institutions.

New 'faith' schools flourished with federal government funding. The Malek Fahd Islamic School was often in the news as it sought distinction in public examinations and negotiated its relationships with Islamic and wider communities. A classroom scene, Sydney, 2004. (National Library of Australia, nla.pic-vn3123464)

Also in 2008, the state and federal Ministers of Education counted the development of early childhood education as a policy priority in their Melbourne Declaration on Educational Goals for Young Australians (MCEETYA, 2008). The early childhood sector comprises several different kinds of institutions, which among them provide a mix of day-care and pre-schooling. Many charge high fees, and there is considerable variation in supply from place to place—especially outside the cities and larger towns. Access is far from universal, especially for Indigenous children and the children of poorer parents. The sector is highly privatised, but governments operate strict regulatory frameworks for accreditation and registration, and are major providers themselves. The provision of early childhood education has been intimately connected with debates about participation in the paid workforce of mothers of young children at least since the 1970s, but currently the rationale for the expansion of access is usually framed in human capital terms, with an emphasis on 'school readiness'. For example:

> Children who participate in quality early childhood education are more likely to make a successful transition to school, stay longer in school, continue on to further education and fully participate in employment and community life as adults. (MCEETYA, 2008, p. 11)

This is a similar rationale to the one that has underpinned state and national government policies since the 1980s: encouraging young people to remain at school beyond the age of compulsion. In the twenty-first century, it seems, there is no such thing as too much education.

The remainder of this chapter identifies a number of current issues in schooling, beginning with the much-discussed topics of 'teacher quality' and 'quality teaching'.

In February 2012, the flagship ABC TV program *Four Corners* aired an episode titled 'Revolution in the Classroom', for which a team of filmmakers documented aspects of the daily life of three high schools. We describe the documentary in a little detail here because of the way in which it illustrates some current preoccupations about school teaching (see Carney and Cohen, 2012), and also because it provides a snapshot of school life in the early twenty-first century.

The first school we see in the documentary is Toronto High School, in regional New South Wales. It is a public school, looking a little run-down. A teacher is making announcements through a microphone above the chatter of students who are sitting on the ground under a large shade awning. The acoustics are bad, but she presses on. Despite its unprepossessing appearance, this is apparently a school in which a new principal has effected a dramatic turnaround. Toronto High, we are told, was out of control just a few years ago, its playground so violent that there was a designated car space for police vehicles. And the examination results were woeful. Things are better now: one student admits that she looks forward to going to school each day. Another has achieved good enough results in her Higher School Certificate to study law at university.

The second school is Knox Grammar, a wealthy boys' school in Sydney. Here the camera shows us impressive buildings and grounds, including a spacious assembly hall. The smiling boys arrive at school, apparently unselfconscious in their crazy uniform of khaki shorts, blue blazers and straw boaters. This school too was under-performing, if only in relation to the schools at the top of the Year 12 league tables—schools with which its fee-paying parents, and therefore the school itself, compared it. The featured student is a boy in his final year who is good at mathematics but struggles with his English results. (He is not from an immigrant background; over 80 per cent of Knox's students come from an English-speaking background.) He manages to do well enough in his worst subject to achieve entry to his desired university course.

The third site, Hume Central Secondary College in Victoria—another public school—is a new foundation that replaced three high schools in an economically depressed area of Melbourne. Considered to be without hope, all three were shut down and reopened as a consolidated multi-campus school. The featured student achieves entry to university—the first in his family to do so, as his proud mother attests.

The documentary is built around the idea that, properly run, any school can do well. It partly takes its cue from devolution policies that increased school autonomy and partly from a present concern—international in scope—with classroom pedagogy and teacher 'quality'. Each of the school principals was recruited expressly to provide strong leadership, in the manner of a chief executive officer, and to improve the performance standards of the classroom teachers in the schools. The principal of Toronto High was part of a school autonomy pilot program, given more than usual latitude to manage his own budget, including enough money to hire an extra senior teacher. The principal of Hume Central was appointed as a 'super' or executive principal, headhunted for the position, and given an individual employment contract with a higher than usual salary—although still only a fraction of the remuneration packages given to many principals of the wealthiest rung of corporate schools. A few years ago, it may have been possible to distinguish, simply from appearances, the head of an elite independent school from the head of a public school in a disadvantaged area. The campuses of the three schools in the documentary look very different, but the three men look similarly businesslike in crisp collared shirts and dark suits. This might seem a superficial observation, but it exemplifies the conservative flavour of much school reform in the twenty-first century—not to mention the persistence of a gender imbalance in the top jobs in secondary schools.

The core mission for each of these principals was to raise the standard of classroom interaction. Resources, class sizes and so on are all well and good, runs the argument, but what really counts is good teachers in everyday classrooms—whether in superannuated demountable classrooms or architect-designed postmodern teaching spaces. To some extent, the kinds of student–teacher conversations going on in each of the schools look timeless. The principals, for example, are shown engaging in avuncular, friendly-ironic banter with their students—a kind of talk that is familiar to anyone who has ever set foot inside a school. Each of the schools, however, is engaged in an intensive, management-driven campaign of teacher development.

A sports coaching metaphor is used by the Hume Central principal to describe his approach. A staff member comments:

> He's got such high expectations and he's never satisfied and he's constantly pushing, but he seems to know, you know, how far he can push, and so he's push, push, push with his leadership team . . . and he coaches us and supports us, drives us constantly.

While each of the schools in the documentary displays qualitative evidence of improvement, it is clear that success has to be demonstrated according to Australia's national and state standardised student assessment tests, such as the long-standing New South Wales Higher School Certificate, and the newer National Assessment Plan–Literacy and Numeracy (NAPLAN), established in 2008. Each of the schools had indeed improved its ranking on state or national 'league tables'.

If one significant characteristic of Australian schooling in the twenty-first century is a preoccupation with school effectiveness, another is the persistence of inequality. According to the broad

In the new century the significance of high-stakes testing rapidly grew. The test results of NAPLAN (National Assessment Program: Literacy and Numeracy) formed a major component of the My School website. Here, Year 9 students are tested at Unley High, South Australia, 2008. (Campbell, 2010, p. 277)

measure of social advantage on the Federal government's My School website, Knox Grammar and the two government schools in 'Revolution in the Classroom' have extremely different populations. Seventy-five per cent of Knox's students are categorised in the top quartile of the website's scale of 'socio-educational advantage' and only 1 per cent in the bottom quartile. For Toronto and Hume, the numbers are almost the reverse, with 7 and 4 per cent in the top quartile respectively and 55 and 45 in the bottom quartile. This means that a typical student at Knox will have at least one parent who has experience, skill and success in senior high school, and probably tertiary education. If students stay on at school past the minimum leaving age, a typical student at either Toronto or Hume will likely be a family pioneer of post-compulsory education. At the school for the more educationally advantaged students, there are likely vastly more material and cultural resources. This educationally relevant resource wealth likely occurs in their homes as well.

During the 2000s, Pat Thomson's (2002) teaching fable, 'Vicki and Thanh', became a staple of pre-service teacher education reading lists. It was about social and cultural capital. Two fictional children start school for the first time. One child has parents in well-paid professional jobs, the other is from a non-English speaking immigrant family with limited schooling experience. One of the children arrives at school already equipped with many of the skills and techniques needed to make the most of her first year of schooling. The other has an equivalent or even greater volume and level of knowledge and skills upon starting school—including a working knowledge of three languages—but these are less closely aligned with the curriculum and culture of the standard Australian classroom. Thanh has to work harder. Through 'Vicki and Thanh', Thomson was, among other things, trying to move beyond cultural deficit explanations of schooling inequality. Her account of the two children provided a practical theoretical framework, grounded in sociological facts, for prospective and current classroom teachers.

In the twenty-first century, the well-understood causal connections between relative parental advantage and children's educational fortunes have been confirmed anew through national and international surveys such as those informing Australia's My School website and the OECD's Program for Student Assessment (PISA). Whether or not policy-makers have prioritised educational inequality as an issue in recent times (broadly speaking, Labor governments tend to do so more than Liberal-National Coalition governments), the emphasis on addressing educational problems through the management and 'improvement' of classroom teachers and school principals has dominated policy. Policy-makers of most backgrounds have united around the following approach, here spoken by John Hattie, an expert on school improvement, for the *Four Corners* program:

> Outside of the home environment and the family situation, the biggest impact on a kid's education is teacher effectiveness . . . If you have a teacher, one of the top performing teachers in Australia compared to one of the least effective teachers in Australia, that can be as much as a year's difference.

Such confidence in the measuring of teacher and teaching effects on student achievement is rhetorically powerful. Sometimes the discussion of teacher effectiveness is punitive, with the idea that the 'problem' with public schools in particular is too many bad teachers. On the other hand, the focus on the teacher in the classroom has resulted—positively—in some practical attention being paid to routine teaching work. According to Hayes and colleagues (2006, p. 19), 'Teachers' pedagogical and assessment practices do matter, and . . . they particularly matter for those students from disadvantaged backgrounds'. 'Authentic pedagogy' and 'productive pedagogy' are two of the terms created to describe broadly similar sets of principles developed by education researchers that aim to enrich classroom experience. Probably the most influential pedagogies research in the 1990s came out of the University of Wisconsin. In Australia, this work was taken up and developed in Queensland (Hayes et al., 2006), and has been used widely in teacher education and professional development. Versions of it were adapted and absorbed into Department of Education policies across the country, notably in Queensland, South Australia and New South Wales.

Another element of the focus on the classroom teacher has been the development of 'professional teacher standards'. By the middle of the first decade of the century all states and territories had established teacher registration bodies, under which 'new scheme' teachers in public and non-government schools had to demonstrate their achievement of sets of competencies. (Some states, such as Queensland, converted existing teacher registration systems. For others, such as New South Wales, teacher registration was a new endeavour.) In 2012, a set of national teacher standards was adopted by all states and territories. The rationale was clear:

> Standards contribute to the professionalisation of teaching and raise the status of the profession. They could also be used as the basis for a professional accountability model, helping to ensure that teachers can demonstrate appropriate levels of professional knowledge, professional practice and professional engagement. (Australian Institute for Teaching and School Leadership, 2012)

Despite well-founded criticism (e.g. see Connell, 2009), both teacher registration and the teacher standards documents were accepted without much opposition. This was partly because the new standards were introduced gradually through new teachers, rather than being imposed across the board, and partly because many in the profession identified possibilities within the standards frameworks for better recognition of the complexity and importance of teachers' work.

Australia's public school systems remain highly centralised, especially by international standards, but the current movement is towards increasing the independence of public schools from central office management, and increasing the relative authority of the school principal as the person who will organise, manage and inspire classroom improvement and teacher competence. In Western Australia, for example, so-called 'independent public schools' are funded according to the same formula as other public schools in the state, but given a one-line budget to be managed locally by the principal. While the schools ultimately remain under the control of the Education Department, some of the governance is devolved to a school board comprising staff, parent and business, 'industry and community' representatives. Part of the rationale is to encourage 'choice' and variety in public schooling, and it is assumed that this will be facilitated by community engagement. The independent public schools, it is argued, offer the best of all worlds—local flexibility, but with the support of larger Education Department systems.

In some ways this sounds exactly what successive commentators have been recommending for Australia since the New Education Fellowship visitors in the 1930s. Yet Martin Forsey's (2007) story of devolution gone wrong in a Western Australian public high school is illustrative of the more consumerist and competitive potential of such policies. In this school, a strong attempt was made to screen out or exclude students who had the potential to lower the average academic performance or damage the school's public image. A different approach to community engagement can be found in a South Australian study of a successful multi-racial kindergarten known for its harmony and effectiveness, despite being located in a country town that is, according to one of the study's informants, 'a racial powder keg just waiting to go off' (Imtoual, Kameniar and Bradley, 2009, p. 2). The kindergarten's success is founded on practices that are quite at odds with those described by Forsey. There is a policy not only of open and transparent enrolment but also of active embrace of the families whose children attend—no matter what the difficulty or complexity of their circumstances may be. The kindergarten actively encourages 'problem parents' and their children. The material structure required for supporting this encouragement and engagement—including higher than usual staff:student ratios—is partly the result of expert and dogged lobbying and grant-writing by its director and her teachers.

Differential provision has long been a characteristic of schooling in Australia. In times past, different schools and different curricula within schools were firmly based on a belief that different school populations, marked by gender, class, race and intelligence, naturally required differential provision. While in recent times those old causes of differential schooling for different populations have not disappeared, the new school markets and school funding arrangements have changed the character of the differences and divisions. Where 'provision' was once the key word in explaining difference, now 'choice' and the efforts of individual families to make their way in a schools 'market' add the idea that schools simply meet the needs of the new 'consumers' rather than more deliberately structuring access to different curricula and different kinds of schools.

This has had an effect on school 'communities'. First, children and youth are less likely to attend their nearest school, especially in city areas and especially at the secondary level. A school 'community' may have little meaning in terms of families living in proximity to one another. More importantly, compared with other OECD nations, the Australian school system is more socially segmented. Australian school students are more likely to be found in schools with a narrow socio-economic mix. Only about a third of students are in schools that have an average or mixed socio-economic status, a proportion well outside the OECD norm (Nous Group, 2011). Contributing to this has been a well-documented drift since the late 1970s from public to non-government schools. (Tables 8.1 and 8.2.)

In recent years, governments have argued that parents' ability to choose their children's school is a positive response to family aspirations; this is frequently framed in public debate as a parental entitlement (rarely as a child's entitlement). Yet it is difficult to see how a consumer-driven allocation of enrolments can operate without creating hierarchies of schools, children and youth. This is a major challenge facing those policy-makers who are concerned with both equity and choice. There is a strong and significant correlation between socio-economic status and school type, with many non-government schools enrolling disproportionate numbers of relatively

TABLE 8.1

Students in Australian schools by school sector, 2012

	No.	%
Government	2 342 379	65.2
Catholic	736 595	20.5
Independent	511 012	14.2
Total	3 589 986	*100.0*

Source: ABS, (2012, Table 40).

TABLE 8.2

Change in shares of school sector enrolment (full-time students), 2001–2012 (%)

	2001	2012	Change
Primary			
Government	72.4	68.9	–3.5
Catholic	18.9	19.4	0.5
Independent	8.7	11.7	3.1
Total	*100.0*	*100.0*	
Secondary			
Government	63.7	59.8	–3.9
Catholic	21.2	22.4	1.2
Independent	15.1	17.8	2.7
Total	*100.0*	*100.0*	

Source: ABS (2012, Table 40).

privileged children and public schools enrolling disproportionate numbers of disadvantaged children, especially children with multiple and complex disadvantages (Preston, 2013).

Arguably the most contentious issue in Australian education today is the relative amount of public financial subsidy given to public and non-government schools by federal governments. In 1973, many government school supporters accepted the entrenchment of public funding for non-government schools because of the prospect of increased funding for all schools. Since 1975, however, the federal funding of non-government schools has increased relative to that provided to government schools, despite their different educational responsibilities. The Liberal-National government of John Howard (1996–2007) substantially increased the allocation of federal funding to non-government schools (Watson, 2003). Non-government school subsidies, it was argued, facilitated the consumer's right of choice.

Under Labor in 2013, the funding model continued to favour the non-government sector, despite the blueprint for change developed by a review of national school funding arrangements commissioned by federal Education Minister, Julia Gillard. The Gonski Report (2011) recommended an increase in government investment in all schools, but especially government schools. The panel's terms of reference made it clear that non-government schools should not lose existing levels of government income under any proposed change in funding arrangements. Nevertheless, the review panel advocated a better balance of funding, arguing that the schools most in need were public schools. The report recommended a substantial reinvestment in 'disadvantaged' schools and 'disadvantaged' students, and a more transparent and less complex system of allocation.

At the time of writing, the fate of the Gonski recommendations is unclear. School funding is such a highly charged issue in Australia that its politics overbalance sensible policy-making. One thing that gave the Gonski panel widespread credibility was that enough members of the panel, including its chair, had indisputable non-government—including Catholic—school credentials that their pro-public school funding recommendations were not easily dismissed. A second element was the report's argument that a fairer funding system would benefit the nation as a whole. It had become increasingly apparent in the research literature that those national systems of education that were most characterised by hierarchies of schools based on the wealth and ethno-religious and class characteristics of parents, and academic selection, were not 'performing' as well as more unified systems. The Gonski report summarised this research and reported it as a call to reform in Australia. Drawing substantially on the widely accepted PISA achievement rankings, the report argued that Australia's performance was in decline, and that there was an unacceptable gap between the highest and lowest performing students, as well as an unacceptable link between low performance and socio-economic disadvantage. Those young people in Australia's low-performing 'tail' of students were not even meeting minimum standards.

Government spending on education in Australia is lower than the OECD average. Private spending, on the other hand, is above average, because of the large numbers of non-government schools. All Australian schools are funded by both state and federal governments. Public schools get most of their funding from state governments (in 2011 about 80 per cent on average, with about 15 per cent on average from the federal government). Catholic system schools get the bulk of their funding from the federal government (57 per cent on average, with 20 per cent on average from state or territory governments). The average figures for independent schools make little sense because there is a huge disparity between the wealthiest and the least wealthy independent schools—a much larger gap than in either the public sector or the Catholic systems. However, close to three-quarters of independent schools receive over half of their funding from governments (see Gonski, 2011, pp. 13–16).

Australia does not yet have 'for-profit' schools in the primary and secondary area—in fact, it is contrary to the rules of government funding. The pre-school/child-care sector is very different, however, with a mix of provision reminiscent of schooling in the nineteenth century. It includes informal, unregistered child-minding by neighbours, friends and relatives, not-for-profit and small for-profit pre-schools and child-care centres, and, until 2008, market domination by the stockmarket-listed ABC Corporation, which expanded rapidly during the first decade of the century and then collapsed just as dramatically in the wake of the Global Financial Crisis.

Australia is internationally unusual in its high proportions of students enrolled in non-government schools, most of which are owned by or affiliated with religious organisations. We discuss other aspects of Australia's mix of public and 'private' schooling in this chapter, but it is clear that the numbers of children receiving a religiously influenced schooling have increased since the 1980s, and this trend shows every indication of continuing. It is hard to know what this will mean for the future. How religious are church-owned schools? Will Australia become more religious as a nation? While the church schools seem to be quite full, the traditional Christian church congregations are in decline. Will the churches fill up too? In research we conducted a few years ago, we found that not all parents who enrolled their children in religiously affiliated schools were happy with the religious teaching and school culture; some of them liked other aspects of the schools and were prepared to tolerate the religious teaching in order to access them (Campbell, Proctor and Sherington, 2009).

For the schools and the churches there are some tensions too, including how to negotiate some of the more socially conservative religious teachings while dealing with the diverse realities of modern families. Recently, for example, alongside the annual soft news features about how much girls are spending on their school formal dresses, newspapers have begun to carry reports about teenagers in religiously affiliated schools barred from taking same-sex partners to school socials. And the popularity of Catholic schools amongst non-Catholics is seen as a mixed blessing for some church people if it threatens to dilute the maintenance of the faith (Pell, 2006). In Sydney, the Australian Anglican church's least liberal diocese, the ruling body recently attempted to limit the possible influence of non-church members (including non-Christians) over the management and governance of its schools by introducing a rule requiring school principals and members of school boards to sign formal statements of faith.

One of the trends of the late twentieth and early twenty-first centuries was a rediscovery of school 'values', the moral and citizenship purposes of schooling, in a context of intensive discussions about immigration, race, religion, social conflict and terrorism. The right-wing politician Pauline Hanson had objected to 'Asian' immigration and welfare 'handouts' to Aboriginal people during the late 1990s. Flashpoints in the early twenty-first century included the Al Qaeda terrorist attacks overseas and the so-called 'Cronulla riots' in southern Sydney in 2005, and assaults on Indian tertiary students in Melbourne a little later. Each of these phenomena became, one way or another, matters with which schools had to deal. Schools spent time educating students—and teachers—about Islam, multiculturalism and what it was to be Australian. McLeod and Yates (2006) found in their study of Victorian schools that students had a good understanding of the language of anti-racism and tolerance: 'For some there was a finely tuned sense of answering in the right way, of anticipating our views, and tailoring answers to satisfy, please or shock us.' (2006, p. 158). In another study, Muslim students offered responses like the following, from Perth school student 'Aziz', to questions about what it means to be Australian after the Cronulla riots:

> Well, I think a good Australian is someone who stands up for people's rights and is tolerant and is accepting of other people's cultures and other people's beliefs and isn't afraid to say how they truly feel, and to stand up for what they feel is wrong. (Kabir, 2007, p. 66.)

As part of a broader interest in citizenship and Australian identity and patriotism, during the era of the Howard government, both the Prime Minister and the Education Minister made several interventions into the field of school 'values', including a rather inflammatory comment by Howard in 2004 that public schools had become too 'values-neutral' (Crabb and Guerera, 2004). On Australia Day in 2006, the Prime Minster spoke about the importance of teaching Australian history in schools in order to strengthen citizenship values. Few students, he argued, were being taught enough Australian history,

Primary school children witness and celebrate the national apology to the stolen generations of Aboriginal children, Canberra, 2008. (National Library of Australia, nla.pic-vn3123464)

and when they were it was often 'a fragmented stew of "themes" and "issues"', paying insufficient regard to the nation's achievements. History ought to be compulsory and it ought to better explain the national heritage.' (Howard, 2006) In 2007, federal Education Minister Brendan Nelson instituted a National Values Framework, which sought to codify the values to be taught in Australian schools, including things like 'care and compassion', 'doing your best' and 'tolerance' (DEEWR, 2005).

One trend in the late twentieth-century history of Australian schooling that has continued into the new millennium is the importance of federal governments in schooling. From 2007, the Labor governments of Kevin Rudd and Julia Gillard were ambitious in their desire for an 'Education Revolution', as it was termed in their 2007 election campaign. Early activity included the 'Digital Education Revolution', under which a whole cohort of junior high school students was given laptop computers. The government's Global Financial Crisis response saw massive expenditure on new buildings in government and non-government schools—a means of countering a predicted economic recession. The 2008 Melbourne Declaration on Educational Goals for Young Australians, issued by the Ministerial Council on Education, Training and Youth Affairs (2008), a body that brings together the federal, state and territory Education Ministers, included statements on 'quality teaching and school leadership', 'promoting world class curriculum and assessment', 'improving educational outcomes for Indigenous youth and disadvantaged young Australians, especially those from low socioeconomic backgrounds' and strengthening 'accountability and transparency'.

Apart from commissioning the Gonski review of school funding, the most ambitious action of the Labor government was to establish the Australian Curriculum and Assessment Authority (ACARA), charged with oversight of the new national assessment program (NAPLAN), the development of a national school curriculum and the design and implementation of the My School website (<www.myschool.edu.au>). ACARA is a remarkable organisation with a big influence on the operation of schools (though at the time of writing it was possible that it would not survive a change of government). In mid-2013, its board was chaired by Barry McGaw, whose previous posts included periods as Director for Education at the OECD and Executive Director of the Australian Council for Educational Research. ACARA has been responsible for much of the coordination of the implementation of the Melbourne Declaration. Its ambition to transform Australian schooling is arguably as great as was the Whitlam government's Australian School Commission in the early 1970s, but within a very different global and national context. In addition to an explicit emphasis on social equity, the animating principles are individual choice and international competiveness. In common with other nations, Australia closely watches the annual PISA rankings. The annual full-cohort testing of students and the public reporting of statistical information on levels of educational achievement are essential features of national education policy, including those policies aimed at addressing socio-economic inequality.

A centrepiece of the federal government's reforms is the My School website, which publishes and compares the NAPLAN results of nearly every school in the country. Its establishment in 2010 transformed NAPLAN from diagnostic to 'high-stakes' testing, revealing individual schools to be either keeping up with, moving ahead of or falling behind other schools with similar social profiles, on the basis of their students' aggregate scores in these short annual English and mathematics examinations. Apparent progress from year to year was also measured and graphed. There is some space on the website for other elements of a school's purpose, culture and achievement to be described, but these arguably lack the impact of the colour-coded rankings. Where My School differs from comparable sites in some other countries, however, is in its attempt to contextualise the NAPLAN results for each school in relation to the social and cultural capital of its constituent families. An Index of Community Socio-Educational Advantage (ICSEA) was developed to perform the task. The main data used in the algorithm are parents' occupation and education levels. The site also includes easily compared information about the wealth and income of each school. ACARA refuses to publish statewide or nationwide tables revealing the 'best' and 'worst' schools. Nevertheless, the news media are quick to compile and publish statewide, and sometimes nationwide league tables.

As well as testing and reporting, ACARA has managed the design and ongoing implementation of a national curriculum. This is no small achievement in a nation where major curriculum decisions have been tightly controlled by state government authorities for well over a century. An earlier attempt by the Labor Education Minister John Dawkins in the late 1980s and early 1990s eventually foundered in the process of consultation with the states. By early 2013, however, the states had agreed to common curriculum frameworks for English, mathematics, science and history for the compulsory years of schooling. Curricula were in development for other subject areas and for the senior high school years.

•

Some institutions persist over very long periods. One of these is surely the school. From their beginnings in Australia, high hopes were held for what they might achieve, both by their providers and often their users. Arguments about how schooling might improve individuals, families, communities, colonies, states and the nation have changed over time—sometimes dramatically. It is a plausible hypothesis that the most persistent institutions are those that adapt to changing circumstances. Schools certainly do adapt. Showing how that has occurred is at the heart of the argument in this book. Nevertheless, some schools strain to retain age-old purposes. The ideal school for boys from oligarchic families in Plato's *Republic* had training the future governing class at the heart of its mission. A curriculum required for that purpose would be very different from what was provided for the children of lower class citizens, let alone slaves, metics—and girls. This history of Australian schooling has shown a democratisation of the school experience over its more than two centuries of history, yet curriculum arrangements and the provision of different kinds of schools—more or less difficult to enter—also see a persistence of very old patterns. Schools remain powerful institutions for producing more and less powerful social groups and classes, and hierarchies in society. Sometimes schools transform not very promising lives for the better, and sometimes this occurs deliberately as well as accidentally. Schools are complex institutions that resist easy analysis. Nevertheless, the provision and improvement of schools—including the demand that young people be subject to their disciplines for ever longer periods of time (nearly all states now require young people to be in education or training through to 17 years of age)—remains at the heart of much public policy.

We know that the following things are true in the second decade of the twenty-first century. Australia is a relatively prosperous country and has had lower unemployment rates than many comparable nations. Australians, on average, enjoy good health and have high life expectancies. At the same time, there has also been an overall increase in inequality over the past two decades, measured by income and wealth disparity. Some 5 per cent of adults experience multiple and complex disadvantage according to a number of indicators. This explains some of the possible relationships children from many families have with their schools. In 2011, 14 per cent of children aged under 15 were living in jobless families, and Australia performed no better than average relative to comparable nations in the relationship between educational outcomes and socio-economic background. Although Australia ranked highly in international league tables of student achievement at the beginning of the millennium, its rank declined somewhat between 2000 and 2009 (see Gonski, 2011; Nous Group, 2011; Taylor, Borlagdan and Allan, 2012).

What of the future? There are no easy predictions to make. The characteristics of the Australian population continue to change as immigration continues, and the old working class and its institutions decline. The phenomena summarised by the term 'globalisation', from the restructure of Australia's economy—including its labour market—through to the impacts of new information technologies, continue to change substantial areas of social and individual life. Controversies over the roles that government interventions should play in the sustaining of institutions such as schools will continue. Policy change can occur quite rapidly.

What does seem likely to continue is an increasing need for students to undergo prolonged schooling to obtain satisfactory employment. Schools will continue to structure much of the experience of childhood and youth, although new and ever more intrusive communications technologies and media will do the same, sometimes to greater effect. Families will also adapt their approaches to schooling in order to secure safe futures, where possible, for their children. The school building, and the teacher, appear to be with us for some time yet. But what happens inside the school, and what the teacher does, have changed dramatically over the past several years, and the likelihood of continuing 'change' is one prediction about which we are confident. 'Virtual classrooms', not so long ago a fantasy, exist for increasing numbers of young people. How we arrived at this present and probable future, however, is only explicable by reflecting on its history.

Further reading

Gonski (2011) provides a remarkable analysis of the early twenty-first century in Australian education. See Connell et al. (2013) for comprehensive essays on contemporary Australian schooling, especially the social impact. On school choice, markets and social class, see Campbell, Proctor and Sherington (2009) and Forsey, Davies and Walford (2008) for the global context. On curriculum, see Yates, Collins and O'Connor (2011). On schooling and the 'making of modern lives', see McLeod and Yates (2006) and Taylor, Borlagdan and Allan (2012). On Indigenous issues, including language policy, see Neumann (2012) and also Pearson (2009). On social justice and schooling, see Teese and Polesel (2003). On early childhood, see Elliott (2006) and Brennan (2007). On government secondary schooling, see Campbell and Sherington (2013). For most of the 200-year history of education in Australia, with the voices of the participants to the forefront, see Niall and Britain (1997).

Select bibliography including references

I Collections of documents

Adams, D. 1984, *Non Government Schooling in Western Australia 1829–1903*, WA Institute of Technology, Perth.

Amies, M. and Zainu'ddin, A. 1988, *Gladly would they Learn and Gladly Teach: Australian women and education*, Monash University, Melbourne.

Austin, A.G. 1972a, *Select Documents in Australian Education, 1788–1900*, Pitman, Melbourne.

Austin, A.G. and Selleck, R.J.W. 1975, *The Australian Government School 1830–1914: Select documents with commentary*, Pitman, Melbourne.

Dow, G. and Factor, J. (eds) 1991, *Australian Childhood: An anthology*, McPhee Gribble, Melbourne.

Fletcher, J.J. 1989b. *Documents in the History of Aboriginal Education in New South Wales*, the author, Sydney.

Griffiths, D.C. (ed.) 1957, *Documents on the Establishment of Education in New South Wales 1789–1880*, ACER, Melbourne.

Haynes, B.T. (ed.) 1976, *Documents on Western Australian education, 1830–1973*, Claremont Teachers College, Perth.

Hyams, B. et al. 1988, *Learning and Other Things: Sources for a social history of education in South Australia*, South Australian Government Printer, Adelaide.

Jolly, E. 2001, *A Broader Vision: Voices of vocational education in twentieth-century South Australia*, Michael Deves, Adelaide.

Neal, W.D. (ed.) 1979, *Education in Western Australia*, University of WA Press, Perth.

Niall, B. and Britain, I. (eds) 1997, *The Oxford Book of Australian Schooldays*, OUP, Melbourne.

Turney, C. (ed.) 1975, *Sources in the History of Australian Education: 1788–1970*, Angus & Robertson, Sydney.

II Other works

ACER, 1956, Review of Education in Australia 1948–1954, the author, Melbourne.

——, 1964, *Review of Education in Australia 1955–1962*, the author, Melbourne.

Anderson, D. 1992, 'The interaction of public and private school systems', *Australian Journal of Education*, vol. 36, pp. 213–236.

Angus, M. 2001, Our future: Report of a survey of Australian government primary school principals, Australian Primary Principals Association, Melbourne.

Armitage, A. 1983, *Newcastle High School*, Newcastle High School, Newcastle.

Artarmon Public School, 2010, *Artarmon Public School Centenary, 1910–2010*, the author, Sydney.

Austin, A.G. 1958, *George William Rusden and National Education in Australia 1849–1862*, MUP, Melbourne.

——1966, *The Australian School*, Longmans, Melbourne.

——1972b, *Australian Education 1788–1900: Church, state and public education in colonial Australia*, Pitman, Melbourne.

Austin, A.G. and Selleck, R.J.W. 1975, *The Australian Government School 1830–1914*, Pitman, Melbourne.

Australian Education Council 1989, The Hobart Declaration on Schooling, the author, Canberra.

Australian Institute for Teaching and School Leadership, 2012, National Professional Standards for Teachers: Purpose, http://www.teacherstandards.aitsl.edu.au/Overview/Purpose, accessed 23 October 2012.

Australian Labor Party, 1972, *Policy Speech*, the author, Canberra.
Baker, D. 1998, *Preacher, Politician, Patriot: A life of John Dunmore Lang*, MUP, Melbourne.
Barcan, A. 1980, *A History of Australian Education*, OUP, Melbourne.
——1988, *Two Centuries of Education in New South Wales*, NSWU Press, Sydney.
Bean, C.E.W. 1950, *Here, My Son: An account of the independent and other corporate boys' schools of Australia*, Angus & Robertson, Sydney.
Benjamin, Z. 1950, *The School-child and his Parents*, Angus & Robertson, Sydney.
Beresford, Q. and Partington, G. (eds) 2003, *Reform and Resistance in Aboriginal Education*, UWA Press, Perth.
Bergonzi, B. 2003, *A Victorian Wanderer: The Life of Thomas Arnold the Younger*, OUP, Oxford.
Berndt, R.M. and Berndt, C.H. 1977, *The World of the First Australians*, Ure Smith, Sydney.
Bessant, B. (ed.) 1987, *Mother State and her Little Ones: Children and youth in Australia 1860s-1930s*, Phillip Institute of Technology, Melbourne.
Bessant, B. 1976, 'Domestic science schools and woman's place', *The Australian Journal of Education*, vol. 20, no. 1, pp. 1–9.
——1983, *Schooling in the Colony and State of Victoria*, La Trobe University, Melbourne.
——1991, '"Progress" and revision in the history of education in the 1980s', *Discourse*, vol. 12, no. 1, pp. 67–84.
Bessant, B. and Spaull, A.D. 1976, *Politics of Schooling*, Pitman, Melbourne.
Bigge, J.T. 1823, Report of the Commissioner of Enquiry on the State of Agriculture and Trade in the Colony of New South Wales. *Parliamentary Papers*, Great Britain, no. 119, London.
Blackmore, J. 1992, *Making Educational History: A feminist perspective*, Deakin University, Geelong.
Blake, L.J. (ed.) 1973, *Vision and Realisation: A centenary history of state education in Victoria*, Department of Education of Victoria, Melbourne.
Bongiorno, F. 2012, *The Sex Lives of Australians: A history*, Black Inc, Melbourne.
Bonnor, C. and Caro, J. 2007, *The Stupid Country: How Australia is dismantling public education*, UNSW Press, Sydney.
Boyd, H.V. 1848, *Letters on education*, W. & F. Ford, Sydney.
Bradley (Chair), D. 2008, Review of Australian Higher Education: Final Report, Australian Government, Canberra.
Braniff, J. 2001, *From Cradle to Canonisation: A short history of St Patrick's Marist College*, St Patrick's Marist College, Sydney.
Brennan, D. 1998, *The Politics of Australian Child Care*, CUP, Cambridge.
——2007, 'The ABC of childcare politics', *Australian Journal of Social Issues*, vol. 42, no. 2, pp. 213–225.
Brett, J. 1992, *Menzies' Forgotten People*, Macmillan Australia, Sydney.
Brice, I. 1997, 'Reluctant schoolmaster in a voluntarist colony: William Cawthorne's diary, 1842–44', *Journal of the Historical Society of South Australia*, no. 25, pp. 80–93.
Brook, J. and Kohen, J.L. 1991, *The Parramatta Native Institution and the Black Town*, NSWU Press, Sydney.
Broome, R. 2010, *Aboriginal Australians*, Allen & Unwin, Sydney.
Browne, G.S. (ed.) 1927, *Education in Australia*, Macmillan, London.
Bubacz, B. 2007, The Female and Male Orphan Schools in New South Wales, 1801–1850, Ph.D., University of Sydney.
Bullivant, B. 1987, *The Ethnic Encounter in the Secondary School*, Falmer, London.
Burns, A., Bottomly, G. and Jools, p. (eds) 1983, *The Family in the Modern World: Australian perspectives*, George Allen & Unwin, Sydney.
Butts, R.F. 1955, *Assumptions underlying Australian Education*, ACER, Melbourne.
Caldwell, B.J. and Hayward, D.K. 1998, *The Future of Schools*, Falmer, London.
Campbell, C. 1993, 'Family strategy, secondary schooling and making adolescents', *History of Education Review*, vol. 22, no. 2, pp. 18–43.
——1995, 'Modern adolescence and secondary schooling: An historiographical review', *Forum of Education*, vol. 50, no. 1, pp. 12–27.
——1999a, 'Pioneering modern adolescence: The social significance of the early state high schools of Adelaide' in C. Campbell et al. (eds) *Toward the State High School in Australia*, ANZHES, Sydney, pp. 55–77.
——1999b, 'The social origins of Australian state high schools: An historiographical review' in C. Campbell et al. (eds) *Toward the State High School in Australia*, ANZHES, Sydney, pp. 9–28.
——2001a, 'Inventing a pioneering state high school: Adelaide High, 1908–1918', *Journal of the Historical Society of South Australia*, no. 29, pp. 5–20.
——2001b, 'The state high school in history', *Change: Transformations in Education*, vol. 4, no. 1, pp. 5–18.
——2002, 'Suspending Jacquelynne Willcox: A South Australian episode in the history of youth and the high school, 1973–1974',

History of Education Review, vol. 31, no. 1, pp. 26–38.
——2010, *Unley High School*, Wakefield Press, Adelaide.
Campbell, C. and Sherington, G. (eds) 2007, *Going to School in Oceania*, Greenwood Press, Westport (CT).
Campbell, C. and Sherington, G. 2002, 'History of education', *Change: Transformations in Education*, vol. 5, no. 1, pp. 46–64.
——2013 *The Comprehensive Public High School: Historical perspectives*, Palgrave Macmillan, New York.
Campbell, C., Hooper, C. and Fearnley-Sander, M. (eds) 1999, *Toward the State High School in Australia*, ANZHES, Sydney.
Campbell, C., Proctor, H. and Sherington, G. 2009, *School Choice: How parents negotiate the new school market in Australia*, Allen & Unwin, Sydney.
Campion, E. 1982, *Rockchoppers: Growing up Catholic in Australia*, Penguin, Melbourne.
Carney, M. and Cohen, J. (2012), 'Revolution in the classroom', http://www.abc.net.au/4corners/stories/2012/02/06/3421391.htm accessed 23 October 2012.
Clark, I. and Heydon, T. 2004, A Bend in the Yarra: A history of the Merri Creek Protectorate Station and Merri Creek Aboriginal School, 1841–1851, *AIATSIS report series*, Canberra.
Cleverley, J. 1971, *The First Generation: School and society in early Australia*, Sydney University Press, Sydney.
——1972, 'The state primary school teacher between the wars' in J. Cleverley and J. Lawry (eds), *Australian Education in the Twentieth Century*, Longman, Melbourne.
——2007, 'Schooling in Papua New Guinea' in C. Campbell & G. Sherington (eds), *Going to school in Oceania*, Greenwood Press, Westport, pp. 193–261.
Cleverley, J. and Lawry, J. (eds) 1972, *Australian Education in the Twentieth Century*, Longman, Melbourne.
Collishaw, G. 1999, *Rednecks, Eggheads and Blackfellas: A study of racial power and intimacy in Australia*, Allen & Unwin, Sydney.
Committee on Social Change and the Education of Women 1975, Girls, School and Society: Report by a study group to the Schools Commission, Schools Commission, Canberra.
Connell, R. 1985, *Teachers' Work*, Allen & Unwin, Sydney.
——2000, *The Men and the Boys*, Allen & Unwin, Sydney.
——2009, 'Good teachers on dangerous ground: Towards a new view of teacher quality and professionalism', *Critical Studies in Education*, vol. 50, no. 3, pp. 213–229.
Connell, R. et al. 1982, *Making the Difference: Schools, families and social division*, George Allen & Unwin, Sydney.
Connell, R. et al. 2013, *Education, Change and Society*, OUP, Melbourne.
Connell, R., White, V.M. and Johnston, K.M. (eds) 1991, *Running Twice as Hard: The Disadvantaged Schools Program in Australia*, Deakin University, Geelong.
Connell, W.F. 1980, *The Australian Council for Educational Research, 1930–80*, ACER, Melbourne.
——1987, 'Research and writing in the history of education' in J.P. Keeves (ed.) *Australian Education*, Allen & Unwin, Sydney.
——1993, *Reshaping Australian Education 1960–1985*, ACER, Melbourne.
Connors, L. 2000, Public Education: The next generation, Department of Education, Employment and Training, Melbourne.
Cornwall, C. 1997, *Mitcham School: 150 years of history, 1847–1997*, Mitcham School Council, Adelaide.
Crabb, A. and Guerra, O. 2004, 'PM queries values of state schools', *Age* (newspaper), 20 January.
Crane, A.R. and Walker, W.G. 1957, *Peter Board: His contribution to the development of education in New South Wales*, ACER, Melbourne.
Crotty, M. 2001, *Making the Australian Male: Middle-class masculinity 1870–1920*, MUP, Melbourne.
Cunningham, H. 1991, *The Children of the Poor*, Blackwell, Oxford.
——2005, *Children and Childhood in Western Society since 1500*, Pearson Longman, Harlow.
Cunningham, K.S. (ed.) 1938, *Education for Complete Living*, MUP, Melbourne.
Cunningham, K.S. and Ross, D.J. 1967, *An Australian School at Work*, ACER, Melbourne.
Davison, G. 1983, 'The city-bred child and urban reform in Melbourne 1900–1940' in p. Williams (ed.) *Social Progress and the City*, George Allen & Unwin, Sydney, pp. 143–174.
Department of Education Employment and Workplace Relations, 2005, Values Education for Australian Schooling, Australian Government, Canberra.
Dow, G.M. 1964, *George Higinbotham: Church and state*, Pitman, Melbourne.
Dudley, J. and Vidovich, L. 1995, *The Politics of Education: Commonwealth schools policy 1973–95*, ACER, Melbourne.
Duffield, J. 1990, 'The making of the Wyndham Scheme in New South Wales', *History of Education Review*, vol. 19, no. 1, pp. 29–42.

——1995, '"Blissfully unaware": Gender and secondary education reform, New South Wales, 1953–61', *Australian Studies,* vol. 9, pp. 70–85.
Dunlop, E.W. 1965, 'The public high schools of New South Wales, 1883–1912', *Journal of the Royal Australian Historical Society,* vol. 51, no. 1, pp. 60–86.
Dunt, L. 1993, *Speaking Worlds: The Australian educator and John Dewey 1890–1940,* University of Melbourne, Melbourne.
Elliott, A. 1982, 'The kindergarten experiment at the Crown Street Public School, 1881–1882', *Forum of Education,* vol. 41, no. 2, pp. 5–14.
——2006, *Early Childhood Education: Pathways to quality and equity for all children,* ACER, Melbourne.
Emilsen, S. 2000, *The Lily and the Lion: A history of Abbotsleigh,* Abbotsleigh School, Sydney.
Faye, E. 1998, 'Growing up "Australian" in the 1950s: The dream of social science', *Australian Historical Studies,* vol. 29, pp. 344–365.
Fitzgerald, R.T. 1970, *The Secondary School at Sixes and Sevens,* ACER, Melbourne.
——1976, Poverty and Education in Australia, Australian Government Commission of Inquiry into Poverty, Canberra.
Fletcher, C.M. 1968, The Monitorial System and its Effect on the Development of Colonial Education, MEd, University of Sydney.
Fletcher, J.J. 1989a. *Clean, Clad and Courteous: A history of Aboriginal education in New South Wales,* the author, Sydney.
Fletcher, L. (ed.) 1982, *Pioneers of Education in Western Australia,* UWA Press, Perth.
Flynn, M. 1993, *The Culture of Catholic Schools,* St. Pauls, Sydney.
Foale, M.T. 1989, *The Josephite Story: The sisters of St. Joseph, their foundation and early history 1866–1893,* St Joseph's Generalate, Sydney.
Fogarty, R. 1959, *Catholic Education in Australia, 1806–1950,* 2 vols., MUP, Melbourne.
Forsey, M. 2007, *Challenging the System? A dramatic tale of neoliberal reform in an Australian high school,* Information Age Publishing, Charlotte (NC).
Forsey, M., Davies, S. & Walford, G. (eds) 2008, *The globalisation of school choice?,* Symposium Books, Oxford.
Freeman, A.T. 2009, "Every locality, however remote, and every family, however humble": The formation of the half-time schools of New South Wales 1866–1869, PhD, Charles Sturt University.
Gardiner, L. 1982, *The Free Kindergarten Union of Victoria 1908–80,* ACER, Melbourne.
Gilbert, R. and Gilbert, p. 1998, *Masculinity Goes to School,* Allen & Unwin, Sydney.
Gladman, F.J. 1898, *School Work,* Jarrold & Sons, London.
Godfrey, J. 2004, '"Perhaps the most important, and certainly the most exciting event in the whole history of education in Australia": The 1937 New Education Fellowship Conference and New South Wales examination reform', *History of Education Review,* vol. 33, no. 2, pp. 45–58.
Gonski (Chair), D. 2011, Review of Funding for Schooling: Final Report, Australian Government, Canberra.
Goodman, R. 1968, *Secondary Education in Queensland, 1860–1960,* ANU Press, Canberra.
Gregory, A. 2005, *Strong like its Pillars: Melbourne High School 1905–2005,* Langley, Courtis, Thompson Library Trust, Melbourne.
Grimshaw, P., McConville, C. and McEwin, E. (eds) 1985, *Families in Colonial Australia,* George Allen & Unwin, Sydney.
Gronn, P. 1992, 'Schooling for ruling', *Australian Historical Studies,* vol. 25, no. 98, pp. 72–89.
Grundy, D. 1972, *"Secular, compulsory and free": The Education Act of 1872,* MUP, Melbourne.
——1989, 'The formation of a disordered teaching service in Victoria, 1851–1871', *History of Education Review,* vol. 18, no. 23, pp. 1–20.
Haebich, A. 2000, *Broken Circles: Fragmenting Indigenous families 1800–2000,* Fremantle Arts Centre Press, Fremantle.
Hansen, S. and Jenson, J. 1973, *The Little Red Schoolbook,* trl. B. Thornberry, Thor Press, Sydney.
Harman, G. and Smart, D. (eds) 1982, *Federal Intervention in Australian Education,* Georgian House, Melbourne.
Hayes, D. et al. (2006), *Teachers and schooling making a difference,* Allen & Unwin, Sydney, 2006.
Hayes, J. 1978 'Education and the Lutheran church' in J. Cleverley (ed.) *Half a Million Children,* Longman Cheshire, Melbourne, pp. 189–219.
Healey, K. 1998, *Secondary Education in Australia,* Spinney Press, Sydney.
Henderson, N. 1942, *What Chance has Your Child? Education and opportunity in Victoria,* Left Book Club of Victoria, Melbourne.
Hogan, M. 1978, *The Catholic Campaign for State Aid,* Catholic Theological Faculty, Sydney.
——1984, *Public versus Private Schools,* Penguin, Melbourne.
Holbrook, A. 1987, 'Slotting them in the right niche: Adolescence and vocational guidance in Victoria 1920s-1930s' in B. Bessant, *Mother State and Her Little Ones,* Phillip Institute of Technology, Melbourne.

Horan, R.S. 1989, *Fort Street: The school*, Honeysett, Sydney.

Howard, J. 2006, 'A sense of balance: The Australian achievement in 2006', http://australianpolitics.com/2006/01/25/john-howard-australia-day-address, accessed 24 October 2012.

Hughes, J. 2002, 'Harold Wyndham and educational reform in Australia 1925–1968, *Education Research and Perspectives*, vol. 29, no. 1, pp. 1–268.

——2008, *Reform and Resistance in NSW Public Education*, NSW Department of Education & Training, Sydney.

Hunter, I. 1994, *Rethinking the School: Subjectivity, bureaucracy, criticism*, Allen & Unwin, Sydney.

Hyams, B. 1976, 'Young, John Lorenzo (1826–1881)' in B. Nairn (ed.), *Australian Dictionary of Biography*, vol. 6, MUP, Melbourne.

——1979, *Teacher Preparation in Australia: A history of its development from 1850 to 1950*, ACER, Melbourne.

Hyams, B. and Bessant, B. 1972, *Schools for the People? An introduction to the history of state education in Australia*, Longman, Melbourne.

Imtoual, A., Kameniar, B. and Bradley, D. 2009, 'Bottling the good stuff: Stories of hospitality and yarnin' in a multi-racial kindergarten', *Australasian Journal of Early Childhood Education*, vol. 34, no. 2

Irving, T., Maunders, D. & Sherington, G. 1995, *Youth in Australia: Policy administration and politics: A history since World War II*, Macmillan, Melbourne.

Johnson, L. 1993, *The Modern Girl: Girlhood and growing up*, Allen & Unwin, Sydney.

Jolly, S. 1996, *Behind the Lines*, Global Books, Melbourne.

Jones, D. 1987, 'Cadets and military drill: 1872–1914' in B. Bessant (ed.), *Mother State and her Little ones*, Phillip Institute of Technology, Melbourne.

Jones, H. 1985, *Nothing Seemed Impossible: Women's education and social change in South Australia 1875–1915*, University of Queensland Press, Brisbane.

Kabir, N. 2007, 'What does it mean to be un-Australian? Views of Australian Muslim students in 2006', *People and Place*, vol. 15, no. 1, pp. 62–79

Kaestle, C. 1973, *Joseph Lancaster and the monitorial school movement*, Teachers College Press, New York.

Kalantzis, M. et al. 1990, *Cultures of Schooling: Pedagogies for cultural difference and social access*, Falmer Press, London.

Karmel (Chair), p. 1973, Schools in Australia: Report of the Interim Committee of the Australian Schools Commission, AGPS, Canberra.

——1985, Quality of Education in Australia, Commonwealth of Australia (AGPS), Canberra.

Kennedy, M. 2001, A History of Collingwood Community School, M.Ed., University of Melbourne.

Kentish, G. 1984, *Fritz Duras: The father of physical education in Australia*, ACHPER, Adelaide.

Kenway, J. 1991, 'Conspicuous consumption: Class, gender and private schooling' in D. Dawkins (ed.), *Education, Power and Politics in Australia*, Falmer Press, London.

Kenway, J. and Willis, S. 1998, *Answering Back: Girls, boys and feminism in schools*, Routledge, London.

King, D. and Meagher, G. (eds) 2009, *Paid Care in Australia: Politics, profits, practices*, Sydney University Press, Sydney.

King-Boyes, M. 1977, *Patterns of Aboriginal Culture*, McGraw-Hill, Sydney.

Kirk, D. 1998, *Schooling Bodies: School practice and public discourse, 1880–1950*, Leicester University Press, London.

Knight, R. 1966, *Illiberal Liberal: Robert Lowe in New South Wales, 1842–1850*, MUP, Melbourne.

Kociumbas, J. 1992, *Possessions, 1770–1860*, Oxford History of Australia, vol. 2, OUP, Melbourne.

——1997, *Australian Childhood: A history*, Allen & Unwin, Sydney.

Kringas, P. and Lewins, F. 1981, *Why Ethnic Schools? Selected case studies*, ANU Press, Canberra.

Krug, E. 1969, *The shaping of the American high school 1880–1920*, University of Wisconsin Press, Madison.

Kyle, N. 1986, *Her Natural Destiny: The education of women in New South Wales*, NSWU Press, Sydney.

La Nauze, J.A. 1940, 'Some aspects of educational opportunity in South Australia' in J. D. G. Medley (ed.), *Australian Educational Studies*, MUP, Melbourne.

Laughlin, A. 1997, *Mount Druitt High School: Review of 1996 Higher School Certificate performance*, Department of School Education (NSW), Sydney.

Lingard, B., Knight, J. and Porter, P. (eds) 1993, *Schooling Reform in Hard Times*, Falmer, London.

Logan, L. and Sachs, J. 1997, *Meeting the Challenges of Primary Schooling*, Routledge, London.

Macintyre, S. 1991, *A Colonial Liberalism: The lost world of three Victorian visionaries*, OUP, Oxford.
Macintyre, S. and Clark, A. 2003, *The History Wars*, MUP, Melbourne.
Mackie, A. (ed.) 1924, *The Groundwork of Teaching*, Angus & Robertson, Sydney.
Mackie, A. 1920, 'Education in Australia' in M. Atkinson (ed.), *Australia: Economic and political studies*, Macmillan, Melbourne.
Mackinnon, A. 1984, *One Foot on the Ladder: Origins and outcomes of girls' secondary schooling in South Australia*, University of Queensland Press, Brisbane.
Maclean, R. and McKenzie, P. (eds) 1991, *Australian Teachers' Careers*, ACER, Melbourne.
Malin, M. 1990, 'The visibility and invisibility of Aboriginal students in an urban classroom', *Australian Journal of Education*, vol. 34, pp. 312–329.
Marginson, S. 1993, *Education and Public Policy in Australia*, CUP, Cambridge.
——1997a. *Educating Australia*, CUP, Cambridge.
——1997b. *Markets in Education*, Allen & Unwin, Sydney.
Marr, D. 1999, *The High Price of Heaven*, Allen & Unwin, Sydney.
Martin, A.W. 1980, *Henry Parkes: A biography*, MUP, Melbourne.
Maslen, G. 1982, *School Ties: Private schooling in Australia*, Methuen, Melbourne.
Maslin, J.S. 1948, *Hagley: The story of a Tasmanian area school*, Georgian House, Melbourne.
Matthews, J. 1983, '"Education for femininity": Domestic Arts education in South Australia', *Labour History*, no. 45, pp. 30–53.
May, J. 2006, 'Imagining the secondary school: The "pictorial turn" and representations of secondary schools in two Australian feature films of the 1970s', *History of Education Review*, vol. 35, no. 1, pp. 13–22.
McCallum, D. 1990, *The Social Production of Merit: Education, psychology and politics in Australia 1900–1950*, Falmer, London.
McCalman, J. 1993, *Journeyings: The biography of a middle-class generation 1920–1990*, MUP, Melbourne.
McCarthy, R. and Theobald, M. (eds) 1993, *Melbourne Girls Grammar School*, Melbourne GGS, Melbourne.
McCulloch, G. (2002), 'Secondary education' in R. Aldrich ed., A century of education, Routledge Falmer, London
McDonald, P., Ruzicka, L. and Pyne, P. 1987, 'Marriage, fertility and mortality' in W. Vamplew (ed.), *Australians: Historical statistics*, Fairfax, Syme & Weldon, Sydney, pp. 42–61.
McGrath, S. 1993, 'Catholic girls secondary education 1888–1950', *Journal of the Royal Australian Historical Society*, vol. 79, pp. 33–53.
McLaren, J. 1968, *Our Troubled Schools*, Cheshire, Melbourne.
McLean, D. (ed.) 1969, *It's People that Matter! Education for social change*, Angus & Robertson, Sydney.
McLeod, J. and Yates, L. 2006, *Making Modern Lives: Subjectivity, schooling and social change*, SUNY Press, Albany (NY).
Meadmore, P. 2003, 'The introduction of the "New Education" in Queensland, Australia', *History of Education Quarterly*, vol. 43, pp. 372–392.
Mercurio, A. 2003, *Questions as Answers: Understanding upper secondary selection and certification practices in South Australia, 1950–2000*, SSABSA, Adelaide.
Miller, P. 1986, *Long Division: State schooling in South Australian society*, Wakefield Press, Adelaide.
——1998, *Transformations of Patriarchy in the West: 1500–1900*, Indiana University Press, Bloomington.
Miller, P. and Davey, I. 1988, 'The common denominator: Schooling the people' in V. Burgmann and J. Lee (eds), *Constructing a Culture*, McPhee Gribble, Melbourne.
——1990, 'Family formation, schooling and the patriarchal state' in M.R. Theobald and R. J. W. Selleck (eds), *Family, School and State in Australian History*, Allen & Unwin, Sydney.
Ministerial Council on Education, Employment, Training and Youth Affairs, 2008, Melbourne Declaration on Educational Goals for Young Australians, Curriculum Corporation, Melbourne.
Mooney, C. 1996, 'Securing a private classical education in and around Sydney: 1830–1850', *History of Education Review*, vol. 25, no. 1, pp. 38–53.
——1997, 'Vanquishing the hydra-headed monster: The struggle to establish the classical curriculum in New South Wales schools, 1788–1850', *History of Education*, vol. 26, pp. 335–352.
Moore, K. 1999, *The Noblest of Professions: Schoolmasters at Hastings 1872–1894*, Society for the Provision of Education in Rural Australia, Brisbane.
——2004, *The Other Rebellion: Attacking ignorance and vice on the Ballarat goldfield*, Peter Lang, Frankfurt.
Mossenson, D. 1972, *State Education in Western Australia 1829–1960*, UWA Press, Perth.

Mulvaney, D. and White, J. (eds) 1987, *Australians to 1788*, Fairfax, Syme & Weldon, Sydney.

Musgrave, P.W. 1992, *From Humanity to Utility: Melbourne University and public examinations 1856–1964*, ACER, Melbourne.

National Inquiry into the Separation of Aboriginal and Torres Strait Islander Children from Their Families 1997, Bringing Them Home, HREOC, Sydney.

Naughtin, M. 1981, *A Century of Striving: St Joseph's College, Hunter's Hill, 1881–1981*, St Joseph's College, Sydney.

Neumann (Chair), S. 2012, Inquiry into Language Learning in Indigenous Communities: Report, Parliament of Australia, Canberra.

Northey, H. 1992, 'Saint Mary's convent schools' in B. Dickey (ed.), *William Shakespeare's Adelaide 1860–1930*, APH, Adelaide.

Nous Group, 2011, Schooling challenges and opportunities, Melbourne Graduate School of Education, Melbourne.

NSW Department of School Education 1996, Aboriginal Education Policy, the author, Sydney.

O'Brien, A. 1999, *Blazing a Trail: Catholic education in Victoria 1963–1980*, David Lovell Publishing, Melbourne.

O'Brien, A. 2005, *God's Willing Workers: Women and religion in Australia*, UNSW Press, Sydney.

O'Donoghue, T. 2001, *Upholding the Faith: The process of education in Catholic schools in Australia, 1922–1965*, Peter Lang, New York.

——2003, 'Child-abuse scandals and the Catholic Church: Are we asking the right historical questions?', *History of Education Review*, vol. 32, no. 1, pp. 1–15.

O'Farrell, P.J. 1992, *The Catholic Church and Community: An Australian history*, NSWU Press, Sydney.

O'Neil, W.M. 1979, 'Anderson, Sir Francis' in B. Nairn and G.Serle (eds), *Australian Dictionary of Biography*, vol. 7, MUP, Melbourne.

Ozolins, U. 1993, *The Politics of Language in Australia*, CUP, Cambridge.

Parker, P. 2006, *The Making of Women: A history of Mac.Robertson Girls' High School*, Australian Scholarly Publishing, Melbourne.

Partridge, P.H. 1968, *Society, Schools and Progress in Australia*, Pergamon, Oxford.

Paulson, G.A. 1996, 'The value of Aboriginal culture' in A. Pattel-Gray (ed.), *Aboriginal Spirituality*, Harper-Collins, Melbourne.

Pawsey, M. 1990, 'John Bernard O'Hara: Poet and school proprietor, 1862–1927' in M.R. Theobald and R.J.W. Selleck (eds), *Family, School and State in Australian History*, Allen & Unwin, Sydney.

——1994, 'The introduction of payment by results into Victoria's schools', *History of Education Review*, vol. 23, no. 2, pp. 1–17.

Pearson, N. (2009), 'Radical hope: Education and equality in Australia', *Quarterly Essay*, no. 35.

Pell, G. 2006, 'Religion and culture: Catholic schools in Australia', National Catholic Education Conference, Sydney.

Petersen, R.C. 1969, 1970 'Australian progressive schools', *Australian Journal of Education*, Part I: vol. 13, pp. 241–250; Part II: vol. 14, pp. 1–11.

——1983, 'The Montessorians: M.M. Simpson and L. de Lissa' in C. Turney (ed.) *Pioneers of Australian Education*, vol. 3, Sydney University Press, Sydney.

——1995, 'Nurseries of nostalgia: The history of ethnic schools', *Forum of Education*, vol. 50, no. 2, pp. 47–58.

Petersen, R.C. and Rodwell, G. (eds) 1993, *Essays in the History of Rural Education in Australia and New Zealand*, William Michael Press, Darwin.

Pettit, D. 1980, *Opening up Schools: School and community in Australia*, Penguin, Melbourne.

Phillips, D. 1985, *Making more Adequate Provision: State education in Tasmania, 1839–1985*, Education Department of Tasmania, Hobart.

Portus, G.V. 1937, *Free, Compulsory and Secular*, OUP, London.

Preston, B. 2013, *The social make-up of schools: Family income, Indigenous status, family type, religion and broadband access of students in government, Catholic and other nongovernment schools*, http://www.aeufederal.org.au/Publications/2013/BPrestonApril13.pdf, accessed 17 April 2013

Preston, L.F. 2007, 'The focus wasn't on "Boomsa-daisy": Sex education at Shepparton South Technical School, Victoria,1973–1986', *History of Education Review*, vol. 36, no. 2, pp. 19–32.

Proctor, H. 2002, 'Gender, merit and identity at Parramatta High School, 1913–1919', *History of Education Review*, vol. 31, no. 1, pp. 39–50.

——2004, Gender and merit: A history of coeducation and gender relations at an academically-selective public secondary school, Parramatta High, New South Wales, 1913–1958, PhD, University of Sydney.

——2007, 'Gender and merit: Coeducation and the construction of a meritocratic educational ladder in New South Wales, 1880–1912', *Paedagogica Historica*, vol. 43, pp. 119–134.

——2011, 'Masculinity and social class, tradition and change', *Gender and Education*, vol. 23, pp. 843–856.

Pusey, M. 1991, *Economic Rationalism in Canberra,* CUP, Cambridge.

Radford, W.C. 1939, *The Educational Needs of a Rural Community,* MUP, Melbourne.

Ramsland, J. 1986, *Children of the Backlanes: Destitute and neglected children in colonial New South Wales,* NSWU Press, Sydney.

Reeves, C. 1935, *A History of Tasmanian Education,* MUP, Melbourne.

Reid, J. and Martin, S. 2003, '"Speak softly, be tactful and assist cheerfully . . . ": Women beginning teaching in 1930s NSW', *Change: Transformations in Education,* vol.6., no.1, pp. 48–69.

Rigney, L. (2011), 'Action for Aboriginal social inclusion' in D. Bottrell & S. Goodwin (eds), *Schools, Communities and Social Inclusion,* Palgrave Macmillan, Melbourne, 2011, pp. 38–49.

Rodwell, G. 1992, *With Zealous Efficiency: Progressivism and Tasmanian state primary education, 1900–20,* William Michael Press, Darwin.

——1999, 'The eugenic and political dynamics in the early history of physical education in Australia, 1900–1950', *Melbourne Studies in Education,* vol. 40, pp. 93–113.

Roe, M. 1984, *Nine Australian Progressives: Vitalism in bourgeois social thought, 1890–1960,* University of Queensland Press, Brisbane.

Roper, T. 1970, *The Myth of Equality,* National Union of Australian University Students, Melbourne

Ross, D. 1954, The trend towards the comprehensive school, University of Melbourne, Melbourne.

Ruzicka, L. and Caldwell, J. 1977, *The End of Demographic Transition in Australia,* Australian National University, Canberra.

Ryan, C. and Watson, L. 2004, *The drift to Private Schools in Australia,* Australian National University, Canberra.

Sanders, C. (ed.) 1966, *Technical Education for Development,* University of Western Australia, Perth.

Schools Commission, 1980, Schooling for 15 and 16 year-olds, the author, Canberra.

Schools Council 1990, Australia's Teachers: An agenda for the next decade, National Board of Employment, Education and Training, Canberra.

Select Committee on Transportation 1812, Report and Appendix. *Parliamentary Papers,* Great Britain, London.

Selleck, R.J.W. 1968, *The New Education,* Pitman, London.

——1972, 'Gladman, Frederick John' in B.Nairn, G. Serle and R. Ward (eds) *Australian Dictionary of Biography,* vol. 4, MUP, Melbourne.

——1978, 'The Catholic primary school' in J. Cleverley (ed.) *Half a Million Children,* Longman Cheshire, Melbourne, pp. 77–105.

——1982, *Frank Tate: A biography,* MUP, Melbourne.

Senate Employment, Education and Training References Committee 1998, A Class Act: Inquiry into the status of the teaching profession, the author, Canberra.

Shaw, G. p. 1978, *Patriarch and Patriot: William Grant Broughton 1788–1853,* MUP, Melbourne.

Sherington, G. 1983, 'Athleticism in the Antipodes', *History of Education Review,* vol. 12, no. 2, pp. 16–28.

——1995, 'Education policy' in M. Laffin and M. Painter (eds) *Reform and Reversal: Lessons from the coalition government in New South Wales 1988–1995,* Macmillan, Melbourne.

Sherington, G. and Connellan, M. 1988, 'Socialisation, imperialism and war: Ideology and ethnicity in Australian corporate schools 1880–1918' in J.A. Mangan (ed.) *'Benefits bestowed'?,* Manchester University Press, Manchester.

Sherington, G. and Jeffery, C. 1998, *Fairbridge: Empire and child migration,* UWA Press, Perth.

Sherington, G., Petersen, R. C. and Brice, I. 1987, *Learning to Lead: A history of girls' and boys' corporate secondary schools in Australia,* Allen & Unwin, Sydney.

Silver, P. and Silver, H. 1974, *The Education of the Poor: The history of a National school 1824–1974,* Routledge & Kegan Paul, London.

Smart, D. 1982, 'The pattern of post-war Federal intervention in education' in G. Harman and D. Smart (eds) *Federal Intervention in Australian Education,* Georgian House, Melbourne.

Smith, B. 1990, 'William Wilkins's saddle-bags: State education and local control' in M.R. Theobald and R.J.W. Selleck (eds) *Family, School and State in Australian History,* Allen & Unwin, Sydney.

Smith, R.A. and Knight, J. 1978, 'MACOS in Queensland' *Australian Journal of Education,* vol. 22, pp. 225–248.

Snow, D. 1989, '"But they're only babies": Policies and practice marginalizing the very young from NSW state schools, 1788–1920' in N. Kyle (ed.), *Women as Educators in Nineteenth and Twentieth Century Australia,* University of Wollongong, Wollongong.

——1991, 'Transforming children's labour through

schooling' in J. Martin and K. Taylor (eds) *Culture and the Labour Movement*, Dunmore Press, Palmerston North.

Spaull, A.D. (ed.) 1977, *Australian Teachers*, Macmillan, Melbourne.

Spaull, A.D. 1982, *Australian Education in the Second World War*, University of Queensland Press, Brisbane.

——1998, *John Dedman*, Hyland House, Melbourne.

——1999, 'The end of the state school system?' in B. Costar and N. Economou eds, *The Kennett Revolution*, UNSW Press, Sydney, pp. 214–224.

——2001, 'The constitution, the "nationhood power" and education before 1950', *Change: Transformations in Education*, vol. 4, no. 1, pp. 104–120.

Spearritt, P. 1979, 'Child care and kindergartens in Australia 1890–1975' in P. Langford and P. Sebastian (eds) *Early Childhood Education and Care in Australia*, AIPP, Melbourne.

Spender, D. & Sarah, E. 1980, *Learning to lose: Sexism and education*, Women's Press, London.

Stead, C. 1945, *For Love Alone*. Republished by Angus and Robertson, Sydney, 1990.

Stephens, H. 2012, Reconstruction of the Familiar: A history of Our Lady of Lebanon College Harris Park, Ed.D., University of Sydney.

Strehlow, T.G.H. 1947, *Aranda Traditions*, MUP, Melbourne.

Sullivan, M. 1974, 'Fifty years of opposition to Queensland's grammar schools', *Melbourne Studies in Education*, 1974, pp. 181–221.

Taylor, J., Borlagdan, J. and Allan, M. (2012), *Turning 21: Life chances and uncertain transitions*, Brotherhood of St Laurence, Melbourne.

Teese, R. & Polesel, J. 2003, *Undemocratic schooling: Equity and quality in mass secondary education in Australia*, MUP, Melbourne.

Teese, R. 2000, *Academic Success and Social Power*, MUP, Melbourne.

Teese, R., et al. 1995, Who wins at school? Boys and girls in Australian secondary education, University of Melbourne, Melbourne.

Theobald, M. 1989, 'The PLC mystique: Reflections on the reform of female education in nineteenth century Australia', *Australian Historical Studies*, vol. 23, pp. 241–259.

——1991, '"Mere accomplishments"? Melbourne's early ladies schools reconsidered' in A. Prentice and M. Theobald (eds) *Women who Taught*, University of Toronto Press, Toronto, pp. 71–91.

——1996, *Knowing Women*, CUP, Cambridge.

——1998, 'Educational history' in G. Davison, J. Hirst and S. Macintyre (eds) *The Oxford Companion to Australian History*, OUP, Melbourne.

——2001, 'The Afghan children of Oodnadatta' in G. Sherington and C. Campbell (eds) *Education and Ethnicity*, ISCHE, Gent.

——2006, 'And Gladly Teach? The making of a woman's profession', in E. Smyth and P. Bourne (eds), *Women Teaching, Women Learning: Historical perspectives*, ed. Inanna Publications and Education, Toronto.

Theobald, M. and Dwyer, D. 1999, 'An episode in feminist politics: The Married Women (Lecturers and Teachers) Act, 1932–47', *Labour History*, no. 76, pp. 59–77.

Theobald, M. and Selleck, R.J.W. (eds) 1990, *Family, School and State in Australian History*, Allen & Unwin, Sydney.

Thiele, C. 1975, *Grains of Mustard Seed*, Education Department of South Australia, Adelaide.

Thomson, P. 2002, *Schooling the Rustbelt Kids*, Allen & Unwin, Sydney.

Thornton, K. 2010, *The Messages of its Walls and Fields: A history of St Peter's College, 1847 to 2009*, Wakefield Press, Adelaide.

Tregenza, J. 1968, *Professor of Democracy: The Life of Charles Henry Pearson, 1830–1894*, MUP, Melbourne.

——1996, *Collegiate School of St Peter Adelaide: The founding years 1847–1878*, The Collegiate School of St Peter, Adelaide.

Trethewey, L. 1994, 'Reforming the age-grade structure in South Australian schools', *Melbourne Studies in Education*, vol. 35, no. 1, pp. 114–133.

Trimingham Jack 2003, *Growing Good Catholic Girls*, MUP, Melbourne.

Triolo, R. 2010, '"*Our war and the Pacific*": *Allies and enemies in Victoria's education department publications, Australia, 1914–18*', *History of Education Review*, vol. 39, no. 2, pp. 14–23.

Tsoldis, G. 1986, Educating Voula: A report on non-English speaking background girls and education. Ministry of Education Victoria, Melbourne.

Tully, K. 2002, 'State secondary education in Western Australia 1912–1972', *Education Research and Perspectives*, vol. 29, no. 2.

Turney, C. (ed.) 1969, 1972, 1983, *Pioneers of Australian Education*, 3 vols., Sydney University Press, Sydney.

Turney, C. 1966, 1967 'The advent and adaptation of the Arnold public school tradition in New South Wales', *Australian Journal of Education*, Part I: vol. 10, pp. 133–144; Part II: vol. 11, pp. 29–43.

Turney, C. 1989, *Grammar: A history of Sydney*

Grammar School 1819–1988, Allen & Unwin, Sydney.
——1992, *William Wilkins: His life and work*, Hale & Iremonger, Sydney.
Tyack, D. 1974, *The One Best System: A history of American urban education*, Harvard University Press, Cambridge.
Van Krieken, R. 1992, *Children and the State*, Allen & Unwin, Sydney.
Vick, M. 1994, 'Schooling and the production of local communities in mid-nineteenth-century Australia', *Historical Studies in Education*, vol. 6, no. 3, pp. 19–37.
Waddington, D., Radford, W. and Keats, J. 1950, in ACER, *Review of Education in Australia 1940–1948*, MUP/ACER, Melbourne.
Walker, J.C. 1988, *Louts and Legends: Male youth culture in an inner city school*, Allen & Unwin, Sydney.
Walton, C. 1997, 'Traeger Park School: A case for human rights' in S. Harris and M. Malin (eds) *Indigenous Education: Historical, moral and practical tales*, NTUP, Darwin.
Waters, J. 2000, *The Lady Gowrie Child Centre: The place, the people, the programs, 1939–1999*, Lady Gowrie Child Care Centre, Melbourne.
Watson, L. 2003, A Critique of the Federal Government's Recent Changes to Private Schools Funding, University of Canberra, Canberra.
Watts, I. 1815, *Plain and Easy Catechisms for Children*, Hilliard & Metcalf, Cambridge.
Waugh, M.N. 2005, *Forgotten Hero: Richard Bourke, Irish Governor of New South Wales 1831–1837*, Australian Scholarly Publishing, Melbourne.
Webster, D. 1981, 'Kilgour of Fort Street: The English headmaster ideal in Australian state secondary education', *Melbourne Studies in Education*, pp. 184–206.
Weiss, G. 1993, '"A very great nuisance": Young children and the construction of school entry in South Australia, 1851–1915', *History of Education Review*, vol. 22, no. 2, pp. 1–17.
——1994, 'Three generations of women: Learning and schooling among the Adnyamathanha, *Historical Studies in Education*, special issue, pp. 171–199.
Welch, A. 1996, *Australian Education: Reform or crisis?* Allen & Unwin, Sydney.
White, M. 1997, 'Carnegie philanthropy in Australia in the nineteen thirties—a reassessment', *History of Education Review*, vol. 26, no. 1, pp. 1–24.
Whitehead, K. 1999, 'Lavinia Seabrooke: Gender and state formation in the late nineteenth century', *Women's History Review*, vol. 8, no. 1, pp. 7–25.
——2003, *The New Women Come Along: Transforming teaching in the nineteenth century*, ANZHES, Sydney.
——2007, 'The spinster teacher in Australia from the 1870s to the 1960s', *History of Education Review*, vol. 36, no. 1, pp. 1–17.
——2010, 'A decided disadvantage for the kindergarten students to mix with the state teachers', *Paedagogica Historica*, vol. 46, nos. 1–2, pp. 85–97.
Wilkinson, I. et al. 2006, *A History of State Aid to Non-government Schools in Australia*, Department of Education, Science and Training, Canberra.
Williams (Chair), B. 1979, Education, Training and Employment, AGPS, Canberra.
Williams, B. 1993, 'Cunningham, Kenneth Stewart' in J. Ritchie (ed.) *Australian Dictionary of Biography*, vol. 13, MUP, Melbourne.
Williamson, A. 1994, *Schooling the Torres Strait Islanders 1873 to 1941*, University of South Australia, Adelaide.
Windschuttle, E. 1980. 'Educating the daughters of the ruling class in colonial New South Wales, 1788–1850', *Melbourne Studies in Education*, pp. 105–133.
Wright, K. 2011, *The Rise of the Therapeutic Society*, New Academia Publishing, Washington.
Wyatt, R.T. 1941, *The History of Goulburn, NSW*, Lansdowne Press, Sydney.
Wyeth, E.R. 1955, *Education in Queensland*, ACER, Melbourne.
Wyndham (Chair), H.S. 1957, Report of the Committee appointed to Survey Secondary Education in New South Wales, Government of New South Wales, Sydney.
Yashchenko, A.L. 2001, *Australian Journey 1903: The travel diary of Aleksandr Leonidovich Yaschenko*, University of Melbourne, Melbourne.
Yates, L. 1993, *The Education of Girls: Policy, research and the question of gender*, ACER, Melbourne.
Yates, L., Collins, C. and O'Connor, K. (eds) 2011, *Australia's Curriculum Dilemmas: State cultures and the big issues*, MUP, Melbourne.

Index

Abbotsleigh School, 87, 89, 153
Abbott teaching family, 52–3
Aboriginal education and schooling, 2–6, 21–2, 24, 27, 37, 53–6, 67–73, 103, 120, 127–30, 137, 142–3, 163–4, 182, 203–5, 226, 233, 241–4, 250, 265
  missions and missionaries, 36, 46, 51–2, 53–7, 67–73
  policy development, 203, 242–3, 250
  protection policies and era, 54, 58, 69–70, 128–30, 163
  racism and eugenics, 9, 67, 71–2, 108, 120, 127–30, 164, 264
  self-determination, 143, 203–5, 233
  see also Indigenous schooling, Native Institution
academies
  Australia, 15, 22, 24, 28, 34, 46, 75, 87, 114
  United Kingdom, 6, 8
  see also private venture schools
Accelerated Christian Education, 232
access, equal opportunity and equity, schools and, xi, 61, 79, 95, 111, 113, 116–17, 143, 189, 202–3, 209, 214, 219–20, 224–5, 235, 244–5, 252, 260, 267
  see also poverty and schools
Adey, William, 121–2, 139, 152
adolescence and schooling, 64, 109, 114, 117, 121–4, 138–40, 146–7, 154, 176, 187, 220, 249
  teenagers, 181–2, 186, 191–2, 264
Advanced School for Girls, 93–4
Afghan-Australians, schooling, 103, 120
agricultural schools and colleges, 46, 94, 115, 146, 160
alternative schools, 113, 131–2, 231–2, 234
Anderson, Francis, 109–10, 117
Anderson, John, 115–16
Andrews, Cecil, 113
Anglican schooling *see* Church of England and schools
Anzac Day, 126–7
Arbor Day, 102, 118
architecture and buildings, school, xi, 25, 96, 103, 137, 198, 220, 229, 238, 254, 266, 270
area schools, 159–60
Arnoldian schooling culture, 91–2, 130, 139, 166, 230
Arthur, Gov. George, 48–9
assessment, student
  before 1860, 10, 22, 27
  1861–1960, 110, 112–13, 116–17, 133–4, 136, 139, 155, 157, 161, 163, 165, 184
  1961–2000, 205, 209, 219, 230, 235, 245
  after 2000, 253, 255, 257, 266–7
  see also NAPLAN, public examinations
athleticism, 92, 130
attendance, student, 8, 14, 16, 17, 36, 38, 47, 49, 54–7, 62, 71–6, 80–2, 85, 97, 103, 120, 122, 138, 175
  see also compulsory schooling *and* retention, student
Australian Broadcasting Commission/Corporation (ABC), viii, 195–6, 252–3
  school broadcasts, 172
Australian Capital Territory, schooling, 161, 182, 215, 231, 255
Australian constitution and education, 106, 198, 208, 227
Australian Council for Education Research (ACER), 144, 161–2, 176, 183, 203, 267
Australian Curriculum and Assessment Authority (ACARA), 266–8
Australian federal government and education,
  before 1965, 106, 173–6, 208
  after 1965, 180, 182–3, 196–202, 211, 214, 224–8, 244, 249, 252, 261–3, 266–7
  see also state aid
Australian Teachers Federation, 194
baby boom and schools, 179–81, 188, 192, 199, 209, 212
Ballarat, schooling, 32, 36, 94, 150
  see also goldfields in Victoria
Baptist church and schools, 6, 34, 55, 80

Bathurst, schooling, 27, 36, 93, 131, 150, 228
behaviour management *see* discipline and punishment
Bell, Andrew *see* monitorialism
Bigge inquiry and Report (1819–1821), 12, 15–17, 25–6
Blackburn, Jean, 201, 206, 234
Bligh, Gov. William, 10, 13–14
Board, Peter, 103, 106, 110–13, 115, 119, 128–9, 131–2, 135, 138
boarding schools, 14, 15, 34, 35, 49, 75, 88, 96, 130, 153
Bonwick, James,49, 56
Bourke, Gov. Richard, 38–40, 61
boy crisis *see* boys schooling, after 1961
boys schooling
  before 1901, 3, 6, 8, 14–15, 22, 28–9, 32–6, 38, 43–4, 51, 58–9, 63, 65, 69, 71, 88–93, 102
  1901 to 1960, 108, 118–19, 121, 123–4, 126, 128–32, 134, 139–40, 143, 146, 152, 157–60, 165–7, 173
  after 1961, 182, 186, 193, 206, 215, 219, 228, 230, 235–7, 238, 240, 244–6, 250, 253, 268
Brighton-le-Sands Public School, 131–2
Bringing Them Home Report 1997, 243–4
British Empire and schooling, 65, 100–1, 114, 125
Broughton, William, 33, 38–42, 48–9
Browne, G. S., 144–6, 148–9, 172
bushrangers, schooling and, 79
Butts, Freeman, 181–4
Carnegie Corporation, 144, 173
catechism, role in education, 6, 17, 23, 24, 40, 51, 110, 133, 165, 196
Catholic church and schools, xiii, xvii
  before 1901, 6, 25, 27–8, 31, 34, 37–40, 42, 44–47, 49, 50, 52–4, 59–61, 72–3, 75, 77–80, 83–5, 90, 93
  1901–1970, 125, 131, 132–5, 145, 149, 153, 158, 164–5, 172, 179, 180–1, 183, 189, 191, 194
  after 1971, 195–201, 208, 213, 218, 221–2, 224, 227–9, 242, 249, 260–4
Catholic Education Offices, xvii, 165, 179, 191, 228
Catholic religious orders and schooling, 34, 45–6, 60, 61, 84–5, 92–3, 133, 135, 165, 196, 153, 222, 227–9
  see also names of particular orders
Cawthorne teaching family, 58–9
central schools, 113, 146, 158, 253
centralisation and systematisation, educational, 37, 44, 64–5, 73–78, 80–2, 84–5, 106, 110, 133, 145, 163, 170, 183–4, 187, 193, 212–13, 228, 258
charity schools, 6–8, 20
children, childhood and schooling, xiv, xv, 2, 8, 249–50
  before 1901, xii, 1–10, 12, 16–22, 24–9, 31–6, 41–2, 44, 47–9, 52–60, 62–73, 75, 79, 82–3, 85–6, 93, 95–6, 100–104
  after 1900, 108, 110–12, 117–8, 120–4, 126–30, 132, 135, 137–40, 142–3, 146, 148, 150–1, 155–60, 163–70, 172–3, 175, 179, 181, 190, 195, 200, 203–5, 207–11, 214, 216–20, 223, 231–2, 239, 241–6, 249–50, 252, 256, 260–1, 263
Children's Hour, The, 100–1, 126
Chinese-Australians, schooling, 86, 103, 122, 246
Christian Brothers, schools of, 84, 85, 228
Christian schools, 230–2
Church and School Corporation, 37–8, 51
Church of England and schools, 6–8, 11–12, 16–17, 23, 26–28, 33–43, 45–6, 48–55, 60–1, 70, 77–8, 80–1, 89–91, 93, 153–4, 213, 230, 264
Clark, Donald, 119
Clarke, Marian, 87, 89
class, social, and schooling, 8–9, 61, 75, 81, 139, 171, 182, 187, 191, 207–8, 215, 246
  see also working class; middle class; ruling class children and youth
coaching colleges, 246
Cold War and schooling, 178, 199–200
Cole, Percival, 146–8
colleges of advanced education, 181, 235
commercial and English schools and academies, 6, 15, 22–3, 28, 35, 87–8, 111, 113, 116, 118, 158–9, 235
Commonwealth government *see* Australian federal government and education
Como High School, WA, 223–4, 259
comprehensive high schools, 187–91
compulsory education and schooling, xiii, 8, 32, 62, 71, 73–4, 76, 80–4, 96, 103–4, 117, 122, 138, 142, 156, 164, 250, 252
  truancy, 82, 107
computers, teaching and learning, 215, 219, 238–9, 266
  see also information technologies, new
Congregational church and schools, 6, 14, 21, 46, 80
Connell, R., 212, 216, 239, 258
Connell, W. F., 183, 232
convict children and children of convicts, 9–12
Coranderrk settlement school, 70–1
corporate schools, xvii-xviii, 165–7, 187
  see also nongovernment schools
correspondence lessons *see* distance education
Council of Education, NSW, 71, 78–9, 84
credentials and credentialism, xi, 65, 88, 112, 139, 184, 215, 249, 251
Crook, William, 14–15, 22, 24
Cunningham, Ken, 144, 161–2
curriculum (1), xiii, xv-xvi, 259
  before 1821, 6, 7, 13, 22–4, 19, 21, 26

1821–1900, 35, 42, 46, 52, 54, 59, 65, 71–2, 76, 79, 82, 84, 87, 91, 93, 95, 97, 99–103
1901–2000, xv, 108, 110–13, 115–20, 126–8, 131–3, 136–7, 146–7, 155, 157, 159–60, 165, 170–4, 181, 184, 188, 190, 195–6, 205–7, 209, 211–12, 214, 218–20, 223, 225–6, 228, 232–9, 242
after 2000, 249, 251, 256
curriculum (2)
Aboriginal and indigenous studies, 2–9, 21, 24, 52, 56, 70–2, 128–30, 137, 142–3, 163, 204–5, 226, 233, 242–5, 251, 259–60, 266, 268
accomplishments, girls', 47, 51, 59, 85, 87–8, 91, 133
agricultural *see* agricultural schools and colleges
arithmetic, 15–17, 23, 26, 35, 40, 57–8, 72, 88, 98, 102, 136, 160, 249; *see also* numeracy *below*
Australian, 49, 205, 243, 265–6, 100
citizenship, 77, 101, 111, 114, 126, 160–1, 170, 233, 265–6
classics-based, Latin and Greek, xviii, 6, 22–3, 28, 34–5, 46, 88, 90–2, 113, 115
English, 17, 22, 24, 49, 54, 57, 66, 69, 101–2, 168, 206, 234–5, 251, 253, 267–8; *see also* literacy *below*
geography, 35, 58, 100, 102, 110, 135–6, 172
health, 123, 161, 187, 220, 226, 235
history, 76, 100, 102, 136, 172, 205, 233–4, 243, 265–6, 268
home economics and domestic science, 119–20, 123, 126, 129, 131, 133, 139, 146, 158–9, 189
languages other than English, 15, 47, 87, 113, 115, 184, 218, 220, 222, 235, 242, 244, 251; *see also* classics-based *above*
literacy, reading and writing, xv, 6–7, 13, 15–19, 23–6, 33, 35, 40, 48, 54–5, 62, 71–2, 80, 92, 100–1, 160, 163, 249–50, 219, 222, 225–6, 238, 249–50, 255
mathematics, 6, 15, 35, 90–1, 119, 170, 184, 195, 220, 234–5, 253, 267–8
morals education, 4, 13, 15, 17, 21, 23–4, 35, 60, 65–6, 77, 81, 99–100, 102, 120, 148, 264
nature study, 116–8, 151
numeracy, ciphering and arithmetic, xv, 163, 219, 222, 225–6, 234, 238, 255; *see also* arithmetic *above*
physical education, games and sports *see main entry* physical education
religious, 6, 17, 23, 26, 28, 33, 35, 39, 46, 52, 55, 74, 76–80, 88, 132–3, 165, 196
science, 6, 42, 77, 110, 113, 119, 135, 198–200, 221, 234, 268
sex education, 132, 174, 235
social studies, 171–2, 179, 195, 232–3
technical and vocational, 8, 42, 88, 94–5, 106, 111, 114–15, 117–19, 127, 133, 139, 154–5, 157–9, 184, 187, 198, 214, 220–1, 224–5, 234–7
values education, 13, 77, 201, 233, 264–6; *see also* morals education *and* citizenship *above*
curriculum development, 195, 226, 232, 234–5, 251
curriculum wars, 232–7, 265–6
Dalton Plan, 132, 149
dame schools, 8, 9, 29, 33, 46–8, 85–6
Darling, James, 166
Davey, Constance, 138–9
Dawkins, John, 225, 268
de Lissa, Lilian, 122, 134
Deakin, Alfred, 114
Defence Act 1910, Australia, 123
demographics, population and schools, 31–2, 64–5, 67, 119–20, 142–3, 175, 179–80, 184–6, 191–2, 214, 216, 251, 269
Denominational Schools Board, 34, 42, 45, 49, 52, 55, 60, 62, 74, 79–80
Depression 1890s, 81, 96
Depression 1930s, 143–4, 149–53, 156–7, 159, 168, 170, 176, 180
devolution policy, school, 201, 223, 227, 234, 254, 259
Dewey, John, educational influence, 107, 149, 195
disabilities, schooling children with, 96, 117–8, 145, 148, 202, 219, 221–2, 249
Disadvantaged Schools Program, 201, 208, 212, 221, 238
discipline and punishment, school,
before 1901, 7–8, 18–19, 24–28, 34, 57, 59, 63, 99
after 1900, 120, 219, 231, 269
distance education, 59, 112, 245
DOGS, Council for the Defence of Government Schools, 202, 227–8
domestic science secondary schools *see* curriculum (2) home economics
drugs, illegal and legal, 181, 216–7
Drummond, David, 173
Duncan, William, 53, 55
early childhood education, xvii
before 1901, 8, 33, 37, 43, 46, 48, 67, 76, 95–6
1901–1960, 99, 107, 117, 122–3, 127, 134, 138, 140, 142, 146, 148–9, 155, 162
after 1960, 214–5, 179, 252, 181, 208, 239, 259
see also kindergarten movement
Education Act 1872, Victoria, 74, 76–8
Education Act 1875, Queensland, 81, 102
Education Act 1875, SA, 80–81
Education Act 1961, NSW, 189
education departments, founding of state, 65, 71, 76, 77, 97, 98, 118
Elementary Education Act 1871, WA, 75

Emilian, Bro., 92–3
Empire Day, 125
equal opportunity *see* access, equal opportunity and equity
ethnic and Saturday schools, 244, 246
eugenics, 107–8, 120–1, 123, 127, 173–4
Ewart, David, 94, 116
experimental education, 21, 107, 109, 127, 131–2, 145, 148, 155, 158, 201, 209, 238
Fairbridge sponsored schools, 124
families, parents and schools, xii, xiv, xvi
  to 1901, xiii, 2, 8, 15–18, 21–4, 29, 31, 33–6, 43, 46–8, 53–4, 56, 58–9, 61, 63–5, 67, 71–3, 75, 79–81, 83–9, 94–5, 102–3
  after 1900, xi, 108, 115, 120–2, 126, 128–30, 138, 140, 142–3, 148, 154, 163–4, 168, 170–1, 175, 179–80, 195, 197, 202–3, 205, 208, 211, 214, 216, 218–19, 221–4, 228–9, 231, 233, 245–6, 250, 259–60, 267–70
feminist influence on schooling, xiv, 109–10, 179, 206–7, 216
Fenner, Charles, 119
Fink Royal Commission, 114
Forsey, Martin, 223, 259
Fort Street schools, 43–4, 52, 84, 110, 113, 139, 143, 191
Fraser coalition government, 202, 224
free, compulsory and secular acts, colonial, 65–7, 73–4, 82–4, 103–5
  New South Wales, 74, 78–80
  Queensland, 74, 81–2
  South Australia, 74, 80–1
  Tasmania, 74, 80
  Victoria, 74, 76–8
  Western Australia, 74–6
Froebel, Friedrich, educational influence, 95–6, 100, 123, 148
gay and lesbian students and teachers, 217, 228–9, 264
gender and schooling *see* boys schooling; gay and lesbian students and teachers; girls schooling; teachers (3); teachers (5) marriage bar
Geoghegan, Patrick, 84
German-Australians, schooling, 32, 47, 51–2, 54, 64, 127–8
  see also Lutheran churches and schooling
gifted and talented students and programs, 218–19, 244
Gillard Labor government *see* Rudd and Gillard Labor governments
Gilmore, Mary, 98–99
Gipps, Gov. George, 40–1, 54
girls schooling
  before 1901, 3, 6, 8, 13, 15, 18–20, 22–3, 29, 31–6, 44, 46–7, 51, 58–9, 65, 71, 85, 87–8, 90–5, 102, 104
  1901–1960, 113, 119–22, 126, 128–31, 133, 138–9, 146, 153, 155–6, 158, 160, 173, 182–3
  after 1960, 186, 196, 206–7, 215, 230, 235–8, 245
Girls, School and Society, 182–3, 206–7
Gladman, Frederick, 99–100
gold fields in Victoria, schooling, 50, 60, 63, 216
Golden Grove schools, SA, 221–2, 224
goldfields in WA, schooling, 76, 81
Gonski Report, 261–3
Goulburn, schooling, 32–6, 89, 93
  Catholic school strike, 196–8
government schools *see* public schools
grammar schools, xviii, 6, 8, 22, 28, 34–5, 37, 46, 48–9, 51, 60, 65, 81, 87, 90–1, 114–16, 132, 166, 187, 230, 253, 256
grammar schools, Queensland, 81, 90–1, 116
Greek-Australians, schooling, 181, 244
Greiner government, NSW, 226–7
Gulargamborne Public School, 72, 237
Hadow Report, UK, 186–7
Haines, William, 50, 78
Hartley, John, 81, 93–4
Hawke and Keating Labor governments, 224–5
Headmasters and Headmistresses conferences, 167
Herbart, Johann, educational influence, 100
high school, public, foundations, 89–90, 93–5, 113–118, 121–2, 126–7, 130, 138–9, 146–7, 151
Higher School Certificate, 190, 253, 255
Higinbotham, George, 78
Hindmarsh Public School, 85–6
historiography of education and schooling, xi-xvii, 51, 107, 233
history wars, 233, 265–6
Hobart, schooling, 17, 27, 49, 115, 118–19, 161, 189, 244
Howard coalition governments, 226, 233, 261, 265–6
Howard, John, 265–6
Human Rights and Equal Opportunity Commission, 242, 244–5
Hume Central Secondary College, Victoria, 253–5
Hutchins School, 49, 60
immigrant children and schooling, 179, 181, 228, 264
immigration policy, 119, 142, 206, 214, 222, 264
independent schools *see* nongovernment schools
information technologies, new, 220, 245, 269
  see also computers, teaching and learning
inspectors of schools, 17, 27, 37, 41, 44, 47, 49, 53, 56, 61, 65–6, 71, 75–6, 78–9, 81, 96–9, 102, 110–12, 114–16, 119, 128, 138, 164–5, 184, 193, 209
intelligence testing, 108, 127, 138, 140, 144, 155–6, 182, 187–8
  see also streaming, tracking and setting

intermediate certificate, 111, 159
intermediate high schools, 94, 109, 118, 133, 158, 160
Irish National curriculum and readers, 39–40, 42, 46–7, 59–60, 75, 100
Irish-Australians, schooling, 9–10, 27–8, 31, 34, 64, 85, 92–3, 108, 134, 136, 195–6,
Italian-Australians, schooling, 181, 205, 218, 244
Jackson, Cyril, 103, 106, 113
Jewish families and schooling, 28, 33, 35, 142, 173, 205–6
Johnson, Richard, 7, 10–11, 13, 18, 21
Joyner, Roma, 232–3
Kandel, Isaac, 162–3
Karmel Report (1973), xvii, 182, 191, 195, 201–2, 208
Kay Shuttleworth, James, educational influence, 100
kindergarten movement, xvii, 76, 95–6, 99, 107, 110, 117, 122–3, 127, 134, 138, 140, 142, 146, 148, 162, 179, 181, 208, 214, 239, 259
  see also early childhood
Kindergarten Union, 122, 146–7, 149
King, Gov. Philip, 19, 20, 27–8
Knibbs and Turner reports, 110, 113, 117
Knox Gramma School, NSW, 132, 230, 253, 256
labour market and schools, ix, 88, 111, 138–40, 149, 155, 157, 184, 209, 211, 213, 215, 217, 220, 245–6, 249, 251–2, 269
ladies schools and academies, 8, 15, 32, 34–5, 46–7, 51, 85, 87–88, 91
Lady Gowrie Child Centres, 175, 214
Lancaster, Joseph, 14, 25–6
Lang, John Dunmore, 37, 42
languages, policy and schooling, 28, 35, 47, 54, 68–9, 72, 87, 90–1, 113, 115, 127, 205, 218, 222, 235, 242, 244, 251
  see also curriculum (2) languages other than English
Launceston, schooling, 27, 36, 115, 118–19, 160, 189
Layard, Albermarle, 34–5
leaving certificate, 111–2
Lebanese and Syrian-Australians, schooling, 222
London Missionary Society (LMS), 12, 14, 21, 67–9
Lowe, Robert, 41–2
loyalty, Empire and nation, 6, 65, 101, 125, 127, 137, 140
Lutheran churches and schools, 32, 47, 52–4, 64, 72
  World War I, 127–8
Macarthur, Elizabeth, 12–13
Mackie, Alexander,137, 150
MacKillop, Mary, 84
MACOS (Man: A course of study), 232–3
Macquarie, Gov. Lachlan, 12–13, 21, 25–6
Malek Fahd Islamic School, 230, 255
Maloga Mission and school, 71–2
Mannix, Daniel, 133, 165
Marist Brothers, schools of, 85, 92–3, 133, 227–9
Marsden, Samuel, 7, 10, 14–16, 19–21, 28–9
McCoy, William, 106, 115, 117–18, 159
medical examinations in schools, 118, 122–3, 207
Melbourne Declaration on Educational Goals for Young Australians, 252, 266–7
Menzies coalition governments, 173, 176, 198–9, 208
Menzies, Robert, 176, 198
merit and meritocracy, schools and, 93, 103, 116–17, 138–9, 145
Methodist and Wesleyan teachers, churches and schooling, 7–8, 15–16, 25, 33–4, 36, 40, 42, 45, 54, 80, 87, 91, 130
middle class children, 9, 15–16, 59, 64–5, 109, 114, 132, 134, 138, 176, 208, 218
military influence on schooling, 9, 16, 18, 51, 102, 123–6, 168, 173
missionaries as teachers, 12, 14–15, 21, 32, 36, 45, 51–7, 67–70, 72, 134
Mitcham Primary School, SA, 218–19
Modern School, The, WA, 113, 189
monitorialism *see* teaching and pedagogy, monitorialism
Montessori, Maria, educational influence, 122–3, 148
moral panics and education, 140, 181, 240
Moreton Bay, schooling, *see* Brisbane
Mount Druitt High School, NSW, 222–4, 239, 246
multicultural policy and schooling, 206, 214, 222, 264
Murray Island, schooling, 67–8
Muslim families and schooling, 33, 103, 120, 230, 264–5
My School (web-site), 251, 256–7, 266–7
NAPLAN (National Assessment Plan Literacy and Numeracy), 251, 255, 266–8
national curriculum, 268
national fitness movement, 173
National Schools Board, 36, 42–3, 52–3, 55, 61
National schools
  Australia, 35, 38–45, 47, 49, 50–3, 55, 59, 61–2, 75, 78–81, 97
  England, 7, 8, 25
Native Institution, 21–2, 24, 54
Neale, William, 106, 117–18
neoliberalism, xi, 212, 223, 225, 227, 230, 231, 246
  see also school choice
Neville, Auber Octavius, 129–30, 163–4
New Education Fellowship and conference, 161–3
New Education, 26, 97, 100, 103, 106–8, 110, 113–14, 116, 117–18, 131–2, 134, 135, 137, 140, 145, 161–3
New South Wales Teachers Federation, 193, 241

New South Wales, schooling,
before 1901, 7–29, 31–48, 54, 62, 71–2, 74, 78–80, 83–6, 89–90, 92–6, 100
after 1900, 109–14, 121, 128–9, 131, 146, 149–50, 152–3, 158–9, 163, 167, 172–3, 189–91, 193, 196–7, 222–3, 226, 241, 243, 245, 253, 258
new vocationalism, 225–6, 234, 235, 237
Newcastle High School, 190–1
Newling, C. B., 150–1
Nicholson, Charles, 53, 81
Nimbin Community School, 231–2
nongovernment schools, xiii, xvii-xviii, 109, 130–4, 176, 191, 198–9, 201–2, 209, 212–14, 224–32, 240, 244, 260–3
see also academies; Catholic schools; Christian schools; dame schools; private venture academies and schools
Norfolk Island, schooling, 1, 19
Northern Territory, schooling, 72, 168, 203–4, 241–2, 250
O'Connor, Janet, 90–1
O'Hara, John Bernard, 130
O'Shanassy, John, 50, 78
OECD, influence on schooling, 225, 257, 260, 262, 267
orphan schools
Catholic, 40, 59
female, 12–13, 18–21, 24, 32, 37, 59
male, 19–21, 25–6, 32, 37, 59, 63
Protestant, 40, 59
Our Lady of Lebanon College, NSW, 222
paedophilia in schools, 58, 228, 240
parents *see* families, parents and schools
Parkes, Henry, 45, 60, 79–80
Parks Community Education Centre, SA, 221, 224, 239
Parramatta, schooling, 13–14, 16, 20–2, 27, 60, 154, 158, 168, 222
payment by results, teacher, 75–6, 97–8, 100, 102, 114
Pearson, Charles Henry, 91, 94
Pestalozzi, Johann, educational influence, 8, 43, 95, 100
physical education, 24, 91–3, 95, 102, 123, 130–1, 137, 139, 171, 173–4, 220
drill and military, 24, 102, 123, 137, 173–4
modern, 171, 173, 220
see also sports and games, school
Piddington, Marion, 173–4
PISA (Program for Student Assessment), 257, 262, 267
Polding, John Bede, 34, 40, 85
Poonindie Anglican Mission, school, 56, 70
poverty and schools, 57, 61, 71, 80, 83–6, 103, 108, 130, 135, 142, 148, 150, 153, 175, 182, 186–7, 201, 208, 216, 221, 223–4, 228, 241, 243, 251–2
Presbyterian church and schools, 31, 33–4, 37, 40, 42, 45, 51–2, 76, 80, 91–2, 132
Presbyterian Ladies College, Melbourne, 91–2
primary and elementary schooling, xiii, 122, 249
before 1900, 28, 37, 46–8, 64, 66, 73, 75, 77–8, 84–7, 89, 94, 101, 103
after 1901, 109–14, 117, 122, 124, 126–7, 132–3, 136, 142, 151, 153, 155–9, 165, 167, 169, 172, 179–81, 185–6, 192–4, 196–7, 215–16, 218–20, 222, 237, 240, 246, 250–1, 255, 261
principals, school, 35, 48, 88–93, 98, 121, 139, 153, 164, 166–7, 193, 215–16, 223, 226–7, 229–30, 253–5, 257–8, 264
private schools *see* academies; dame schools; nongovernment schools; private venture schools
private venture schools, xvii, 8, 13, 15, 29, 31, 34, 42, 46, 59, 51–2, 60–2, 75, 83, 85–91, 93, 109, 118, 130–2, 138, 146, 153, 176
progressive education, 8, 25, 96, 107–8, 143, 156, 161, 166, 172, 174, 181, 195–6, 207
see also New Education
provisional schools, 69, 72, 79, 98, 103, 111–12
psychology and student administration, 26, 104, 107–8, 127, 137–9, 146, 148, 154–6, 161, 171, 175, 181–2, 203
see also intelligence testing
public examinations, 27, 65, 87–8, 90–1, 112, 116, 130, 133–4, 139, 157, 161, 163, 170, 184, 209, 219, 230, 245, 265
see also assessment; credentials and credentialism; merit and meritocracy
Public Instruction Act 1880, NSW, 79–80, 96
public schools, xviii, 13, 224
to 1901, 28, 36–53, 60–2, 65–7, 71–91, 93–6, 100, 102–5
1901–2000, 106, 109–15, 120, 125–9, 134–5, 140, 143–6, 151–60, 164–5, 176, 179, 184, 186–91, 198–9, 202, 212–16, 223–4, 227, 231, 233, 246
after 2000, 249, 257–63
punishment of students *see* discipline and punishment
pupil teachers, 43–4, 75, 84, 97–8, 100, 110, 114, 149, 170
qualifying certificate, 111–12
Queensland, schooling, 40, 43, 51–4, 68–70, 74, 81–2, 85, 90–1, 94, 96, 102, 106, 112, 115–16, 124, 127–8, 137, 145–6, 161, 168, 170, 189, 209, 232–3, 235, 257–8
racism and schooling, 67, 120, 127–30, 241, 243, 264–5
Reddall, Thomas, 25–6
religion, churches and schooling *see names of churches and* curriculum (2) religious
retention, student, 165, 184, 191, 209, 212, 217–18, 240, 242–3

Richardson, Henry Handel, 75, 91
Robertson, Thomas, 189
Roe, Reginald, 106, 116
Rosson, Isabella, 9
Rousseau, J.-J., educational influence, 8
Rudd and Gillard Labor governments, 261–2, 266
ruling class children, xviii, 38, 48, 61, 65, 108, 132–3, 191, 229–30, 253–4, 263
rural and remote schools and communities, xii, 61, 67, 73, 76, 79–82, 85–6, 98, 102–4, 111–12, 115, 117, 127, 145–6, 150–1, 159–60, 167, 169, 203, 207–8, 213, 241, 244–5, 250–1, 259
  see also distance education
Rusden, George, 42–3, 50, 52
Saint Josephs College, Sydney, 92–3
school efficiency movement, 57, 73, 81, 84, 98, 114, 127, 156
school choice, 33, 221, 259–61, 267
school fees, 60, 80, 81, 84, 110, 113, 117
  abolition of, 32, 73, 76
school libraries, 198, 202, 218, 221
school magazines, 91, 100, 126, 139, 147, 168, 172
school of the air *see* distance education
school registration, 114, 165, 176, 222, 232, 242
school, significance of, xiii, xv-xvii, 1, 249–50
Schools Commission, Australian, 182–3, 200–2, 205–8, 212, 218, 221–2, 224–5, 234, 245,
Schools in Australia see Karmel Report
Scotch College, Victoria, 51–2
Scott, Thomas Hobbes, 36–8, 59
Scottish-Australians, schooling, 31–2, 37, 51–2, 59
  see also Presbyterian church and schools
secondary schooling, xiii, 88, 93–5, 109, 111, 113–20, 122, 133, 138–9, 142, 146, 156, 165–7, 170, 176, 179–80, 184–91, 198, 209, 211–13, 226, 235, 240, 250, 261
SEMP (Social Education Materials Project), 232–3
Shelley teaching family, 21–2
social darwinism, 67, 120, 127
social reconstruction, post World War II schooling, 144, 170, 175, 183, 248
Society for the Promotion of Christian Knowledge (SPCK), 6, 12, 24, 33, 48
Society for the Propagation of the Faith, 84
Society for the Propagation of the Gospel (SPG), 12, 33
Society of the Sacred Heart schools, 133–4
South Australia, schooling, 46–8, 54–7, 61–2, 70, 72, 74, 80–1, 84–5, 88, 90, 114, 116–7, 119–21, 126–7, 138, 152, 159, 171, 184, 189, 192, 219, 231, 235–6, 259
special education *see* disabilities, schooling children with
sports and games, school, 89, 91–3, 121–2, 130–1, 139, 165, 169, 201, 230
  see also physical education
St Patrick's Marist College, NSW, 227–8, 229
St Stanislaus College, NSW, 131, 228
state aid to schools, xi, 7, 39–40, 49, 72, 74–8, 80, 84–5, 133, 173, 180, 196–202, 225, 227
state schools *see* public schools
States Grants (Science Laboratories and Technical Training) Act 1964, 198, 202
streaming, tracking and setting, 144, 156, 187, 220
student activism, 180, 235
sunday schools, 7, 16, 33, 48, 87, 102, 204
Sydney Grammar School, 60, 90, 230
Sydney Teachers College, 137, 149–50
systems of schools *see* centralisation and systematisation
Tasmania, schooling, 1, 9, 12, 15, 17, 48–9, 60, 74, 80, 90, 106, 108, 117–19, 148, 159, 189, 244–5
Tate, Frank, 106, 108, 113–15, 119, 127, 130, 138, 145
teacher training and education, 25, 34, 40, 43–5, 52, 57–8, 61, 65, 68–9, 84, 95–7, 99, 103, 110, 116–17, 134, 137, 146, 149–50, 175, 181, 184, 192, 214, 243, 257
  see also pupil teachers
teacher unions, 97, 117, 134–5, 151, 170, 180, 192–4, 226–7, 234, 239–41
teachers (1), xiv
  infant, kindergarten and preschool, 95–6, 134, 214
  primary and elementary, 11, 13–14, 16, 25, 42, 44–5, 57–8, 61, 64, 69, 76, 85, 96–9, 110, 114, 134–8, 150–3, 162, 191–4, 196
  secondary, 91, 99, 192–4, 221
teachers (2)
  before 1821, 11, 13–14, 16–17, 25
  1821-1870, 33–4, 42, 44–5, 57–8, 61
  1871-1950, 64–5, 69, 76, 85, 91, 96–9, 106, 110, 114, 149–53, 162, 169–70
  1951-2000, 180, 191–4, 216–17, 221, 227, 231, 238–41
  after 2000, 257–8
teachers (3)
  female, 9, 65, 76, 84, 96, 99, 131, 135, 153, 193, 240
  male, 65, 126, 193, 228, 240
  marriage bar and married women, 65, 76, 96, 152–3, 169, 192–3
  see also gay and lesbian teachers and students; teaching families
teachers (4)
  Aboriginal, 243
  Catholic religious and lay, 196, 222, 228, 238; *see also* Catholic religious orders and schooling
  convict, 9, 12–14, 17, 49
  governesses and tutors, private, 29, 35, 59, 86, 52
  missionary *see main entry* missionaries as teachers

teachers (5)
inspection of, 37, 41, 44, 53, 61, 65–6, 76, 79, 97–9, 102, 110–11, 115, 165, 184, 193, 209
professional development, 219, 238, 243
professional standards, 57, 102, 149, 254, 258
promotion, 43, 76, 134, 240
registration, 258
salaries and wages, 10, 12, 43, 53, 65, 76, 85, 96, 98, 127, 134–5, 151, 153, 169–70, 196, 224, 239–40, 254
teachers colleges *see* teacher training and education
teaching and pedagogy, xiv, 22–7, 54, 56–60, 65, 95, 99–103, 110, 123, 132, 134–8, 145, 149, 151, 165, 172–4, 184, 194–5, 209, 221, 238–41, 245, 254, 257, 266
class and simultaneous, 43, 56, 84, 99
individual method, 24, 56, 58–9, 99
monitorialism, 14–16, 25–7, 33, 37, 43, 49, 51, 56–7, 84, 87, 100, 152, 194
new information technology, computers and, 215, 219–20, 238–9, 245, 266, 269
project and small group based, 132, 149, 181, 238
teaching aids, 25–6, 57, 151, 137, 195; *see also* computers, teaching and learning
timetables, 26, 65, 84, 99, 102, 136, 160, 220
teaching families, 9, 13, 21–2, 35, 52–3, 58–9, 65
technical secondary schools, 94, 111, 114, 118–19, 127, 133, 139, 146, 154–5, 157–9, 184–5, 187, 189, 194, 234
Thebarton Boys Technical High, 117, 159
Theosophical schools, 132
Therry, Joseph, 37
Thomson, Pat, 256
timetables, school *see* teaching and pedagogy
Toronto High School, NSW, 253–4, 256
Torres Strait Islander schooling, xiii, xv, 2, 67–9, 182, 243–4, 250
truancy *see* compulsory schooling
Tufnell, Edward, 53, 81
University of Adelaide, 90, 116, 138
University of Melbourne, 51, 95, 114, 173
University of Sydney, 53, 60, 90, 109, 112
Unley High School, SA, 147, 162, 219–21, 236, 239, 251
values, school, 77, 231, 233, 264–6
see also moral panics; curriculum (2)
Victoria, schooling,
before 1901, 36, 40, 50–1, 55, 60, 62, 70, 74–8, 90, 93–5, 97–8, 100
after 1900, 107, 113–5, 119, 127, 136, 138, 150, 159, 165–7, 170, 172–3, 180, 189, 192, 194, 196, 217, 227
Vietnamese-Australians, schooling, 218, 244, 256
Vocational and Educational Training (VET), 225, 237
vocational guidance, 139, 154, 156, 159, 170, 187
Wakefield, Edward Gibbon, 38, 46
Warwick district, schooling, 52–3
Wentworth, William Charles, 15, 37, 136
Wesley, John, 7–8
Western Australia, schooling, 32, 45–6, 61, 73–6, 81, 85, 90, 97, 103, 106, 113, 116, 123–4, 127, 129–30, 135, 148, 151–2, 163, 168, 189–90, 204, 223–4, 258, 259
Whitlam Labor governments, 183, 200–2, 204, 206, 267
Wilkins, William, 43–5, 52, 56, 78, 100
Williams, Alfred, 106, 114, 116–7, 119, 138
Wollongong, schooling, 40–1
Woods, Julian Tenison, 84–5
working class children and youth, 6, 8–9, 23, 28, 33, 36, 63, 73, 81–2, 93, 103, 139, 208, 217, 269
World War I, 109, 113–14, 133, 140
World War II, 143–4, 154, 167–70
Wyatt, William, 47, 56–8
Wyndham Committee and Scheme, NSW, 189–90
Yashkenko, Alexandr, 135–7
Yass, schooling, 34, 71–2
Young, John Lorenzo, 88
youth unemployment, 211–12, 217–8
see also labour market and schools